D0627531

THE NORTH WILL RISE AGAIN
Pensions, Politics and Power in the 1980s

THE NORTH WILL RISE AGAIN
Pensions, Politics and Power in the 1980s

Jeremy Rifkin and Randy Barber
Peoples Business Commission

BEACON PRESS Boston

Peoples Business Commission Staff:
Mary Murphy
and
Noreen Banks, Ted Howard, and Dan Smith
With Special Research Assistance by Bruce McWilliams, Larry Roth,
and Arthur Girasole

Copyright © 1978 by the Center for Urban Education
Beacon Press books are published under the auspices
of the Unitarian Universalist Association
Published simultaneously in Canada by
Fitzhenry & Whiteside Limited, Toronto
All rights reserved
Printed in the United States of America

(hardcover) 9 8 7 6 5 4 3 2 1
(paperback) 9 8 7 6 5 4 3

Library of Congress Cataloging in Publication Data
Rifkin, Jeremy.
    The North will rise again.
    Includes bibliographical references.
    1. Trade-unions—United States. 2. Pension
trusts—United States. 3. Regional Planning—
United States. I. Barber, Randy, joint author.
II. Title.
HD6508.R52   1978   331.88′0973   78–53652
ISBN 0–8070–4786–4
ISBN 0–8070–4787–2 pbk.

Acknowledgments

During the preparation of this book, we interviewed over one hundred and fifty people—labor leaders and organizers, public officials, pension administrators and advisors, academics and other informed observers. Our discussions ranged from ten minute telephone calls to in-depth interviews ranging over several sessions. Needless to say, many of those we interviewed will disagree with our conclusions. We wish to thank the following—plus more than a score of others who requested anonymity—for their cooperation:

David Allen, legislative aide, Senator Lloyd Bensten; Russ Allen, coordinator of pension courses, AFL-CIO Labor Studies Center; Jack Baltes, International Foundation on Employee Benefits; Dan Beller, Bureau of Labor Statistics; Jack Bigel, president, Planning Associates; Al Bilik, organizing director, International Union of Electrical Workers; Dean Birch, Program on Regional and Neighborhood Change; Bill Brennan, Education-Instruction, Hartford, Connecticut; former Governor Edmund Brown, Sr.; John L. Brown, Genesco, Inc. pension plan; Sam Brown, director, ACTION; Nick Carbone, Hartford, Connecticut City Council; Michael Clowes, executive editor *Pensions & Investments* magazine; Ralph Conant, TIAA-CREF; Robert Connerton, general counsel, International Laborers' Union; Nelson Cruikshank, presidential advisor on senior citizen issues; Robert Daley, Union Labor Life Insurance Company; Richard Days, administrator of welfare and pension funds, UAW Local 259, New York City; Larry DiCara, Boston City Council; Henry Dillon, international vice-president, Graphic Arts Industrial Union; California Senator John Dunlap, chairman, Select Committee on Investment Priorities and Objectives; John English, Tom Judge and Don Raymond, AT&T pension system; Henry Foner, president, Joint Board of Furriers and Leather Makers Union; Massachusetts Representative Barney Frank; Esmond Gardner, former vice-president for the pension trust department, Chase Manhatten Bank; Woodrow Ginsberg, Center for Community Change, and consultant to union pension funds; Mel Glasser, UAW Social Security Department; Reese Hammond, director of education and training, secretary to the Central Pension Fund, Operating Engineers International Union; Paul P. Harbrecht, S.J.; Doris Hardesty, AFL-CIO Labor Law Reform Taskforce; John Harrington, consultant, California State Senate Select Committee on Investment Priorities and Objectives; Representative Michael Harrington, (D-Mass); Bob Kalman, Policy Department, American Federation of State, County and Municipal Employees; Kevin Kistler, AFL-CIO Organizing Department; Jack Kittredge, Massachusetts Social and Economic Opportunities Council; Howard Kline, House Pension Taskforce; James La Fleur, executive secretary, Wisconsin State Pension System; Ian Lanoff, administrator, Pension and Welfare Benefits Program, U.S. Labor Department; Murray Webb Latimer, union pension advisor; Leonard Lesser, Center for Community Change, and union pension consultant; Noel Arnold Levin, past president, International Foundation on Employee Benefits and pension consultant; Bob Levy, president, Computer Direction Advisors; Jean Lindberg, vice president, Chase Investment Management Corporation; Mike Locker, Corporate Data Exchange; Representative Ed Markey (D-Mass); Andrew Martin; John L. Martin, vice president, Litton Industries, president, Association of Private Pension and Welfare Plans; James McKeon, Salomon Brothers; Andrew Melgarde, U.S. Chamber of Commerce; Paul Merrion, Washington editor, *Pensions & Investments* magazine; John Moriarty, staff director, Congressional Northeast/Midwest Economic Advancement Coalition; Jack Morris, vice president for public relations, Morgan Guaranty Trust Company; Barbara Muldouer, United Mine Workers of America; Jack Orben, president, American Pension Management Services; Tom Palay, Wisconsin Center for Public Policy; David Preminger, pension attorney, New York City Legal Services; Dick Proston, AFL-CIO Industrial Union Department; Senator William Proxmire, (D-Wisc), chairman, Senate Banking Committee; Representative Henry Reuss (D-Wisc), chairman, House Banking and Currency Committee; George Roach, international organizing representative, Oil, Chemical and Atomic Workers Union; Pat Roach, Dayton, Ohio, City Council; Ray Rogers, Amalgamated Clothing and Textile Workers Union; Jim Rosapepe, Public Interest Opinion Research; Henry Rose, general counsel, Pension Benefit Guarantee Corporation; Mel Ruben, president, Retail Clerks Local 1371; Murray Sabrin; Jim Savarise, director, Policy Department, AFSCME; Henry Schecter, AFL-CIO Mortgage Investment Trust; Roy Schotland, Georgetown University Law School; John Schulter; Ohio State Senator Mike Schwartzwalder; Bob Seltzer, Corporate Data Exchange; Ted Silvey; I. Philip Sipser, union pension attorney; Lawrence Smedley, associate director, AFL-CIO Social Security Department; Harrison Smith, executive vice president for trusts, Morgan Guaranty Trust Company; Richard Smith, vice president, Thorndike, Doran, Paine & Lewis; Tim Smith, Inter-Faith Center on Corporate Responsibility; Representative George Starr, Oregon State Legislature; Elliot Stein, Jr., Lehman Brothers; Sol Steten, vice president, Amalgamated Clothing and Textile Workers Union; Wallace Sullivan and Joe Russo, Teachers Retirement System of the City of New York; Joe Swire, union pension expert; John Thompson, Bureau of Labor Statistics; Robert Tilove, vice president, Martin E. Segal and Associates; William Winpisinger, president, International Association of Machinists; Richard Witmer, secretary, Pennsylvania State Public Employees Retirement Fund; Pam Woywod, Amalgamated Clothing and Textile Workers Union; Martha Yohalem, Social Security Administration.

We would like to thank the following people for their comments on the manuscript of this book: G. William Dumhoff; Erwin Knoll and John Buell of *The Progressive* magazine; Charles Pillsbury; Vic Reinemer, staff director, Senate Sub-committee on Reports, Accounting and Management; Prof. William F. Whyte, New York State School of Industrial and Labor Relations, Cornell University.

Most of all, we would like to gratefully acknowledge the constructive criticism and support we received from Bill Behn, Center for Economic Studies, Palo Alto, California, and Karen Ferguson and Jay Tower, Pension Rights Center, Washington, D.C.

Contents

Chapter 1: The Crisis and the Opportunity

Just ten generations have come and gone since Adam Smith published his 441-page tract entitled *The Wealth of Nations.* Two hundred years is certainly not a very long period of time. For the anthropologist, it represents an eighth of an inch of dirt on any standard archaeological dig. For the astronomer, it means just three sightings of Halley's comet. For the geneticist, not even enough time to detect a microscopic new bud on the evolutionary tree.

During this brief span of history an entire economic epoch has run its course. From the clanking sound of textile mills in eighteenth-century Manchester to the electronic whiz of computer storage banks in downtown Houston, capitalism, the driving force of the Industrial Revolution for these past two centuries, is casting its final mark on the unfinished business of civilization. For better or for worse, the system first extolled by Adam Smith is about to take its place as one of the more interesting chapters in humanity's rather short and turbulent existence.

Capitalism is not likely to exist anywhere in the world a hundred years from now. Our children's children will read about it in history books, but they will probably not live under it. In Western Europe, demands for various socialist alternatives are already challenging the capitalist economies. In Italy, nearly half the population voted their preference for either communist or socialist economic programs in the 1976 parliamentary elections. The Italian Communist party now controls the municipal governments of Italy's largest cities. West Germany is already ruled by a mildly socialist party (the Social Democrats), and its youth wing, the Young Socialists, is applying increased pressure to hasten the transition from capitalism to community and worker control over the economy. Meanwhile, the concept of public ownership of industry is by now well established, with the national government owning outright many key business operations, and unions already holding one-third of the representation and control on the boards of major domestic industries.

France's left, comprised of socialists and communists, received slightly less than half of the vote in the last national legislative elections and controls a majority of the country's municipalities. There is no doubt that they are a force to be reckoned with and will need little additional support to gain power. Like other Western European nations, France has already nationalized a number of key businesses and will certainly pursue an even more ambitious campaign to take over many of the remaining large privately owned enterprises if and when the left comes to power.

In Britain a powerful labor movement is fast pushing the nominally socialist Labour party government leftward with demands that unions participate in 50 percent of the control of all major British companies. While the trade unions still face formidable opposition from Britain's dwindling middle class and Conservative party, their strategic control over key sectors of the economy gives them the leverage to make their demands for socialization heard.

The Scandinavian countries and the Netherlands are already well on the way to complete socialization of their economies. Although the voters in several recent elections seemed to favor a more conservative approach to socialization, there is no serious talk of reverting to an earlier capitalist-dominated system.[1]

The powerful economic changes that are sweeping through the Western European continent are a bellwether for what will soon take place in the last great bastion of capitalist strength, the United States. According to a survey conducted by the *Harvard Business Review* in 1975, America's top business leaders are convinced that an economic transformation of dramatic proportions is also about to take shape in America. The publication asked its high-level corporate readership which of two ideologies—capitalism or socialism —will prevail in the United States by the mid-1980s. Over 73 percent of the business community responding believe that the capitalist system will be largely replaced by a de-centralized socialist order within a decade.[2] Whether this will happen in such a short period of time and what the re-sults of such a change will look like in practice are matters for speculation. What is clear, however, is that the percep-tion of an historical transformation from one economic sys-tem to another is based on certain truths which business leaders here, in Japan, and in Western Europe can no longer ignore; truths that provide convincing evidence of the de-cline in power of the capitalist countries of the world.

From the mid-40s to the late 60s, "western" capitalism enjoyed a sustained, broad-based period of economic expan-sion. Even with the inevitable boom-and-bust cycles, growth continued at record levels. In the early 70s, however, this growth reached its peak and the major capitalist nations entered a new period of chronic economic stagnation. None of the major capitalist nations has substantially recovered from the 1974–1975 recession; and most experts fear another strong recession in the near future. Although there is plenty of capital available, growth in investments has proceeded at a snail's pace: France experienced almost no increase in 1977, Japan had minimal growth, and in the United States invest-ment levels are still below those of 1974. Structural unem-ployment has reached crisis proportions in Japan, all the Western European nations, and the United States. Excess productive capacity has now become endemic, and many of the aging plants and factories are no longer being modern-ized or replaced. Inflation remains abnormally high in all Western industrial nations and there are predictions of an across-the-board return to double-digit inflation. At the same time the cost of energy has quadrupled since 1973, and many other crucial raw materials are also in short or dwindling supply. Most economists agree that all of these problems signal, in one way or another, the beginning stages of a long-range economic decline for the advanced capitalist nations.[3]

In this country, the American people are just now becoming aware of this emerging economic reality. According to one major national opinion poll, a plurality of Americans now believe that "the capitalist economic system has already reached its peak in terms of its performance as a system and is now on the decline."[4] Reports that America is fast depleting its natural resources, running out of energy reserves, and fighting a losing battle against foreign competition are hastening that awareness.

In Europe the awareness that capitalism is no longer a viable economic system has long since given birth to major social movements for the transformation of economic power. For years, ideologically oriented unions and left-wing political parties have fought to win popular support for fundamental economic changes. Their partial victories over the years are now adding up to major defeats for the once dominant capitalist ethic.

The battle between capitalism and socialism in Europe has been a battle for control over capital itself. Little by little, the European left has been successful in wresting this control from the private sector. While more attention has generally been focused on instances where productive capital (plants, equipment, and firms) has been put under some form of public regulation or ownership, it is also important to recognize that finance capital itself has come increasingly under the control of these European governments.

State-owned and controlled banks in West Germany, Sweden, Britain, France, Italy, and other Western European nations have increasing domination over economic planning and the allocation of capital resources. Although in many cases they still act as an aid to the private sector, these government-owned banks have taken over more and more of the basic prerogatives which have long been considered essential to maintaining the hegemony of the private capitalist sector.[5]

In this country, while the federal government has assumed a larger role in the regulation and flow of money, the private corporate/banking community continues to enjoy near-absolute control over capital investment decisions. Today banks control 75 percent of America's money supply—some one hundred banks alone account for 45 percent of all bank deposits.[6] Two hundred giant corporations own two-thirds of the manufacturing assets of the United States.[7] As a result, America's major banks and corporations dominate the economic planning and capital allocation decisions of the entire nation.

Although the powerful corporate/banking establishment has never really been popular with the American people, it has, nonetheless, been tolerated over the years. There are two main reasons for this. First, the public has come to accept the notion that what's good for the banks and corporations is ultimately good for the people: if they prosper it will inevitably mean more jobs and greater economic prosperity for everyone. Secondly, the American people have never seriously considered the possibility of alternative ways to structure economic planning and capital allocation policies. For most people, capitalism has represented more than just a set of economic rules. It has come to be looked upon as a part of the natural order of things.

As long as the capitalist economic pie has continued to expand, and along with it everyone's individual little slice, the legitimacy of the corporate/banking establishment has been relatively secure. The people have been willing to remain dependent on the private sector for their economic survival, even though it meant a captive relationship with a small elite of enormous unelected power. Now, however, that pie has begun to shrink and most of the experts agree that the shrinkage will continue virtually unabated in all advanced capitalist economies. There is no doubt that the United States and other industrialized nations are entering a period of economic contraction, highlighted by energy crises and overall resource depletion. Short of some major technological breakthrough comparable to the introduction of the steam engine or assembly-line automation, the capitalist countries will be unable to substantially reduce this downward economic trend.[8]

While a shrinking economic pie has already come to mean smaller slices for everyone, two major power blocs find that they are being increasingly denied even a meager portion of what still remains. Organized labor and the local and state governments that comprise the midwest/northeast region of the continental United States[9] are being systematically abandoned by the private capital market. Industry is turning away from the northern quadrant to avoid the higher costs of union shops, taxes, and the other expenses that go with maintaining plant operations in this older and more antiquated industrial corridor. At the same time, the banking community has begun to turn off the vital flow of finance capital in a regional "redlining" campaign that is effectively blocking any further economic development in this already hard-pressed area of the country.

The unions, whose membership is overwhelmingly concentrated in this northern tier, and public officials of the sixteen states affected, are becoming increasingly desperate. In an effort to lure back private capital, both power blocs have begun to make sizable accommodations. Labor has lessened its bargaining demands and state governments have attempted to shower public subsidies, gifts, and special favors on the private investment community. While such panic maneuvers have won both blocs a few minor reprieves, they are unable to reclose the financial floodgates that are pouring jobs and capital out of the region to more lucrative areas in the Sunbelt and overseas. This mass exodus of capital is wreaking havoc on union membership rolls as hundreds of thousands of displaced workers file into unemployment offices. Meanwhile, the region as a whole is collapsing and there are fears that the next great economic downturn for the country will result in economic catastrophe for the Northeast.[10]

Time is running out for the unions and what we call the Graybelt corridor (the sixteen states that make up the northeast/midwest quadrant of the United States). In 1982 Congress will be reapportioned on the basis of the 1980 census. According to a detailed *New York Times* study, the Sunbelt states will gain fifteen seats in the House of Representatives and, for the first time since the founding of the Republic, will be the dominant force in Congress. The northeast and midcentral states, which have dominated national politics for close to two centuries, will move from their present majority of 225 seats to a minority-bloc status of 210 seats.[11]

The political shift of power in Washington is much more than just a reflection of the shift in population from North to South. At the root of this massive migration is a shift in economic power as historic as that experienced during the early stages of the Industrial Revolution when millions of rural Americans were forced, by new economic realities, to abandon their small farms and become a part of America's new urban industrial proletariat. Today, those same urban areas that became the center of the Industrial Revolution are themselves falling victim to this newest shift in economic power and are becoming a new industrial Appalachia. But unlike the rural migration to the cities over a century ago, today's population shift is much more selective. Millions of white middle-class professionals are moving south, leaving behind them a population heavily weighted with semiskilled and unskilled white ethnics, blacks, and browns. Not coincidentally, those left behind also happen to comprise the bulk of unionized workers in the country. Over 60 percent of all unionists are concentrated in the northeast/midwest corridor; in contrast, only 15 percent of them are in the Sunbelt. This is obviously a key reason why capital and production are abandoning the North for the South.[12]

For organized labor and the Graybelt states, the long-range implications of this historic shift of economic and political power are so monumental that even seasoned political observers are hesitant to draw more than a few tentative conclusions. However, this much is clear at the outset. With this power shift, the liberal ideology which has dominated federal policies since the New Deal era is likely to give way to an increasing conservatism, reflecting the attitudes of the new power centers in places like Orlando, Houston, Phoenix, and Albuquerque. A second and related assumption is that organized labor and the industrial states will suffer growing political and economic losses after 1982 as their traditional clout is significantly reduced in Washington.

At AFL-CIO headquarters on 16th and I streets, and across the Mall on Capitol Hill, where northern politicians have opened up a special Coalition Taskforce office, both groups have been huddling. Out of weeks and months of strategy sessions have come the initial battle plans which each of these two beleaguered power blocs hope will reverse their fortunes over the next several years.

For the unions, the strategy is a two-pronged assault designed to open up the South to union shops and to make it easier for labor to recruit new members in general. This emphasis on organizing the unorganized represents a dramatic break from the business-as-usual lethargy which has characterized the labor movement over the past several years. It is a sign that organized labor is beginning to understand both the impact of its present situation and the implications of the power shift from North to South. To accomplish their new organizing goals, labor leaders are concentrating their efforts on a massive nationwide boycott of one of the leading anti-union companies in the South, J.P. Stevens, and on the effectiveness of new labor-reform legislation.

Northern politicians are focusing their attention on legislation to reverse the disproportionate flow of billions of dollars of tax money out of their region to the Sunbelt and on measures to secure federal funds for various capital development programs for their respective states and cities. Two coalitions, one comprised of governors from the Northeast, the other of congressional representatives of the region, have been formed to press their demands in Washington.

As they are presently conceived, both strategies are likely to have only a marginal impact at best, leaving both power blocs in an even more weakened position in the foreseeable future. To understand why, it is first necessary to trace the recent histories of organized labor and the states that run along America's northern tier. Both have been experiencing a dramatic decline in economic and political clout for two decades. It is not so much that history has passed these once powerful entities by, as some observers would like to believe. It is more that private capital has begun to leave the region and the organized work force behind as it seeks other regions and countries with large pools of cheap nonunion labor, untapped resources and lenient regulatory policies. At the same time, it would be incorrect to assert, as some have done, that the power shift from North to South has been mostly a geographic phenomenon, as if the southern states had become the actual repositories of a new economic power. The economic power has not shifted at all. It still resides in the same private sector. The fact that the business community has begun to shift its base of operations to the Sunbelt (and abroad) has, of course, meant greater economic benefits for these regions. But economic power itself, that is, control over economic planning and capital allocation decisions, is still firmly embedded within the private capital sector.

While the private sector is the primary cause of the economic crisis facing organized labor and the North, neither of these blocs is entirely without responsibility for the situation that now confronts them. Through a combination of misguided loyalties, internal lethargy, and lost opportunities, unions and the industrialized states have allowed themselves to fall prey to the uncompromising demands of an unelected corporate elite.

Confused, disoriented and partly cast adrift by the private capital sector, organized labor and northern state governments find themselves in a difficult position. Some politicians and labor leaders still hope they can patch up their relationship with the private sector, even though it would mean becoming even more of a captive dependent; others now realize that the terms of such an arrangement would simply be too harsh to bear. On the other hand, no one is quite ready to throw in the towel altogether and become a ward of the federal government. This leaves one final option: developing their own independent economic base. There is talk now about labor unions and northern state governments assuming a new role as investors, owners, planners, and participants in the economic process. It is the kind of talk that would have shocked all but a handful of left-wing activists and academics just a few short years ago. Though still unfocused and only vaguely understood by even those who have begun to consider the possibilities, the concept of labor and public control over economic planning and production has finally crossed the Atlantic and reached American shores.

Of course, any serious discussion of developing an alternative economic base inevitably raises the basic question of where the capital will come from. Without an independent source of abundant capital readily available to them, organized labor and the northern industrial states will never be able to fill the economic vacuum left by the exodus of the private capital sector. Fortunately for them, such a capital pool does exist—in the form of the employee pension fund. Pension funds are a new form of wealth that has emerged over the past thirty years to become the largest single pool of private capital in the world. They are now worth over $500 billion and represent the deferred savings of millions and millions of American workers.[13] Pension funds at present own 20 to 25 percent of the equity in American corporations and hold 40 percent of the bonds.[14] Pension funds are now the largest source of investment capital for the American capitalist system.[15] And most importantly, pension-fund capital is neither privately owned nor publicly owned. It is a unique new form of wealth to which three major parties have potentially competing claims: the private financial community, the unions, and the state and local governments.

Today over $200 billion in pension-fund capital comes

from the combined deferred savings of 19 million union members and the public employee funds of the sixteen states that make up the northeast/midwest corridor.[16] The unions and the states have, over the years, relinquished control over this powerful capital pool to the financial establishment. The banks, in turn, have used these capital assets to shift jobs and production to the Sunbelt and overseas, thus crippling organized labor and the northern economies of the United States. Increasingly unwilling to see their own funds used against them, some labor leaders and northern state officials are beginning to see the value in pressing their claims for control over this great pool of pension capital. For these two beleaguered power blocs, pension funds offer a partial way out of their economic bind. It is the only large pool of capital which is potentially available to them. It is also the only source of funds that is large enough to provide them with the beginnings of their own independent economic base. With control of these moneys, unions and public authorities can begin to take over more and more of the economic-planning and capital-allocation decisions that have, for so long, been the exclusive prerogative of the private capital sector.

On the other hand, the financial community is not likely to give up control over this pool of pension capital without a fight. Pension funds have increasingly become its lifeline to economic suvival. Without ready access to pension-fund assets, the private capital system in the United States would be in serious trouble.*

---

* As we will show in Section II, this fact has not gone unnoticed within the corporate and financial communities. For example, Peter Drucker, the management consultant and capitalist guru, has attempted to diffuse any potential counterclaims for control of pension capital by asserting that workers already control the American economy simply through their pension ownership. Drucker calls this "socialism," but socialists vehemently disagree with his definition of socialism. Responding to Drucker's book, *The Unseen Revolution: How Pension Fund Socialism Came to America,* the late Senator Lee Metcalf charged that Drucker's "contention that employees already own, control, and direct

This book is about the competing claims of unions, northern industrial states, and the corporate/banking community for control over this giant pool of capital. Section I will examine the internal policies and external pressures that have led to the decline of organized labor and the Graybelt states, and the loosening of their ties with the private sector. Such an examination is essential to understanding both the urgency of the present crisis and the reasons why both these power blocs might begin to press their claims for control over hundreds of billions of dollars of pension capital. Section II will examine the historical development of pension-fund capital, the ways in which it is presently being used, and the claims and counterclaims by the unions, states, and financial community to control over it. The final section of this book will focus on the potential for using pension capital as an opening wedge in the development of basic economic alternatives within the United States.

With pension-fund capital, the American economy has entered a new stage. American workers are now a major new ownership class. Whether control over their pension capital and, ultimately, over the American economy is transferred to them will depend on many factors, including which initiatives organized labor and the industrial states choose to take. For union workers facing unemployment lines and for the

---

large amounts of pension fund capital is a major, monstrous myth." [17] There is, in fact, a big difference between ownership and control of pension assets.

Drucker's vision is profoundly conservative. He gleefully predicts that the emergence of "pension fund socialism" will be the death blow for the labor movement, since workers will now be more loyal to their "capital" than to their unions. He envisions inevitable conflict between young and old, working class and poor—all as a result of his "socialism." Writing in *Working Papers*, James Henry replies: "Perhaps the sole point on which socialist writers would agree is that the transfer of economic ownership to workers, the state or anyone else is by itself irrelevant, and is at best a means to an end. That end is not ownership but control: the extension of democracy to the production process and the elimination of artificial inequality." [18]

Graybelt states facing severe economic hardships, the question is whether they will continue to allow their own capital to be used against them, or whether they will assert direct control over these funds in order to save their jobs and their communities. Behind this very practical question, however, lies an ideological question that has, in one form or another, long been the central issue for all advanced industrial nations: who should control the means of production? The dramatic growth of private- and public-sector pension-fund capital, and the crisis of organized labor and northern state economies have made that ideological question both timely and immediate.

Chapter 2: Unions in Turmoil

The year: 1939. It's early evening in lower Manhattan. A barely perceptible breeze curls its way up 14th Street, cooling off the heat that has soaked the heart of the clothing district since just after mid-morning. A young socialist, moustached, wire-rimmed glasses neatly affixed, steps up onto a lettuce crate at Union Square Park to address an after-work assortment of young workers; the kind of melting-pot crowd that sociologists of a later period would become so fond of eulogizing. "Which side are you on?" the bespectacled young conductor yells out into the crowd. "The union," chants the chorus, with that clear tone of defiance that comes of knowing that one is about to taste that first lick of unqualified power. . . .

A picket line outside the Ford plant in Detroit, Michigan. Again the exhortation, "Which side are you on?" Again the tough, no-nonsense rejoinder. "The Union makes us strong," rings back and forth along the entire line.

Repeated over and over again, at a thousand factory gates, it was a new religion itching to spread its missionary gospel to all those seeking salvation, justice, dignity. And they listened. One million, two million, five million. All sold, one by one, on the union. The union would organize the unorganized. The union would provide a united voice for the working man and woman. The union would fight for a decent wage for a decent day's work. The union would prevail over the greed and avarice of the capitalist bosses. The union would make them strong.

The year: 1972. An interview in the businessman's magazine, *U.S. News & World Report*, with George Meany, the head of the AFL-CIO.

Question: Mr. Meany, what is the state of the union movement today? Why is total membership not growing as fast as the country's labor force?

Mr. Meany: I don't know, I don't care.

Question: You don't care? Why not?

Meany: We have never had a large proportion of the work force in this country, nothing like Britain, nothing like the Scandinavian countries, nothing like the Germans.

Question: Would you prefer to have a larger proportion?

Meany: Not necessarily.... We've done quite well without it. We've delivered more to the American worker than any labor movement that ever existed, yesterday or in the past. ... Why should we worry about organizing groups of people who do not want to be organized? If they prefer to have others speak for them and make the decisions which affect their lives, without effective participation on their part, that is their right.

Question: If unions do not keep pace with the growth of the work force, will organized labor's influence be reduced?

Meany: I used to worry about the size of the membership. But quite a few years ago I just stopped worrying about it, because to me it doesn't make any difference.[1]

What Mr. Meany stopped worrying about are numbers; numbers that tell the story of what was once an almost unstoppable army of workers, now being slowly whittled down over the years, through attrition, through arrogance, through benign neglect.

In 1945, 35.5 percent of all workers in nonagricultural jobs were members of a labor union. Today less than 25 percent of the labor force carries union cards.[2] Twenty years ago, American workers voted for union representation twice as often as they voted to keep unions out. Now organized labor is losing 52 percent of all the elections that are held. Even where unions already represent workers, the number of elections to withdraw recognition of a labor union have increased three-fold in the past ten years. (Elections to with-draw from a union can be initiated only when at least 30 percent of the employees involved petition for a decertification election.)[3]

According to the Labor Department, unions lost almost 600,000 members between 1974 and 1976 alone.[4] "Part of the trouble," contends veteran CIO organizer Joe Swire, is that "many of the guys who have been union organizers for years and years have slowed down."[5] George Brooks, professor of Labor and Industrial Relations at Cornell, is a little more graphic. "The typical union leader hates to organize. First, it's a terrible job. Today, the workers insult you, they spit on you, they throw the cards in your face." The union leader would much rather have a cocktail at lunch with manage-ment, says Brooks, than be at the factory gates organizing at 6 A.M.[6]

Even when they are out at the factory gates there's a fair to good chance that the workers they're organizing are al-ready members of other unions. In fact, much of the orga-nizing effort that the unions undertake is raiding one an-other's rank-and-file membership. "I don't think there's any statistic anybody could compile that would give an accurate picture of the time and energy and everything else that's wasted and lost in these jurisdictional fights between unions," says Joseph Beirne, former president of the Communications Workers of America.[7] Because the AFL-CIO has no effective mechanism for consolidating unions or resolving jurisdic-tional disputes, internal squabbling between unions continues to drain valuable resources and energies that "should be de-voted to seeking out and signing up nonunion workers."[8] This constant internal warfare reflects the fact that the AFL-CIO has become more of an association of self-interested businesses than the united voice of organized labor. Until these jurisdictional jealousies are resolved, says Irving Blue-stone, vice-president of the UAW, "the labor movement as a whole will continue to represent fewer than one out of four workers."[9]

Still, this doesn't even begin to account for the dramatic decline in union membership over the past twenty years. Organized labor is losing its strength for a number of reasons, some of which are of its own making. Of those which can be laid directly at labor's doorstep, none is more important than the loss of crusading zeal within the union leadership itself. The great prophets of social reform and economic justice that inspired millions of working Americans to stand up and be counted in the early days of the labor struggle are now long gone. The few aging patriarchs that still remain are huddled away deep inside the inner sanctums of the giant union bureaucracies, untouchable and out of touch with their own rank and file. Thomas W. Gleason of the Longshoremen is seventy-seven. Matthew Guinan of the Transportation Workers is sixty-seven. Max Greenberg of the Retail, Wholesale and Department Store Union is seventy, and, of course, the Godfather himself, George Meany, is now eighty-three. "We definitely have a problem," said Jerry Wurf of AFSCME a few years ago, "when you stop to think that at fifty-two, I'm the youngest V.P. of the AFL-CIO." The fact of the matter, says Wurf, is that "a lot of my colleagues are products of an era and an environment that is no longer in existence." [10] He might have added that the old labor chieftains of today are much more comfortable sitting around a pool in Bal Harbor, Florida, reminiscing about the battles of a bygone era than in dealing with the incredible changes that are now taking place on the American labor scene; changes which threaten to dislodge an already feeble union bureaucracy.

When George Meany and his closest friends were in their prime, a "worker" was narrowly defined as a white male who toiled on an assembly line or built a house, or labored down in the mines. In those days, the woman's place was still in the home, blacks were thought of as errand boys and maids, and it went without saying that young people were to be seen but certainly not heard. A lot of things about the American work force have changed dramatically over the past thirty years. By failing to recognize and embrace these changes, unionism in this country has come to look more and more like a fraternal order and less like the movement it once claimed to be.

Changing Collars

Lane Kirkland is the Secretary Treasurer of the AFL-CIO and heir apparent to George Meany. Every morning Mr. Kirkland passes through the outer lobby of the AFL-CIO building on 16th Street in Washington, D.C., on the way up to his eighth-floor suite. In that lobby are giant ceiling-to-floor murals (à la WPA era) depicting scenes of American laborers at work, complete with hammers, chisels, and hard hats. Equally important, there are secretaries, lab technicians, and sales clerks on the walls as well. Evidently these murals haven't much influenced Mr. Kirkland's views on which kinds of workers should be organized. To quote Mr. Kirkland:

In many industries, there has been a declining percentage of production workers and an increased percentage of people employed in sales, advertising, clerical, managerial and research. Well, those haven't been areas we've found particularly responsive to organizational appeals. Nor have we felt much compulsion to make a major effort at it.[11]

Mr. Kirkland's comments reveal a great deal about the future prospects for organized labor. Given the changing composition of the American work force, the prospects are not bright. Between 1950 and 1970, white-collar employment in America rose by 70 percent while blue-collar went up only 19 percent.[12] Some of the biggest advances in white-collar categories were in clerical work, technical jobs, and sales. By 1980 the number of white-collar workers will be greater than the number of blue-collar, service, and farm workers combined.[13] At the same time, in the two areas where organized labor is highly concentrated, construction and manufacturing, substitution of machines for people is expected to reduce further the number of blue-collar jobs. According to employment projections, manufacturing and construction jobs will only grow by .4 percent between now and 1980 and not at all from 1980 to 1985.[14] Leonard Woodcock, former president of the UAW, is alarmed by the statistics. "The groups of workers we generally have represented are growing smaller. There has been a union breakthrough among white-collar employees," concedes Woodcock, "but mainly in government." One reason why white-collar workers don't join the union, contends Woodcock, is because management gives them the same raises that unions win for the production workers inside the plant. "Office workers have told us frankly that they are content to stay out of the union because they don't have to pay dues or go on strike but get the same raises. They admit it's the union that wins them their raises," says Woodcock.[15] There are other reasons as well for not joining a union. First, there is the tendency of many white-collar workers to identify more with the management team. Correspondingly, there is the feeling that being in a union is somehow a step down in status since unions are generally associated with blue-collar work. Most important, however, is the unwillingness and inability of organized labor to tailor an aggressive organizing strategy suited to the particular needs of this expanding group of workers in the American labor force.

Until there is a recognition of the need to organize the unorganized white-collar worker, especially in the private sector (AFSCME has made inroads in the public sector), union membership rolls will continue to decline as the traditional blue-collar base gives way to an increasingly technological and service-oriented economy.

The New Worker

One out of every four workers in the United States is under thirty years of age.[16] Two out of three of these young workers have completed high school and nearly one out of seven has a college degree. By 1985, over 75 percent will have high-school diplomas and 20 percent will have finished college. They're smart, they think critically, and they have high expectations. Nevertheless most are channeled into dead-end jobs that could just as well be performed by a ten-year-old. It's no wonder that the Labor Department has warned that "the job mix and education mix are already out of balance." That imbalance is now spelling big trouble.[17]

For millions of young workers, job alienation is more than just a phrase out of a college sociology text. It's a living hell eight hours a day, week in and week out, without any hope of reprieve. For the statisticians it's a set of grim facts and figures. Alcoholism now claims millions of workers each year. Absenteeism costs management $3 billion in lost productivity, and mental-health problems have reached near-epidemic proportions among the working-class population.[18]

Organized labor has been slow to recognize the problems of the young worker and even slower to address them. For the worker of forty years ago who had little education and an empty stomach, the union demand for a living wage was enough to secure his loyalty. Today, the young worker has come to expect a decent wage. It makes no difference how much I. W. Abel and other labor leaders lament the fact that "the young workers don't appreciate what the unions have built." [19] Over and over again, like a broken record, comes the familiar phrase: "They didn't go through the Depression, they didn't know the rough times." What the aging leadership of organized labor fails to comprehend is that young workers are going through their own depression, their own rough times. Except that now it's not just a matter of low wages, although making ends meet is still a big problem. But it's more than that. It's about the nature of work itself. It's about a mind that has absorbed twelve or fourteen years of education and ends up tightening a bolt on a widget as it travels down a conveyer belt. It's about working in a deadly environment of toxic chemicals and fumes. It's about a system that technologizes and computerizes and robotizes every aspect of production, including the workers themselves.

While labor leaders give occasional lip service to these problems, usually in speeches before academic audiences, seldom do they make them an integral part of their contract negotiations. As a result, labor leaders are not only failing to win over new workers but are having an increasingly difficult time getting the respect of their own younger rank and file, a rank and file that is expressing very real needs that the leadership simply refuses to deal with substantively. Sam Geist, secretary-treasurer of a large UAW local in Detroit, complains that young workers "don't have the consideration toward the union like they did in the past. Talk union to them," says Geist, "and they'll say, 'What'd the union ever do for me?' They just take $8 or $9 and that's all." [20]

But instead of asking these young workers what kind of things they want of the union, the leadership continues to act as if they were representing the GI Joes of three decades ago. And when wildcat strikes increase and members continue to overturn contract recommendations, union honchos scratch their heads in disbelief as if to say that there's no way of pleasing these kids no matter how hard you try. Fred Di Sisto, a young sewage-treatment worker and shop steward of his local union in New York City, says the trouble is the unions just don't listen to what young workers are telling them.

You keep pounding your head against the wall and you don't get anywhere. It's the nature of the work ... they've made it so the guy doesn't worry or doesn't care or have pride in his work. The union just says look at what we've done for you. We've doubled your salary in ten years. They push for the money, money, money. And they seem to think that'll keep us happy....[21]

Angered by the antiwar protesters a few years ago, George Meany took time to respond to the young Fred Di Sistos of the country in a Labor Day address:

By what stretch of the imagination can you say that a twenty-year-old kid knows what is wrong with the world and what should be done about it. Especially when you see the behavior of the kids. There is more venereal disease among them than there was in my time, and it's going up all the time. There are more of them smoking pot, and to say that because they have long beards, and look dirty and smell dirty, that they are better qualified to run the world than the older generation, that to me is a lot of baloney.[22]

The Fred Di Sistos vs. the George Meanys. They both have union cards in their wallets, but they live in two completely different worlds. The gap between young workers and old leadership is now so great that one critic has aptly observed that "the union that once protected the men from the bosses has become the union that protects the bosses from the men." [23]

Women in the Work Force

"We have a message for George Meany. We have a message for Leonard Woodcock. We have a message for Frank Fitzsimmons. You can tell them we didn't come to Chicago to swap recipes." [24]

The gauntlet down, Myra Wofgang, vice president of the Hotel and Restaurant Workers of America, stepped off the podium amidst the stamping and clapping of over 3,000 women unionists who had come together in Chicago to launch the Coalition of Labor Union Women (CLUW). The coalition was formed in response to organized labor's long history of failure aggressively to organize women workers and its equally dismal neglect of women trade unionists.[25]

Today women make up over 43 percent of the total work force. Despite the fact that 33 million women are presently employed, only 4.2 million, or slightly more than 13 percent, are members of labor unions. Even more disquieting to the women who came together to form CLUW is the fact that while the number of women in the work force is increasing each year, the proportion who are union members is declining at an even faster rate than the decline of male union members.[26] One of the main reasons why such a small percentage of women are in unions is that they are concentrated in low-wage white-collar and service industries, which have traditionally been low-priority areas for union organizing drives.[27]

Another reason for such a small union membership among women is the sex discrimination within the leadership hierarchy of organized labor. There is not one woman representative on the thirty-three-person executive board of the AFL-CIO. When asked why, George Meany admitted that he "hadn't thought of that." After a pause he added, as an afterthought: "We have some very capable women in our unions but they only go up to a certain level. They don't seem to have any desire to go further." [28] That level Mr. Meany referred to is barely above ground zero. Today, not one of the 113 AFL-CIO unions has a female president and of the 173 officers of state AFL-CIO central bodies, women hold a grand total of eight positions. While women make up over half the membership of twenty-six unions, they only hold 4.7 percent of the leadership positions. In fact, of the 4,800 positions on union governing boards, only 350 are held by women.[29]

The exclusion of women from leadership positions within organized labor has been explained in a number of different ways. First, there is the time element involved. Married women in the work force, especially those with children, usually have a "job" waiting for them at home after work, and their husbands are not likely to fill in so they can attend to union business in the evenings. Also, there is the confidence factor. Being part of a male-dominated environment that actively discourages female participation presents a formidable barrier, one that often takes a tremendous amount of stamina and willpower to overcome. Then too, the women's movement has by and large not provided much backup support for union women, preferring instead to concentrate its energies on issues of more concern to professional women and middle-class housewives.[30]

Explanations aside, a study done several years ago found that 68 percent of the union women polled said they'd be willing to run for a top union office or support another woman for the position.[31] For these reasons labor-union women have come together to form CLUW "to strengthen the participation of women in union policymaking positions" and "to encourage unions to be more aggressive in efforts to organize unorganized women." The prevailing mood among CLUW supporters is that if women are to get "More!" as old Samuel Gompers was so fond of saying, then they'll have to organize together and demand more because the existing male leadership of organized labor has shown little inclination on its own to speed up the process of full participation for women in the American trade-union movement.[32]

Blacks and Unions

Just two years before the women trade unionists first met, another contingent of union members converged on Chicago to form its own coalition. In September 1972, some 1,200 black union officials and rank-and-file members met to form the Coalition of Black Trade Unionists. Like the women, their complaints centered around exclusion from policymaking roles within the trade-union community and long-standing union practices that discriminate against black workers both inside and outside the labor movement. Three years later, at the coalition's third annual convention in Detroit, the black assemblage, whose stated purpose from the beginning was to work for change from the inside, was forced to acknowledge its lack of progress. In a warning designed to put union leadership on notice, the coalition said it would no longer tolerate a second-class status within organized labor.[33]

According to William Lucy, the president of the coalition and the secretary-treasurer of AFSCME, even though blacks now make up over 15 percent of the total union membership, only two of the thirty-five members of the AFL-CIO Executive Council are black and they both represent tiny unions with little real clout. While black trade unionists remain somewhat cautious in their criticism of the labor movement, others outside organized labor have been much more vocal.[34]

The NAACP, for one, charges that "increasingly . . . big business and big labor [are] working together in a unified manner against the interests of . . . primarily the great mass of nonwhite workers, who are the most exploited and the most oppressed." [35]

While the interests of black workers are still getting short shrift in the house of labor, changes in the composition of the organized work force are likely to force an accommodation. With unskilled and semiskilled jobs in steel, auto, and other major union industries becoming increasingly the domain of black workers, black union leaders feel they will be in a better bargaining position in the future to push for changes that reflect the interest of black rank-and-file union members.

The New Unionism

Despite the internal warfare, the bureaucratization, the lack of organizing zeal, the insensitivity to young people, women, and blacks, and a host of other sins too long to enumerate, there is still only one labor movement in the United States. If all the labor unions in the country were to decide to fold up their tents and disband tomorrow, the vacuum would soon be filled by new organizations with many of the same characteristics, although perhaps without as many of the faults. The point is that if there were no unions, workers would merely reinvent them. Without some kind of strong institutional voice to represent them, millions of individual workers would be completely at the mercy of giant corporate bureaucracies whose only interest is to maximize profits by minimizing the cost of labor. With all their shortcomings, the unions are the only organized voice in America that working people have. All the Common Causes, Ralph Naders, and public-interest groups together might have a marginal impact in Washington, but they have even less influence when it comes to direct dealings with the nation's corporate giants. Their power is more illusory than real and more geared to the concerns of middle-class professionals than working-class America. When it comes down to fighting for such basic concerns as minimum-wage laws, expanded social security and health benefits, disability and unemployment compensation, organized labor has been and continues to be the only real mechanism available. For this reason, it is even more unfortunate that union leadership has become so ossified and lethargic over the years. Their insensitivity has not only cost them dearly in terms of loss of membership and clout, but has also cost the American worker dearly in terms of loss of economic rights and benefits.[36]

There are growing signs, however, that the intransigence of the present union hierarchy is about to be challenged. A new and more militant rank-and-file leadership is beginning to emerge in union locals and district councils across the country. Weaned on the antiwar and civil-rights politics of the 1960s, this new breed of union organizer more closely resembles the firebrand reformers of the 1930s. These young leaders are far from willing to forgive the aging patriarchs for their past transgressions. What's more, they fervently believe that from now on aggressive and militant action is the only true path to redemption. These are people who remain strong believers in the concept of unionism while skeptical and above all impatient with existing leadership. This new unionism is making itself heard throughout the labor movement. In New York City, Local 1199, a hospital workers' union, has been organizing poor black, brown, and white unskilled workers with a fervor reminiscent of the early CIO organizing drives. In Washington an incipient reform movement has captured the district offices of the powerful Teamsters Union. In Gary, Indiana, a young radical socialist, Ed Sadlowski, was elected president of the largest steel-union district in the United States and went on to challenge the establishment's hand-picked choice for president of the international union. Although he subsequently lost the national election in a long and bitter campaign that attracted national attention, the reform issues he raised are expected to increase the momentum for substantial internal policy changes within the United Steel Workers. In the United Mine Workers, a similar reform

movement, Miners for Democracy, was successful in dis-
lodging the corrupt Tony Boyle regime and replacing it with
a reform ticket headed by Arnold Miller. The process of insuring both union democracy and a responsive leadership is
still very much under way in the UMW. Miller himself has
now become a target of increasingly dissatisfied rank-and-
file miners. Contrary to many news reports, the monumental
1977–1978 coal strike was not the result of union anarchy
and disintegration. Rather, it reflected new strength and
unity at the local level as the union continued the reorgani-
zation begun by the Miners for Democracy.

At the same time, new unions (like District 65, which represent office workers) are beginning to make substantial inroads into the untapped reservoir of white-collar workers
who have, for so long, been largely ignored by the trade-
union establishment. Nowhere has the new unionism been
more successful than in organizing the millions of workers
now employed in the public sector. Over the past decade,
the American Federation of State, County and Municipal
Employees has been organizing the unorganized at such an
incredible rate that it has become one of the most powerful
unions in the labor community.[37]

While still in an embryonic state of development, the
new unionism represents the first stirrings of what many observers foresee as a major revolt-in-the-making within the
ranks of organized labor. Concern for democratizing the
union machinery, becoming more responsive to the needs of
the rank-and-file membership, and organizing the unorganized places these up-and-coming union dissidents at direct
loggerheads with many of the most powerful men in labor's
inner circle. In fact, the pressure they are bringing to bear
has already had a marked impact on some of the thinking
within that circle. New faces and even some old ones around
labor's executive table—men like Murray Finley, president
of the Amalgamated Clothing and Textile Workers, Robert
Georgine of the AFL-CIO Building and Construction Trades
Department, and William Winpisinger of the Machinists[38]—

are, for the first time, voicing concern over shrinking membership rolls, loss of clout in Congress, and a deteriorating public image and they've begun to do something about it. Georgine is finding ways to meet the growing challenges of nonunion building construction throughout the country. Finley is responsible for spearheading a drive to organize southern workers. Perhaps the most militant of the group is William Winpisinger, the new president of the giant Machinists Union. Winpisinger believes the labor community should lead a new left-wing movement to redistribute the wealth in America.[39]

However, even as the new unionism has begun to focus attention on the internal problems that have seriously weakened organized labor, an external threat, every bit as dangerous to the future survival of the union movement, has begun to pick up tremendous momentum. Beginning in the mid-1960s with the great wave of corporate mergers and the rise of the giant multinationals, the American business community embarked on a new concerted drive to rid their operations of union employees and effectively break the back of organized labor in this country. The basic premise behind this strategy was not only simple, but has proven to be quite effective in practice. The strategy can best be summed up in two words: "runaway shop."

Chapter 3: Uprooting Union Jobs

In the old days, if company bosses wanted to break the union, they'd hire Pinkertons or a local goon squad to come down to the factory gates and bust a few heads, usually those of the ringleaders. Today, things are done much more antiseptically and efficiently. The bosses merely hire a moving company to pack up the whole operation and ship it out lock, stock, and barrel to some other community—one far enough away so the union workers can't get to it. Or, in many other instances, they merely leave their older plants in the region, but locate all new facilities elsewhere. So effective is this new exodus strategy that it has succeeded in virtually decimating the membership rolls of entire unions and has seriously weakened the union movement itself within the span of just two decades.

Over 60 percent of all trade-union membership is concentrated in sixteen northeast and midwest states. It's no coincidence that these are the very states from which the multinationals are pulling up stakes and moving out. The extent of the exodus is phenomenal.

Between 1960 and 1975, manufacturing employment declined by 9.9 percent in the New England states and by 13.7 percent in the midwest states. In the Great Lakes states manufacturing jobs increased only by 3.2 percent while employment in the nation as a whole was growing by 8.3 percent.[1] Translated into numbers of jobs, the statistics are even more grim. In Massachusetts alone, the old textile, leather, and food-processing industries have lost more than 200,000 jobs in less than three decades.[2] In less than seven years, New York City has lost a whopping 647,000 jobs of different kinds and in less than five years, Philadelphia has lost nearly one-

fourth of all its factory jobs.[3] In city after city along an industrial corridor stretching from Back Bay to Chicago's lake
front, factories are being padlocked and boarded up as company after company takes off for new industrial parks both
overseas and in the nation's emerging Sunbelt. Whether relocating in Hong Kong or Roanoke Rapids, North Carolina,
the one common denominator that these new sites all have
in common is the absence of card-carrying union members.

Shifting Jobs Overseas

Some people might be surprised to learn that two out of
every ten GM vehicles and three out of every ten Chryslers
are made abroad, or that 95 percent of all radios and tape
recorders and 50 percent of all black-and-white television
sets are assembled in other countries. Smith-Corona makes
typewriters in Italy; NCR makes much of its equipment in
Taiwan and Japan; Sears, Roebuck makes shoes in Spain;
and H. J. Heinz now makes tomato paste in Portugal.[4]

Industry by industry, the pattern is the same. U.S. global
corporations are shifting their industrial base to other countries. For example, 33 percent of the total assets of the chemical industry, 33 percent of the pharmaceutical industry, 40
percent of the consumer-goods industry, and 75 percent of
the electrical industry are located abroad by American global
corporations.[5] The magnitude of this exodus is without paral-
lel. American companies established over 8,000 subsidiaries
abroad (mostly in manufacturing) between 1945 and 1970.[6]
The effect on domestic employment and particularly on union
jobs has been staggering. Between 1966 and 1970, U.S.-based
global firms had an employment growth rate abroad that was
3.5 times that of domestic employment.[7] Today one out of
every three employees of American global corporations is
located outside the United States. At the same time the
capacity of the manufacturing sector to provide jobs for
Americans is declining at a rate of six times that of the 1950s.[8]

Behind these abstract statistics lie thousands of individual
human tragedies brought about by exiting industries and

permanent unemployment: unpaid medical bills, foreclosures on mortgages, broken families. Former electrical workers in Cincinnati and Memphis have felt this firsthand. RCA closed down plants in both cities in 1971, forcing over 6,000 workers into unemployment lines. The company then moved its entire television production to Taiwan—where wages are 14¢ an hour and strikes are illegal.[9]

For the corporations who relocate abroad, the prospects of slave wages, no unions, and no strikes is a dream come true. For American unions it is a nightmare of frightening proportions, especially since there is virtually no effective international mechanism by which American unions can fight back. First, because the corporations often locate in right-wing countries where union activity is minimal or not tolerated at all, the prospect of any international cooperation between workers or joint collective-bargaining strategies is almost nil. Secondly, American trade-union leadership has steadfastly opposed international unionism since the early days of the Cold War when the AFL split from the United World Federation of Trade Unions (WFTU). While the AFL-CIO later helped form a counterfederation, the International Confederation of Free Trade Unions (ICFTU), it later broke from it as well when the new federation moved to unify with the older WFTU. As long as this kind of go-it-alone mentality permeates the top echelons of the American labor establishment, multinational corporations will continue to enjoy a union-free ride abroad, and American trade unionists whose jobs are displaced throughout the northern industrial states will continue to join the ranks of the unemployed.[10]

Shifting Jobs South

Between 1970 and 1975, more than 2.5 million Northerners packed up their bags and headed for the Sunbelt.[11] They did so partly because that's where the corporations are relocating their facilities and that's where the jobs are. While the Midwest and Northeast have been losing jobs left and right since 1960, manufacturing jobs in the Southeast have risen by 43.3 percent, and in the Southwest by 67 percent in the same period.[12] The Sunbelt is no longer just a string of little redneck gas stations along Route 1 in Georgia, tobacco patches in the Carolinas, or cattle grazing just outside town in El Paso. The Sunbelt is now one big business boomtown. In fact, manufacturing jobs in the South now outnumber those in the Northeast.[13] And the new neighbors in towns like Winston-Salem, Waco, and Jacksonville, the multinationals, are putting out the welcome mat. The only condition for becoming a part of this grand new corporate South is an antiunion loyalty pledge. In other words, corporations are moving south for the same reason they are moving abroad: no unions, no strikes, and cheap wages. They mean to keep it that way.

"The South is just waiting to be organized." So said Samuel Gompers, the founder of the AFL, in 1898.[14] Sam would still be just as right if he said that today. Only 13 percent of southern workers belong to labor unions as opposed to a national average of 25 percent. In North Carolina, the most heavily industrialized state in the South, only 6.9 percent of the work force is organized as compared to 38 percent in New York. Moreover, the unions' share of the southern work force is continuing to shrink. According to the Bureau of Labor Statistics, unions lost ground in eight of eleven states of the South between 1964 and 1974.[15]

The absence of a strong labor movement is reflected in the low wage scales of the region. In 1970 wages in the South were 20 percent lower than the national average.[16] While the average hourly wage for production workers outside the South was $4.40 in 1974, it was only $3.60 in the Confederacy.[17]

Nowadays even such giants as GM, which has long pursued a semicooperative union policy in its northern plants, are now opening up new divisions in the South and fiercely resisting union organizing. For example, in its Clinton, Mississippi, plant, GM has taken a hard line against UAW attempts to organize the operation. Although corporate vice-

president George Morris in Detroit terms charges of antiunion activities as "nonsense," Leonard Woodcock, former
president of the UAW, accused GM of having developed a
"Southern strategy" to keep unions out and wages down.
Irving Bluestone goes further and suggests that "GM may be
hoping to eventually shift operations to the South and build
a competitive factor on the same basis multinationals do in
low wage countries." It is not hard to understand why GM
and other firms are interested in building a nonunion operation in the Sunbelt; the average hourly wage of a GM worker
in the nonunion Clinton plant is $1.05 an hour less than a
similar worker's in its Packard Electric Division in Warren,
Ohio. That adds up to a $2 million savings for one company
in just one plant.[18]

GM and other large corporate employers aren't alone in
their antiunion bias. If there is one thing Southern hospitality
has never really warmed to, it's union organizing. A key feature in keeping unions out of the South has been the decision
to locate plants in small rural towns and away from the big
cities. In fact, while manufacturing jobs increased by 43.7
percent in the metropolitan areas of the South in the 1960s,
they increased 61 percent in the rural counties fifty miles or
more from the metropolitan areas. Being the largest employer in a small town gives the company a tremendous
amount of economic and political power; the kind which is
hard, if not impossible, to buck.[19]

Finally, nothing is more important to maintaining a nonunion South than the so-called right-to-work laws which
which have been passed in every single state in the Sunbelt.

Right-to-Work Laws and the South

"What's all this that's in the paper about the open shop?"
asked Mr. Hennessy.

"Why, don't you know?" replied Mr. Dooley. "Really, I'm
surprised at your ignorance, Hennessy. What is the open
shop? Sir, 'tis where they keep the doors open to accommo-

date the constant stream of men comin' in t' take jobs cheaper than the men what has the jobs. 'Tis like this, Hennessy: suppose one of these free born citizens is working in an open shop for the princely wages of one large iron dollar a day. Along comes another son-of-a-gun and he sez t' the boss, 'I think I could handle the job nicely for ninety cents.' 'Sur,' sez the boss and the one dollar man gets the merry jinglin' can and goes out in the crool world t' exercise his inalienable rights as a free born American citizen an' scab on some other poor devil. And so it goes on, Hennessy. An' who gets the benefit? True, it saves the boss money, but he doesn't care no more for money than he does for his right eye. It's all principle with him. He hates to see men robbed of their independence. They must have their independence regardless of anything else."

"But," says Hennessy, "these open shops you mention say they are for the unions if properly conducted."

"Sure," says Dooley, "if properly conducted—and how would they have them conducted? No strikes, no dues, no contracts, hardly any wages and damned few members." [20]

Labor's right to organize, strike, and close a shop was engraved into the law with the passage of the Wagner Act in 1935. Twelve years later, however, a Republican Congress rammed through legislation—the Taft-Hartley Act—over President Truman's veto that had the effect of seriously weakening portions of the earlier legislation.[21] Among other provisions in the new act was Section 14(b), which allowed individual states to circumvent federal statutes with the enactment of so-called right-to-work laws. As Dooley explained to Hennessy, these right-to-work laws, which are now in effect in twenty states, mainly in the Sunbelt region, make the closed union shop (compulsory union membership) illegal—even if a majority of the work force votes for a union to bargain for it. As a result, even in those plants where the unions have won a certification election, they are often decertified

shortly thereafter, as management replaces union employees
with nonunion scabs who then vote the union out. Even if
the workers don't decertify the union, since paying union
dues is voluntary, many workers will let the union bargain
better pay and other benefits for them but then refuse to
contribute to the union—thus getting a free ride at the
union's expense. More often, however, right-to-work laws are
an effective barrier against unions getting any kind of an
organizing foothold in the first place.[22]

The National Right-to-Work Committee—the twenty-
three-year-old antiunion organization that now boasts a
multi-million dollar budget and a staff of nearly a hundred—
claims that right-to-work laws have been enacted to uphold
the sacred principle that each worker should have the right
to choose. Cesar Chavez and Bayard Rustin, in their report
on right-to-work laws, come to a different conclusion about
what rights are involved:

As the *evidence* shows, contrary to guaranteeing the right to
work, what these laws do is to guarantee the right to work
long hours, the right to discriminate, the right to pay sub-
standard wages, and the right to destroy organized unionism.[23]

The evidence Chavez and Rustin refer to is underscored
by a study done for the state of North Carolina in 1975. According to the report, the two most important factors in
accounting for the depressed wages in the state, and the
region as a whole, are right-to-work laws and the low degree
of unionization of workers.[24]

In short, then, right-to-work laws mean keeping the
unions weak or out. And keeping the unions weak or out
means employers are able to get away with paying lower
wages for their workers. All in all, right-to-work laws are an
ideal lure for those northern companies who are looking for
a way to kiss the unions good-bye.

Chapter 4: Labor's Chief Weapons

The union movement owes its success over the years to two related phenomena. First, through the use of the strike, unions have been able to win recognition from the employers as the exclusive bargaining agent for the workers. Secondly, by amassing their power as the bargaining representatives for the workers, unions have been able to transport their clout into the political arena. The passage of federal legislation, especially the Wagner Act, has served to legitimize the right of the trade-union movement to act on behalf of the American worker.

The Strike and the Law! Organized labor's major weapons for over forty years are, in its most critical hour, becoming increasingly ineffective as a means of advancing the interests of unionism in America.

The Strike

"Show me a country in which there are no strikes and I'll show you a country in which there is no liberty." [1] Seventy years after Samuel Gompers uttered that historic phrase, his contemporary, George Meany, in an interview with the press, stated his conviction that the day of the strike is ending. Mr. Meany hopes to substitute binding arbitration instead. The United Steel Workers, in fact, have already gone so far as to sign a contract with the steel industry which prohibits industrywide steel strikes. Other unions are expected to follow suit. [2]

What has happened to undermine labor's chief weapon? First, says Kevin Kistler, field representative for the AFL-CIO organizing department, "with the increasing conglomerate picture, it's more difficult to hurt an employer who has places all over the country and the world. He can shift work, he can close down one plant, but has dozens more to turn to." [3] Then too, there is the effect that sophisticated technology has. Henry Dillon, vice-president of the Graphic Arts Industrial Union, explains that in the old days a strike could effectively close a plant. With production shutdown, employers would eventually have to come to some kind of agreement. Today, says Dillon, "technological developments have changed all that. It's much easier to operate, to some degree, in the face of a strike these days." [4] While there are still some industries that can be effectively shut down by a strike, like steel, coal, and auto, there are others, like utilities, gas, chemical, oil refining, telephone, and electronics, where the technology is so advanced that a handful of supervisory personnel can virtually maintain the operation, even if the workers stay out on strike indefinitely.

Advanced technology and the ability of multinationals to shift production to some other location at a moment's notice are not the only factors undermining the strike as an effective weapon. Public opinion has also had an impact. People have come to see the strike as a disruptive force, one that threatens to hurt the company and perhaps their own jobs. This fear of the secondary effect of the strike is very real in the minds of many Americans despite the fact that total working time lost due to strikes during 1976 amounted to a minute .19 percent.[5] Underlying this public psychology is the notion that strikes usually only help the greedy self-serving interests of labor unions. This antistrike mood has been fueled in recent years by public employee strikes. People don't like it when sanitation workers, police, and teachers go out on strike. It's not only disruptive to their daily lives, but costly because it's their tax dollars, they figure, that will be bargained away in any settlement.

This antistrike, antiunion psychology has its effect on the picket line. Years ago, people were more inclined to honor a picket line. It was considered a matter of principle, of solidarity, of empathy with the plight of those on strike. Honoring a picket line even became the chic thing to do among America's salon set. In the old days the popular definition of a scab went something like this:

After God had finished the rattlesnake, the toad and the vampire, he had some awful substance left with which he made a scab.... Esau was a traitor to himself; Judas was a traitor to his God; Benedict Arnold was a traitor to his country; a scab is a traitor to his God, his country, his family and his class.[6]

A lot of people don't see it that way anymore. In their view, the union is just another special interest group, often making unjustified demands. Crossing the picket line, then, is no longer a moral decision. Sometimes it's even done with relish, as if to say "Screw the union bosses." Often it's done just because individuals need a job and figure every worker's got to look out for number one first.[7]

The Law

When he walks into a corporate boardroom, all eyes are glued on his every move, his slightest gesture. He is the messenger, and the reverence which he is shown attests to the great height which only he has reached. The powerful study his countenance. He has the answer. Listen carefully, please, to what he has to say.

All [young people] know about unions is the student unions, or that the union was the people who made their jeans. So you've got to get your message out first. People are very impressionable then.... [Unions] think we're standing there teaching people to cheat, steal, shaft the people and all that stuff and I'm not doing that. I'm just saying that if you decide you're going to run nonunion, here's how you do it.[8]

Meet Charlie Hughes. He's forty-three and a psychologist by training. Mr. Hughes is the Muhammad Ali of a new profession called labor/management consultants: a collage of lawyers, advertising men, public relations experts, and psychologists whose mission is to manipulate human psychology and the law to keep unions out, or if already in, to

drive them out. They are so good at what they do that the
AFL-CIO Executive Council has declared: "Today's union
busters wear business suits and carry attaché cases. Sharp
lawyers and Madison Avenue propagandists have carefully
calculated devices to destroy, without leaving any visible
bruises, the desire of workers to organize." [9]

For Kevin Kistler, the AFL-CIO organizer, the emergence of the labor/management consultants is fast becoming
the major roadblock to union organizing efforts. "They've
become experts in legal and illegal ways of thwarting the
rights of the workers to organize. Charlie Hughes is the best
but there's any number of them." [10]

Again Mr. Hughes: first change the job names. "Workers like it because it sounds better in bars. Put out some titles
that have some good strokes." In other words, if you have an
oil-tank cleaner, make him a petrochemical technician instead. If you want to get a little more variation of the theme,
lectures Hughes, then move to "multi-crafting," which elim-
inates all craft titles once and for all. No more carpenters,
painters, or electricians; instead teach each of them all three
tasks, then call them technician, grade one, technician, grade
two, etc. Hughes guarantees that his multi-crafting tech-
nique will drive the unions up the wall. "They want to organize your plumbers and they can't find any." [11]

The name of the game is psychological warfare, and the
labor/management consultants have it down to a science.
For example, if you want to impress your workers with the
financial burden they'll incur by joining the union, then issue
their weekly paychecks for $6 less than usual. Take the extra
$6 and put it in cash in a little envelope marked union dues
on it. Then hand both to them at the same time. [12]

The labor/management consultants have concocted an
elaborate bag of tricks specifically designed to thwart the
union, ranging from personalized letter campaigns to workers' families to heart-to-heart chats and "touchy-feely" en-
counter-group sessions, with top management participating
right alongside the workers.

Of all the weapons at their disposal, the most effective in the labor/management consultants' arsenal is the outright manipulation of the law and particularly the National Labor Relations Act. According to Alan Kistler, director of the AFL-CIO organizing department, "the upshot of the increasing use of labor/management consultants by companies with union problems is a phenomenal increase in what are known in the trade as 8A3 violations (cases where employees involved in union organizing are discharged unfairly)." [13] In the past fifteen years, the number of charges of such violations has increased by two and a half times, from 6,240 cases in 1961 to 15,090 in 1976. In the past year alone, over 7,000 workers received back-pay awards from the NLRB for illegal employer discrimination, such as firing, passing over for promotion and downgrading.[14] As far as the company is concerned, it's a cheap price to pay to get union troublemakers out of their plants—a lot cheaper than having to pay union wages, which might be the result if ringleaders were allowed to stay in the plant to organize their fellow employees.

Another area where labor/management consultants have been extremely effective is in delaying the collective-bargaining process once the union wins a certifying election. Refusal-to-bargain charges—known as surface bargaining—have skyrocketed at the NLRB. Again, even if found guilty of such charges, the fines mean nothing to management, especially if, through the delaying process, they have been able to rid themselves of the union. A study conducted by the Industrial Union Division of the AFL-CIO shows exactly how effective surface bargaining and lengthy NLRB and court procedures can be. In more than one out of every five cases in which the union won a certification election in 1970, the union did not obtain a contract. Of those that did, one out of six no longer had a contract by 1975. "In other words," according to the AFL-CIO, "five years after certification, one third of the certified units had become nonunion." [15]

While labor/management consultants can take a good deal of credit for breaking union organizing drives, there are also other factors which seriously hamper labor's efforts. None is more important than the psychology of unemployment. "The company that can take advantage of the unemployment situation can, in almost any instance, beat a union," says Al Bilik, organizing director for the International Union of Electrical Workers. When jobs are scarce, workers are understandably unwilling to jeopardize their own security by becoming involved with a union organizing drive. That's why full employment has been a number-one priority on labor's agenda for over three decades. Says Bilik: "There's no question that when we have a relatively high level of employment, that's the time when organizing has been most effective." [16] With unemployment continuing to hover at near 8 percent nationally and over 10 percent in many northern states, organized labor is finding it increasingly difficult to convince workers to risk their jobs by fighting for union shops.

In surveying the decline of organized labor in America, it becomes clear that the critical problems facing the trade-union movement fall into one of two categories. First, there are the problems that the unions have in part created for themselves because of their own misguided policies; for example, their neglect and, in some cases, outright hostility toward organizing certain unorganized groups within the labor force, like women, blacks, white-collar workers, and youth. Second, there are the problems created for unions by the corporations; the runaway shops and capital, and the manipulations (and violations) of the law, all are part of a new concerted drive by the business community to destroy organized labor in this country.

The first set of problems is something that the labor community can begin doing something about on its own. To a large extent, their solution will depend on the emergence of a new leadership that is sensitive to the needs of these unorganized constituencies and anxious to expand the base of organized labor support. That leadership is just now beginning to emerge. The second set of problems, however, requires a frontal attack on the business community itself. Organized labor has finally started that attack with a two-pronged offensive which it hopes will neutralize the runaway shop strategy and eliminate the legal loopholes which have allowed the business community to maneuver around, and on occasion to violate, existing labor laws. The unions are concentrating their efforts on a nationwide boycott campaign against the South's leading antiunion employer, J. P. Stevens, and on the effectiveness of major labor reform legislation. Unfortunately, both strategies play more to labor's present weaknesses than its strengths. And even if the unions are completely successful on both fronts, it is doubtful that these victories, in and of themselves, will provide organized labor with the openings it desperately needs to survive and expand its base. A detailed examination of these two major union offensives reveals some of the inherent problems in labor's strategy.

Chapter 5: Organized Labor's Strategy

The J. P. Stevens Boycott

One old-timer likes to tell the story about the great strike of 1929. The whole thing took place in the sleepy little town of Marion, North Carolina. One afternoon angry workers walked off their jobs in the textile mill there to protest an order by the boss extending the twelve-hour workday by another twenty minutes. Picket lines formed. The militia was brought in and finally violence erupted when the sheriff and his men threw tear-gas bombs into a crowd of peaceful picketers. As the strikers began to run from the choking fumes, the police opened fire. Six strikers were killed and twenty-five wounded—all shot in the back, according to eyewitnesses.

At the mass funeral a few days later, an old mountain preacher presided:

"Oh Lord, Jesus Christ. Here are men in their coffins, blood of my blood, bone of my bone.

"I trust, Oh God, that these friends will go to a better place than this mill village or any other place in Carolina.

"Dear God, what would Jesus do if he were to come to Carolina?"

The police who murdered the protesters were tried and found not guilty. Several of the ringleaders of the strike were sentenced to six months of hard labor on a Carolina chain gang.[1]

The old storyteller lives in Roanoke Rapids, North Carolina, and these days it seems that he's never without an audience eager to hear about these ancient labor battles. Except this time they're not listening to be entertained, but to learn something; something about unions and organizing and bosses. They are workers at the J. P. Stevens mill, and they've joined the union. What makes that special is that they and 3,000 other workers at the Roanoke plant are the only Stevens workers anywhere in the South who are unionized. That singular act has turned this mill town into a battleground. Opposing forces have taken up their positions on opposite ends of Main Street, in two little storefronts. On one side is the Amalgamated Clothing and Textile Workers Union of America and on the other the antiunion J. P. Stevens Employees' Education Committee. Unlike neighboring Marion forty-eight years ago, the weapons being used in Roanoke are ideological; it is a battle of words, of persuasion, and of legal maneuvers. It's the union vs. J. P. Stevens, and the issue has completely polarized this tiny textile town.[2]

"We didn't even know we had any rights before the union came," says Carolyn Brown, a twenty-nine-year-old quiller.

"We always worked hard and the company knows that and they appreciate that. We don't want nobody to give nothing to us, and that includes the union," says Jack Watkins, a thirty-five-year-old machinist. . . .[3]

The arguments on both sides are emotional and intense. And since J. P. Stevens is the largest employer for a hundred miles around, everyone considers that they have a personal stake in the outcome. "I believe it is incumbent on a man of God to speak out," says Reverend Marvin Faile, minister of the First Baptist Church, "but Stevens is another matter. I know of no situation where people were treated unfairly." Ethel Woodruff, who's worked in the mill for over twenty years, has a very different story to tell:

Some days I was so tired when I got to the door that I thought my heart would stop. You didn't get paid when your machine stopped. So, instead of taking time off for lunch, you'd just pick up your sandwich and lay it down while you were working. Most of the time it would get so much lint on it, it would end up in the trash can.[4]

For this, Mrs. Woodruff was paid $137 per week. When she retired last year after two decades of service, she received a lump sum of $1,153 to live on for the remainder of her life.

Mrs. Woodruff's story is not unique. She is one of nearly 600,000 textile workers who suffer the distinction of being the lowest-paid industrial workers in the country. Hourly wages in southern textile mills average around $3.46 an hour, compared with $6.73 in basic steel. Her employer, J. P. Stevens, is the second-largest textile firm in the United States (Burlington Industries is first), and as far as organized labor is concerned it is the most important symbol of antiunionism in America today.[5]

In the summer of 1976, the ACTWU announced a nation-wide boycott of J. P. Stevens products and pledged $1.5 million a year for the next ten years in a campaign to pressure the company to accept unionization. The boycott, which labor leaders contend will be the largest in the history of America, has the all-out support of the AFL-CIO, which sees it as the key to its long-range goal of unionizing the South. Says James Sala, director of the southern region for the AFL-CIO: "As long as we've got J. P. Stevens we'll never really succeed in organizing the South, not because of textiles but because of the example it sets for antiunion resistance." That example is legend.[6]

Stevens began as a small family-owned textile firm in New England in 1813. After World War II it merged ten companies and began shifting its plants down South, where labor was cheaper and nonunionized. Other textile plants then followed the J. P. Stevens lead, closing down mills in Fall River, New Bedford, Lowell, Lawrence and elsewhere, and moving south to avoid having to pay for union labor. The concept of the runaway shop, which J. P. Stevens helped to popularize, has, in just twenty-five years, resulted in the wholesale displacement of some 372,000 textile workers and the collapse of small mill towns throughout New England and the Mid-Atlantic states.[7]

Today southern mills employ 75 percent of the country's textile workers and have become the South's number-one industrial employers. Only 10 percent of all southern textile workers are unionized, making it the least-organized major industry in the United States. J. P. Stevens, still a front-runner in the industry, now claims sales of $1.4 billion and assets of $825 million. It employs over 46,000 people.[8]

J. P. Stevens has also set the tone for working conditions in southern textile plants. Its employees receive wages that are 31 percent below the average received by other factory workers across the country. Its facilities are so unsafe, according to inspectors from the North Carolina Department of Labor, that one out of three workers is likely to develop a disabling respiratory disease known as brown lung (from illegally high concentrations of cotton dust) and half are likely to suffer hearing losses from the illegally high noise levels in the plants.[9]

Given J. P. Stevens's track record, the ACTWU and the rest of labor believe they can turn the nationwide boycott into a moral crusade, enlisting the support of millions of Americans who are concerned with the principles of elementary justice. "We look at this as not just a question of unionization but of the basic principles of this country. [It is] a struggle for industrial democracy, a fulfillment of the civil rights revolution, a moral issue," says Jacob Sheinkman, secretary-treasurer of the textile workers union.[10]

To show they mean business, the union and some 3,000 supporters took their boycott crusade right into the annual meeting of the J. P. Stevens stockholders, at Stevens Tower in New York City in 1977. In front were such notables as Coretta King and Paul O'Dwyer, president of the City Council of New York. The meeting quickly turned into a combination debate and shouting match with James D. Finley, chairman of the board of Stevens, claiming that the boycott would have "no discernible effect" on the company and would "only hurt the people who work at Stevens." In response, William M. DuChassi, executive vice-president of the ACTWU, vowed: "If it takes ten, fifteen, or twenty years, J. P. Stevens is going to be made to live up to the law." [11]

The question of which side will eventually win is of equal concern to the American business community and to the labor movement. If J. P. Stevens falls, then labor is in a better position to fulfill its goal of organizing the Sunbelt. The business community is well aware of what's at stake and is likely to do all it can to support Stevens in its campaign to keep the union out. In the final analysis, the success or failure of the boycott campaign will rest more on the effectiveness of the strategy employed by the unions than with the reaction by J. P. Stevens. To bring J. P. Stevens down will be no easy matter. To mobilize the public behind the boycott will be extremely difficult.

First, unlike the lettuce and grape boycotts, where the United Farm Workers Union could claim the loyal support of the workers themselves, the ACTWU only represents 3,000 of the 46,000 employees at J. P. Stevens. The company is already taking advantage of this fact in its public-relations program by asserting that big unions are attempting to force unionization on unwilling employees through the boycott. To back up its claims it points to the fact that workers have voted against union representation in thirteen of the fourteen elections held in J. P. Stevens plants since 1963. Of course it conveniently omits the fact that the company has been charged with repeated violations of labor law and National Labor Relations Board (NLRB) orders, for illegally interfering in those elections, for coercing workers and for firing prounion sympathizers. Nevertheless, for public-relations purposes this will be a strong card to play in neutralizing public opinion or in even turning it against the boycott altogether.

At the same time, Stevens is telling its workers that the boycott being waged by "outside union agitators," if effective, will result in a curtailment of operations and the loss of thousands of jobs. Already such dire warnings have spurred the development of the company-sponsored Employees' Education Committee, whose purpose is to spread the warning

among the workers in an attempt to isolate further any pros-
pective prounion sympathizers.[12]

Then there is the all-important question of whether the
nationwide boycott will have any effect at all on company
sales. Says one labor analyst: "I have some real doubts about
whether *any* nationwide boycotts have any effect on sales.
The good union man may insist on another product, but I'm
not sure there are many like him in the consuming public." [13]

The sex appeal of the product is another major factor.
When people were asked not to eat grapes on Thanksgiving
to help support the struggle of impoverished Chicano farm
workers, it touched an emotional chord, especially within the
liberal community. Most products just don't conjure up the
same kind of image identification. *Industry Week*, the voice
for management, put the problem in perspective: "The
chances of the general public becoming excited enough
about the Monroe shock absorber or the Dal-Tex optical
wear boycotts to crawl under the family auto or to contest an
optician's choice of glass frames are considerably slim." With
Stevens draperies, yarns, and fabrics, a similar problem
exists.[14]

One of the most important stumbling blocks facing the
campaign is the confusing array of brand names and private
labels under which J. P. Stevens products are sold. The list is
almost endless: Hockanum, Boldeena, Wash Ease, Wool
Press, Worumbo, Forstmann, Appleton, Twist Twill, Wefta-
matic, 20 Below, Gesture, Coachman, Lady Consort, Carou-
sel, Stevetex, Beauti-Blend, and dozens more. The union is
attempting to solve the problem by printing up wallet-sized
cards listing all the names, but the chances that the average
consumer will take the time to check the entire list every
time he or she buys any item made from textiles is sheer
wishful thinking.[15] Mr. James Finley, chairman of Stevens,
understands this very well. Speaking to some Wall Street
analysts, he said that there was little reason to believe the
boycott would work "because of the diversity of the com-

pany's product mix, the nonidentifiable nature of a large portion of our goods and the wide geographic distribution of our customers." [16] What Mr. Finley might have added is that even if the consumer boycott were to make some appreciable dent, it would only have an effect on about 33 percent of the company's business which is oriented to the consumer market. Over 48 percent of Stevens sales are directly to apparel makers and another 18 percent are for industrial and sporting use. Legally, the ACTWU cannot "attempt to force these manufacturers to stop using Stevens fabrics." [17]

The hard truth is that Stevens is not likely to be easily influenced by the union's boycott pressure, especially when its record shows that it has not even been influenced by the law and the courts. In the last twenty-two years, Stevens has been cited fifteen times by the NLRB for violating labor law. Among the many charges were bad faith bargaining, illegal firing of employees for union activities, and coercing workers. Other charges of which it has been found guilty by the courts include tax fraud, price fixing, wiretapping, violation of health and safety standards, and racial discrimination.[18] The company's past and present performance led Boyd Leedon, former chairman of the NLRB, to remark: "J. P. Stevens is so out of tune with a humane, civilized approach to industrial relations that it should shock even those least sensitive to honor, justice, and decent treatment." [19] J. P. Stevens is not, then, the kind of firm to lie down and roll over in response to union pressures.

Some boycott leaders privately admit they are worried about their present campaign strategy. In fact, as an alternative strategy, there has been a move to apply pressure on the financial community to withhold loans from Stevens. Union supporters have organized letter-writing campaigns and have overwhelmed the annual shareholders meetings of several companies that have ties with Stevens through loans or interlocking directors. This strategy has already been successful in forcing two J. P. Stevens directors off the Manufacturers Hanover Trust board. But it remains to be seen whether this new approach will be able to effectively isolate Stevens from the rest of the corporate community and deprive it of loans and credit from the major financial institutions.[20]

As it stands, George Meany and his colleagues at the AFL-CIO have at least given their blessing to a massive boycott drive designed to break Stevens and open up the South to organized labor. While no one is expecting too much more from the top leadership in light of their past record of organizing the unorganized, some of the up-and-coming new presidents of large industrial unions are sincerely and energetically behind this campaign, so much so that they have publicly gone out on a limb by placing much importance on the success of the boycott for the future of organized labor. Still, this is not the first time that labor has mounted an all-out campaign to open the South. A similar effort by the CIO in the late 40s flopped completely, as did another $13 million campaign by the Industrial Union Department of the AFL-CIO in the 60s, which only netted an embarrassing 93,000 new members.[21] This time prospects look equally dim—that is, if labor continues to hold to the notion of an orthodox consumer boycott against Stevens as the opening wedge. Of course, union leaders committed to this effort are hoping that the second half of their strategy, the passage of new labor-reform legislation in Congress, will provide the cutting edge which will allow this southern strategy really to take off. On this count, they are once again on very shaky ground in their calculations.

Labor-Reform Legislation in Congress

In February 1977, George Meany and the executive council of the AFL-CIO, at their mid-winter meeting in Florida, announced plans to launch an unprecedented $800,000 lobbying campaign to win approval of sweeping changes in the nation's labor laws. The intent behind the proposed changes is to help improve organizing efforts for the unions. In announcing their plans, Mr. Meany remarked that organizing is "a major responsibility and a continuing obligation" of the federation.[22] This is certainly a far different George Meany from the one who told *U.S. News & World Report*, just a few years earlier, that he didn't care if union membership was growing or not.

What accounts for the metamorphosis is the emergence of some new faces in and around the executive council of the AFL-CIO. Some of these up-and-coming labor leaders, who have already been mentioned, have been putting pressure on Meany and some of the other patriarchs to begin an all-out organizing offensive before it's too late. The February announcement was an indication that they're having some impact within the labor leadership.

There are several important features contained in the overall labor-reform proposals drawn up by the AFL-CIO. Some of these proposals have already been submittted to Congress, while others are not expected to come up for consideration until later. The most important, as far as the unions are concerned, is the proposal calling for a speed-up in representation elections. A provision in the current NLRB law allows companies to delay elections for a year or more with administrative and court challenges. This tactic has been used repeatedly and with a great deal of success, especially by southern employers. Long delays between the filing of petitions and the actual election work to the disadvantage of the union; organizing momentum is lost, and prounion workers often become dispirited and divided. Under labor's new proposal, representation elections would have to take place within fifteen to seventy-five days of the time a petition was signed.

Related to the problem of election delays has been the widespread practice, again mostly among southern companies, of illegal discharges of prounion organizers and supporters during the long delays before an election is held. Even when workers decide to challenge such dismissals, it often takes two or three more years before the courts make a ruling and, in the meantime, employers are able to eliminate prounion workers during the crucial period leading up to the union election. The new labor-reform proposal calls for the NLRB to seek preliminary injunctions against such illegal labor practices, so that workers will be immediately reinstated. If employees can return to work quickly, the unions believe, it will have an important psychological effect on the outcome of the election, by showing workers that the law will protect them from the employer. Another corresponding proposal calls for double back-pay rewards for workers who have been illegally discharged for union activity. Under the current laws the penalty amounts only to the actual wages lost during the dismissal period. The unions argue that such penalties aren't severe enough to deter management from such firings.

Other proposals call for the expansion of the NLRB board from five to seven members in order to streamline case rulings, and the denial of federal contracts to firms that violate NLRB orders.[23]

The original labor-reform proposals contained several other crucial provisions. All of them were axed within the first 120 days of the Carter Administration. On March 23, 1977, the House voted 217 to 205 to defeat the common situs picketing bill, which would allow a single union to picket an entire construction project. Some labor leaders saw this bill as crucial in their struggle to challenge the rising number of nonunion construction companies across the country.[24] The defeat was only the first of many. Labor has asked for a boost of the federal minimum wage from $2.30 to $3.00. The Carter Administration refused to go along and substituted a mere 35-cent rise instead. Labor wanted to automatically certify a union as the legal bargaining agent when 55 percent of the workers in a plant signed valid union authorization cards. Again, the administration said no. Finally, labor wanted section 14(b) of the Taft-Hartley Act to be repealed by Congress (the provision which allows states to pass right-to-work laws) but quietly dropped the demand when even their supporters on Capitol Hill refused to introduce the proposition.[25]

These initial defeats have had a sobering effect on the labor leadership. Said William Winpisinger of the International Association of Machinists: "The politicians aren't doing a thing for us right now because they perceive the same weakness everybody else does." [26] Fearing that the remainder of their reform proposals will be either watered down, whittled away, or simply defeated, an AFL-CIO spokesman, Thomas R. Donahue, sounded the official alarm in June 1977. "The question of . . . the maintenance of a strong labor movement hangs in the balance, and so we'd best do something about our labor laws." [27]

That something Donahue alluded to is a dramatic shift in labor strategy. In the past the AFL-CIO relied almost exclusively on lobbying activity on Capitol Hill in order to get favorable legislation passed. Now, realizing that it no longer enjoys the clout it once had in the halls of Congress, labor has had to shift focus to a strategy designed to win wide support for its programs among the general public. "This has got a lot of people nervous here," said Doris Hardesty, of the AFL-CIO Labor Law Task Force. "That's not the way we've done things in the past." [28] It's not hard to understand why the unions have the jitters. The thought of appealing directly to a public that has become openly hostile to labor leadership is not very comforting. Nonetheless, union organizers hope to convince the American people that their legislative proposals represent not only the interests of organized labor but of all working Americans as well. To accomplish this task, the federation has set up a special task force to mount a grass-roots organizing drive in every congressional district.[29]

Organized labor's success, then, will depend on whether or not it is able to enlist the active support of the general public. That support, according to the public-opinion polls and political observers, cannot be relied on at this moment in time. A 1977 Harris poll is illustrative. It found that, by a wide majority, the public believes that union leaders have become too arrogant and no longer represent the workers in their unions. More important, at a time when organized labor is trying to expand its membership and influence in the South through strategy and legislation, a majority of the public, 63 percent, believes that "unions have already become too powerful and should be restricted in the abuse of their power by law." Still, some of the findings of the Harris poll offer a ray of hope to union strategists. A majority of the public, though openly hostile to union leadership and its perceived power, still believes unions are necessary and offer the only real protection available for securing the rights of working Americans. Union leaders hope to draw on this residual goodwill in mobilizing popular support behind both the reform legislation and the Stevens boycott.[30]

In order to turn the tables and secure public support, the unions will first have to win over the liberal community, and once again, their chances are not good. "Where was labor when blacks were marching on Selma?" "Where were the unions when young people on the campuses were protesting the war in Vietnam?" "Where was labor when women were fighting to pass the ERA?" To many in the liberal community who pleaded with the union leadership aggressively to take part in the civil rights, antiwar, and women's rights movements, union pleas for help now deserve little if any attention. John Fischer, former editor of *Harper's*, a leading liberal magazine, voices the feelings that many liberals harbor about organized labor:

To us it seemed self-evident that the quickest route to universal reform was to muster all the unorganized workers into strong unions. They would then form the backbone of a liberal movement. . . . Instead of becoming the shock troops of liberalism, the unions (with a very few exceptions) quickly petrified into lumps of reaction and special privilege.[31]

Even as the unions feebly attempt to restore their image among traditional liberals, business and right-wing forces are mobilizing an unparalleled counteroffensive to defeat labor reforms. A coalition comprised of the U.S. Chamber of Commerce, the National Association of Manufacturers, the Association of General Contractors, and several high-powered industry associations, has come together to defeat upcoming labor reform proposals. Right-wing groups like the Right-to-Work Committee, Americans against Union Control of Government, Liberty Lobby, the Christian Crusade, and the Conservative Caucus can be expected to pour additional millions of dollars and grass-roots organizing time into defeating labor's legislative initiatives.[32]

The inherent weaknesses in both the boycott and the labor reform strategies as they are presently constituted are numerous. But let's assume that by some fortuitous set of circumstances organized labor is able to win on *all* scores. What has labor won? Both strategies are based on organizing the unorganized workers in the labor force—especially in the South. Twenty years ago such strategies, by themselves, would have made a lot of sense. Today they don't make as much sense, for two very important reasons. First, by focusing their "exclusive" attention on strategies designed to win new members, the unions have lost sight of the fact that their number one threat at present is the loss of their remaining membership, 60 percent of which is concentrated in the Graybelt. Nowhere are they proposing a serious program to counter the adverse effects on present union membership of massive runaway shops from the North. It might be argued that opening up the South to union shops will tend to discourage the further flow of jobs south since wages in that region will eventually become more competitive with those up North. Still, even if the boycott and the legislation were to succeed tomorrow, it would take ten to twenty years to organize the South. In the interim, the many other problems facing the northeast/midwest quadrant—energy costs, taxes, old and worn-out facilities—will continue to worsen, hastening the departure of more union jobs southward and, to some extent, overseas.

Even with the passage of labor law reform legislation, real questions remain as to how effective it will be in increasing organizing success. It will be years before the real impact of this "fine tuning" of labor law can be evaluated.

Most important of all, whatever gains labor achieves on the legislative front now are bound to be short-lived. After 1982 the Sunbelt states will, for the first time in American history, be the dominant bloc in Congress. It is foolish to believe that when that happens they won't move to weaken or wipe out altogether whatever legislative victories labor is able to secure now.

The cardinal rule of all organizing is never to move out on a flank until your base is secure. By ignoring this central truth, the unions have played right into the hands of their opponents. They face the further loss of their already dwindling base in the northern tier and with that, a further loss in their national political clout, right at the very time in their history when they need to consolidate their existing strength the most.

This does not mean that the South and the unorganized groups within the labor force should not be made an organizing priority for the unions. That is essential, if the trade-union movement is to regain its progressive leadership role as the voice of working men and women in America. But current strategies for organizing the unorganized *must* be combined with an equally ambitious strategy to prevent further losses among the existing rank-and-file membership in the northern industrial quadrant. This will require embarking on new courses of action that are not contained in organized labor's current two-pronged strategy.

Most importantly, it will require the development of some kind of working partnership with the sixteen Graybelt states, where the majority of union members are concentrated. For better or for worse, much of the future hopes and prospects of the union movement will rise or fall with the future economic and political prospects of the northeastern and midwestern states. The long-range fate of the Graybelt states will largely determine whether organized labor itself has a future at all. Both share a common problem: they are each being abandoned by the private corporate sector. Their solution lies in finding new ways to work together to fashion a viable economic alternative to insure their mutual survival. A look at the underlying causes of the economic crisis facing the Graybelt is the first necessary step toward identifying the many intersections where these two declining power blocs can join together.

Chapter 6: The Decline of the Graybelt

One doesn't have to be an economist to observe what's happening to America's northern industrial corridor. A simple train ride on Amtrak's New York to Chicago run provides convincing evidence of the crisis at hand. Passing through towns like Erie, Harrisburg, Cleveland, Toledo, Elkhart, and South Bend, a passenger needs only to take a look out of the window to see what has happened to these once-powerful industrial centers. While each city could once point to some unique feature as its own particular claim to glory, there is now a sameness to them all. Old factories, some a block long or more, dot the sides of the tracks. Mostly deserted, their windows shattered or checker-boarded, they look like a scene from war-torn Europe.

There is a dreariness to these cities; it's not a lazy kind of dreariness, but more a tired kind. There's no life, no anticipation. The squeaks and groans of the train wheels seem to pass judgment on it all.

The northeast/midwest corridor of America is fast becoming a strip of giant industrial ghost towns. Businesses are leaving, jobs are leaving, the tax base of local and state governments is eroding, and public services are being cut back drastically.

There are two immediate causes for the crisis. First, federal tax and spending policies are transferring the wealth of the region to the emerging Sunbelt states. Secondly, the private capital sector—the banks and corporations—has begun to redline the entire region from Chicago to Boston. Private capital, like federal funds, is being transferred from the Graybelt largely to the Southwest and Southeast sections of the country.

Federal Funding Policies

In 1975 alone, the sixteen northern industrial states contributed $29.3 billion more to the federal treasury than they received back in contracts, grants, and payments from the federal government. At the same time, the nineteen Sunbelt states received $17.1 billion more in federal funds than they paid in taxes. The reasons for this inequity go back to the New Deal era, when the government decided to undertake a long-range development program designed to bring the poverty-stricken South up to par with the rest of the country. As a result, for the last thirty years the more affluent northern states have been underwriting, with their tax dollars, a long list of development projects in the South ranging from TVA to highway construction, irrigation, rural electrification, and the building of defense and aerospace plants. Now the tables have turned; the South is booming economically while its once-rich northern neighbors find themselves in the throes of an ever-worsening economic decline.[1] This turn of events angered a lot of northern politicians. As Indiana's lieutenant-governor, Robert Orr, says: "We are now actually subsidizing the states that are successfully competing against us."[2]

The unequal distribution of federal dollars has had a profound effect on every aspect of local and state economic development. Take federal employment policies. In its 1976 report, the Joint Economic Committee stated that federal (nonmilitary) payrolls are often three to four times higher in the states of the South, where business is thriving, than in the economically depressed northern region.[3] In fact, between 1963 and 1973, federal civilian employment grew by only 9,000 in the Northeast while 118,000 workers were added to the federal payrolls in the South Atlantic states.[4] The same pattern exists in assistance from the Economic Development Administration. In the past ten years the depressed Graybelt states only received 26.5 percent of EDA funds for public works, business loans, and overall economic development, while the Sunbelt received over 42 percent.[5]

Of course, when it comes to federal expenditures for

military and aerospace work, the South has consistently enjoyed a favored relationship. For example, in 1975 NASA awarded 60 percent of its one hundred largest contracts to industries in the Sunbelt and a meager 13 percent to the North.[6] Direct military expenditures are even more one-sided. In fiscal 1976, the military spent twenty times more money on improving military installations in the South than they did in the Northeast.[7] A few years ago, northern politicians might have looked away from such imbalances, but not anymore. "There's been a diabolical political conniving in Washington against the Northeast," charges Governor Milton Shapp of Pennsylvania, who, like other northerners, wants to know why his state's tax dollars should be subsidizing military expenditures in a region of the country that's much better off than his own. So far, no one has provided the governor with a satisfactory answer.[8]

A few years ago there was a lot of ballyhoo about the adoption of a community development federal revenue sharing program. But here again, the effect of the program has been to penalize those urban areas of the North where poverty is the most pronounced and to reward the middle-class suburbs of the southern rim. Under this new program, seventeen out of the nineteen largest cities in the Graybelt will actually receive $168 million less than they had under previous programs, while the ten largest cities in the Sunbelt will gain $71 million in assistance.[9]

In their book, *The Abuse of Power,* Jack Newfield and Paul DuBrul point out that the federal government has applied the same standard of favored treatment for the Sunbelt in housing as well. Since FHA and VA insurance and other federal programs are geared toward single-family private homes, the poorer apartment dwellers in the over-crowded cities of the North benefit little if at all. In 1972, for example, Newfield and DuBrul report that private home subsidies accounted for two-thirds of the $15.3 billion in federal housing support. With the high cost of construction and financing of new homes beyond the reach of most people living in northern metropolitan areas, the bulk of federal housing support money has flowed southward. Again using 1972 as an example, in that year alone two out of three new private homes were being built in the Sunbelt, and that region accounted for well over half of all federally insured mortgages.

In health-care facilities, aid to public education and dozens of other areas, the story is the same. Northern tax dollars are being used to subsidize the already thriving Sunbelt, while cities and states along the entire northern rim sink deeper and deeper into debt, decline, and despair.[10]

The Flight of Private Capital

The most basic problem facing the North, according to Albert Rees, former chairman of the Council on Wage and Price Stability, is that it is no longer attracting private capital. No one is disagreeing with Mr. Rees. The Census Bureau figures show that between 1967 and 1972 new capital expenditures in New England went up by only 1.6 percent; for the Mid-Atlantic it was only a slightly higher 4.1 percent. In contrast, new capital expenditures for the South Atlantic rose by 37.8 percent during the same period.[11]

While a few observers hold to the mistaken notion that the northern tier is suffering from a shortage of capital vis-à-vis other regions of the country, the statistics tell a very different story. The irony of the situation, says Representative Michael Harrington of Massachusetts, is that most of the firms which allocate capital for the entire country actually have their headquarters in the North, and still the capital is flowing outward and southward (and to some extent overseas).[12] For example, eight of the top fifteen commercial banks in the nation are based in the Northeast. Together, they hold upwards of $293 billion in assets. And that's just for openers. The region is also the home of fourteen of the fifteen largest insurance companies, with combined assets of another $158 billion. In addition, nine of the top fifteen corporations, with assets of $122 billion, are also headquartered in the northern part of the country.[13] Economic consultant Richard Morris summed up the apparent contradiction in a 1976 report to the Governors' conference.

The wealth of the Northeast is a historical reflection of its prior economic primacy, not a daily tool for survival. The wealth owned by those in the Northeast neither reflects current economic circumstances nor is it at the disposal exclusively of the region. Wealth owned by northern individuals has no particular propensity to be invested where they live.[14]

What is really taking place in the Graybelt is a massive regional redlining campaign undertaken by the financial community, argues John Moriarty, director of the Congressional Northeast/Midwest Economic Advancement Coalition. "Those guys have the money and they know very well where investment dollars go." They're not investing in the region, says Moriarty, because they figure they can get a "better return in Texas or abroad." [15]

Banking and insurance companies will never publicly admit that there is a deliberate policy of redlining the region, but they have done everything short of putting a map on their boardroom walls with a bright red crayon circle marked around the region. A case in point: the Fantus Corporation, a consulting firm and subsidiary of Dun & Bradstreet, has developed a "business climate ranking" for forty-eight states. The ranking is based on fifteen factors considered important to companies looking into alternative locations for their operations. The factors include corporate income taxes as a percent of total state taxes; per capita welfare expenditures; per capita income tax; labor legislation favorable to management, and average workmen's compensation payments. Not surprisingly, nine of the twelve most favorable states for capital investment are located in the South and nine of the twelve worst states are located in the Graybelt.[16] Studies like this are relied on heavily by the investment community in deciding where to place its chips. Bernard Weinstein, professor of economics at the University of Texas, took the time to draw up a correlation study between the Fantus rankings and net manufacturing jobs won or lost by each state over the past seven years. The report, which was delivered in June 1976 before the Western Economic Association, concluded that, in fact, "there is a fairly good correlation" between the Fantus business climate rankings and the shift of jobs out of the Northeast.[17]

Because we operate under the restrictions of a system where economic planning is primarily a function of private capital seeking maximum return for investment, the picture for the Midwest and Northeast is not likely to improve in the future. The reasons are manifold. First, the productive facilities in the North are old and worn out and the supporting infrastructure—sewage facilities, rail, air transport—is antiquated and becoming increasingly expensive to maintain. Then too, public services, which are vital to a healthy economy, are being cut back to adjust to the ever-declining tax base in most northern cities.

A favorite reason given by businessmen for moving plants, jobs, and capital out of the region is their reluctance to continue to work alongside inefficient and overly bureaucratic local governments and elected officials who are perceived as being too critical of the ways of the business community. "To be more specific," says Dr. James Howell, senior vice-president of the First National Bank of Boston, "our governments in the Northeast seem to be unusually characterized by outdated management control and accounting and personnel systems that must somehow attempt to deliver services to a citizenry with a virtually unsatiable appetite for more social services, and to a business community that has become increasingly discontented because it cannot cut through governmental red tape."[18]

Speaking much more candidly before a Rotary Club forum in Boston, Edson de Castro, president of Data General, a Massachusetts-based firm, gets right to the heart of the matter.

At best, the state appears geared for industrial contraction, not for growth. Its enormous expenditures for social welfare, unemployment compensation and the environment are choking the state's existing industrial base and discouraging the start of new industry or transfer of other industry into the state.[19]

Of course, large expenditures for social services requires higher taxes and there is no doubt that the tax burden in the northern states is high when compared to other regions of the country. But here again federal policies must share the blame. For example, the Northeast must pay in more for public assistance, Medicare, and unemployment insurance programs. When these programs were first begun, poor states were only required to pay about one-fifth of the public assistance costs while the wealthy states only received a 50 percent federal reimbursement. At the same time, each state was allowed to set its own standards for welfare payments. As a result, the Sunbelt states set very low standards, so low in fact that a state like Mississippi provides only $60 per month to a family of four on public assistance. And even with this low figure the federal government shoulders four-fifths of the costs. In contrast, Massachusetts provides a family of four with $330 per month, still well below the poverty level but a princely sum in comparison. Still, the government only picks up half the tab for Massachusetts public assistance allotment. So Massachusetts ends up paying fourteen times the amount that Mississippi does for public assistance.[20]

A similar problem exists with unemployment insurance. Although the federal government taxes all employers uniformly to finance its reserve fund, each state sets its own standards in determining benefit levels. Here again northern states, on the whole, provide much more generous benefits than southern states.

In the end, when all the figures for social services are added up, northern states tax the average citizen ten times as much as do southern states. For providing a more humane policy toward the poor and the dependent, the northern states are doubly penalized. First, in having to take over an ever-increasing welfare and tax burden as a result of past migration from the southern states to the North. Second, in having to further increase taxes on those who remain behind as middle-class residents flee from the North to the South in ever-expanding numbers to avoid the high welfare taxes. This vicious cycle is exacerbated still further by the overall tax burden the northern states incur.[21]

By 1975, state and local taxes in the Northeast and Midwest were already 20.6 percent higher than the national average.[22] The alternative to raising them further is to slash basic public services. Either way, the states and localities are damned. When they raise taxes industry pulls out because of the higher costs, and when they lower taxes industry still moves out because of insufficient public services. With industries leaving, the local and state governments are forced to raise personal income taxes to fill the vacuum left by the loss of business taxes. Personal income taxes have risen by 150 percent in cities like Boston and New York in the past eight years, as compared to 80 percent in cities like Dallas. Needless to say, the increase in personal taxes tends to drive even more middle-class taxpayers out of the region and the whole grim cycle is repeated again and again and again.[23]

As if all these problems aren't enough, one final element has been introduced in the past few years which has all but finished off America's aging industrial corridor—energy.

There has been a massive transfer of income and wealth from the importing to the exporting countries. We should observe a similar transfer of this income from New England and the Great Lakes to the Southwest and Border States.[24]

What Mr. Steven C. McDonald, a leading petroleum economist, is getting at is that eleven of the thirteen major energy-producing states are all in the Sunbelt region. "Next to the Arab Sheiks," claims consultant Richard Morris, "it is the South and Southwest which have benefitted most by the rise in oil prices." [25] Morris is right. The costs of energy in the Northeast are more than double those in the South. The reason for this tremendous cost disadvantage is that the Northeast has little natural gas of its own (only 9 percent of the national total). Natural gas is the cheapest of the fuels. In fact, it is only one-third of the cost of the more expensive petroleum oil. Without this cheap natural gas, the Northeast is forced to import over 88 percent of its fuel in the form of expensive petroleum from the Arab countries. By contrast, the Sunbelt is able to meet between 50 percent and 70 percent of its energy needs with cheap natural gas from its tremendous indigenous reserves.[26]

As Paul London, director of the New England Economic Research Office points out, the fact is that "there is no single factor which has hurt the regional economy as much over the past six years as the rapid increase in oil prices relative to the price of natural gas in the Sunbelt." [27] For the business community the additional energy costs involved in continuing to do business in the North is just one more good reason for packing up and heading south.

Flight of federal dollars, flight of private investment capital, the high costs of union labor, energy, taxes, and welfare, antiquated production facilities, dilapidated urban infrastructures, breakdown in public services—the list of crises facing the once-powerful industrial North is mindboggling. For the giant cities that make up the core of the northeast quadrant, the situation is even more desperate than for the region as a whole. The aging cities of Newark, Cleveland, Detroit, Buffalo: their majestic old downtown hotels are nearly deserted now; their magnificent skyscrapers are in disrepair. Their street corners are lined with people, some with tattered union cards in their wallets, all with time on their hands and no place to go. Poor people, blacks, browns, and whites, all trapped within a region of the country without an economic future.[28]

While the capitalist system hasn't as yet let completely go in these older cities and states, it has nevertheless made it more than clear that it doesn't really plan on ever coming back to stay. And what of those who are left behind? Their political representatives in Congress and in the statehouses have belatedly thrown together two regional coalitions in a frantic effort to address the monumental problems facing this dying economic corridor. Unfortunately, like organized labor, these political coalitions have failed to appreciate fully the situation confronting them. As a result, they are proposing Band-Aids when radical surgery is urgently required.

Chapter 7: The Graybelt Strategy

Question: "Have you looked at the potential impact of re-apportionment in 1982?"

Answer: "Absolutely. We really believe that the timing of this whole thing is crucial because of that fact. We in the Northeast and Midwest will be a numerical minority for the first time since Reconstruction. We may be closing the door after most of the horses got out; and there's always that fear. But there's a lot to suggest that a lot can be done right now. . . . We've probably got eight years of a southerner in the presidency; we've got about six to eight years of a northeasterner, Tip O'Neill, as Speaker of the House. The Senate is basically now controlled by the South in its leadership.

"It's even scarier once you go beyond those six to eight years. You have to figure that a southerner is the prime candidate for the next speaker. Take that, plus the net reduction in the number of seats we'll hold, and you've got a substantial problem.

"What we want to do now is pave the way for a more sensitive treatment of our region as our political clout is reduced. We think we can maximize it right now . . . and hopefully pave the way for a more sensitive treatment in the future when our potential clout diminishes. How much it will diminish, I don't know. . . ." [1]

John Moriarty is director of the newly formed Congressional Northeast-Midwest Economic Advancement Coalition (NMEAC). Its membership is composed of 204 Congresspeople from sixteen northern industrial states, who together represent some 90 million Americans. The coalition reflects a belated recognition of the fact, as Governor Reuben Askew of Florida puts it, "that the wheel of power in this nation is turning unmistakably from the North to the South." [2] The coalition hopes to slow that transition by forging a united front in Congress to fight for federal programs that will aid their region. It is this new sense of embattled regionalism which *Business Week* has dubbed the "New War Between the States." The conflict, says the magazine, though bloodless, promises to be every bit as "bitter and devisive because it will be a struggle for income, jobs, people and capital." [3] The commanding general for the northern forces is Michael Harrington, the young democratic Congressman from Massachusetts, who, as coalition chairman, is responsible for formulating overall strategy. Under his leadership, the coalition has set up special task forces to deal with a range of issues from federal welfare reform to a regionwide energy program.

Harrington is aware that the coalition faces serious internal and external problems that must be resolved soon if any headway is to be made before the all-important 1982 reapportionment. First, admits Harrington, "as perhaps the largest coalition ever assembled in Congress, NMEAC's diverse membership reflects every conceivable political and ideological point of view." While they are joining together to address a regional problem of crisis proportions, Harrington acknowledges that "the members nevertheless have varied interests and areas of concern which are not universally shared." In fact, long-standing rivalries among states within the region could seriously weaken the prospect of molding a cohesive coalition offensive. Harrington also realizes that whatever the coalition undertakes, it will still face formidable opposition. "Programs which have an historical bias in favor of other sections of the country will undoubtedly be fiercely guarded by those who view the coalition as a sectional effort which seeks to deny other regions of the country their due." [4]

The Congressional Coalition is augmented by a second coalition made up of the governors of seven northeastern states. Formed in the fall of 1976, the Coalition of North Eastern Governors (CONEG) has pledged to form "a united front in Congress" to secure greater economic assistance for their region. In their first joint statement, the governors contended that they were not coming together to seek advantages but to seek equity. However, behind the lofty phrases is a deep-seated anger and indignation over federal policies which the governors believe have seriously short-changed their region. The prevailing mood among the governors is one of urgency. As one legislative aide remarked: "If we don't do something soon, the federal government is going to have to start an Appalachian Regional Commission for the Northeast." [5]

There are already several areas where the Governors' Coalition and its counterpart in Congress are in agreement, at least in principle. Both coalitions are calling for the restructuring of federal spending programs to reflect the greater needs of the Graybelt region. Both groups have made it clear that they are no longer willing to contribute nearly $30 billion more to the federal government each year than they get back, especially when the bulk of that money ends up subsidizing further economic development in the South. They are also calling for the federalization of welfare programs. The only fair thing to do, they argue, is to raise minimum benefits nationally and relieve the North of the excessive burden of taking care of millions of dependents, many of whom migrated there from the Sunbelt in the first place.[6]

One of the major problems shared by the Northeast and Midwest states is the high cost of energy. Many politicians in the regions are hopeful that this can provide a basis for the first real cohesive partnership between the states. CONEG has already endorsed a proposal to create a regional Energy and Development Corporation to be capitalized initially by the member states to the tune of $50 million, with the hope of securing federally guaranteed bonding to bring capitalization up to nearly $1 billion. The corporation would establish a regional energy plan that might, among other things, finance a regional mass-transportation system, rebuild the region's coalmining industry, construct transmission lines to bring Canadian power South, and extend pipelines to bring natural gas North. The corporation might also finance the modernization of existing power plants and help develop offshore oil reserves.[7] The energy project is already being referred to as a TVA for the North, and in fact, politicians are leaning heavily on the analogy to secure needed federal underwriting. They point out that the federal government made a similar commitment in the Sunbelt by pouring $3 billion in funds to build over twenty dams and power plants in the TVA area. In addition, in recent years the Bureau of Reclamation doled out another $6 billion in seventeen western states for capital-improvement projects and over $79 billion for highway construction throughout the Sunbelt, all of which provided an environment conducive to private investment. Now CONEG wants the same type of commitment to its region. "Without energy parity," said one regional planner, "we will forever remain at a disadvantage with the Sunbelt in luring new private investment into the region." [8]

Here again, the phrase "private investment" enters the picture. Regardless of whether the talk is about taxes, welfare, energy, or differences in the weather, the discussion always gets back to the question of private investment. What is clear is that as long as the investment community continues to redline the region, talk of other reforms is just an exercise in futility. To stimulate an increase in private capital expenditures, several proposals have been set forth. To date, the most important are the one sponsored by the business establishment which calls for a regional development corporation, and Congressman's Harrington's bill calling for the formation of a series of regional public banks.

The New England Capital Corporation is the brainchild of James Howell, executive vice president of Boston's First National Bank. It would be financed with up to $1 billion of private capital and would supply "long-term debt capital to established, profitable, sound, and growing firms at competitive costs." Congressman Harrington is not impressed and argues that this consortium will behave no differently in its investment policy than the individual banks, since its primary concern, as stated by its sponsors, will be to earn the maximum profit possible. This precondition, contends Harrington, already precludes it from placing investment funds where they are most needed, in those companies and localities which are suffering the most financially.[9]

Harrington's proposal, on the other hand, would have the federal government finance a series of ten regional banks, each with $2 billion which could be invested in the equities of locally based businesses. "Banks are private companies and have the right to lend to whomever they want when they want," argues Harrington.

So I propose we establish a public lender.... If a factory in Lynn wants to modernize its plants, let the First National Bank have first crack at lending the capital. But if they'd rather lend their money in Taiwan or Brazil, let's have a public bank in New England to provide the investment money. Because we need jobs in Lynn, and we need capital to create those jobs.[10]

The business community does not like the Harrington bill. They argue that by financing companies that are already marginal, the federal government and the American taxpayer will be the big losers. A doomed company is a doomed company, they contend, regardless of how much capital is poured into it. While there is some truth to this allegation, the business community was remarkedly silent when the same argument was used against bailing out Lockheed and other aerospace giants. In their case, federal subsidies are still keeping them from sinking, but for how long is a matter of conjecture. A more impressive argument is the one put forth by financial expert Frank Comes, who questions the concept of ten regional banks. (Harrington's bill calls for a number of banks throughout the country largely because of a political calculation on his part that a broad proposal of this sort would have an easier time passing both Houses than one that called for just one bank in the Northeast.) The problem with Harrington's strategy, says Comes, is that there would really be no advantage for the southern states to vote for a series of regional public banks, since the Sunbelt already has plenty of private capital available to it.[11] Comes goes on to argue, rather convincingly, that southern taxpayers are not apt to look kindly on any legislative proposal that would pour their money into subsidizing projects north of the Mason-Dixon Line. "The loan guarantees might prove to be as unpopular with voters and representatives outside the Northeast as the special legislation for aid to New York City was in December of 1975."[12] Of course, Harrington and his colleagues in the CONEG and the Congressional Coalition would respond to such charges by arguing that when the South was in need, the North did not turn its back, but instead provided billions of dollars in economic development assistance to bring the region up to parity.

However, it isn't just a question of southern taxpayers bailing out their neighbors in the North. Aside from the financial competition that's involved, there are other factors, often unconscious ones, to predispose people against the Northeast. For one thing, when middle-class taxpayers think of the Northeast and the decline of the cities, there is often in their minds the image of blacks, Hispanics, welfare mothers with eight children, and rampant crime and drugs—some of the very things that caused them to flee those areas in the first place. The question of racism, says Moriarty of the Congressional Coalition, cannot be ignored, and because of that, the battle facing the North in its effort to win concessions from the rest of the country is going to be much more difficult than the one the South faced forty years ago, when it asked for and received aid from the federal government.

The irony is that in spite of all the fury being aroused at the prospect of the federal government going into the lending and investment business—as if they hadn't been doing it for the past thirty years through various subsidies, contracts, and grants to big business—the Harrington bill is still more public relations than real substance. Even Harrington's chief of staff, Moriarty, says unabashedly that $2 billion dollars of proposed public funds for investment in private business equities for the region is "just a drop in the bucket." The question then is why is it being proposed in the first place? Moriarty's answer is revealing of the entire dilemma facing the coalition and the North. The Harrington bill, says Moriarty, "will never be passed, and even if it did, it would only be used to embarrass, to prod and hopefully to leverage private investment by scaring the shit out of them." [13]

Moriarty fails to explain how "a drop in the bucket" is going to "scare the shit out of them," but his remarks do point out the real contradiction facing CONEG and the Congressional Coalition. That is, regardless of what kind of public-development bank is adopted by the coalition, it will still be seen as little more than a leveraging device to stimulate the private capital market. Even the much-touted Urbank proposal being advanced by the Carter Administration is designed to serve the same ends. While this development bank would provide cities with low-interest loans, its other major purpose would be to provide loan subsidies to businesses as an inducement to locate their operations in depressed communities.[14] In the final analysis, then, it is still the private business sector that the northern politicians continue to fall back on to solve their problem, hoping against hope to find the appropriate lure to convince those who are primarily responsible for creating the problem in the first place to now solve it as well. In fact, it is this almost complete dependency on the private sector that threatens to undo the northern coalitions before they even get off the ground. Eighty years ago, John D. Rockefeller remarked that he could use "one half of the working class to destroy the other." His grandson David, who is chairman of the board of Chase Manhattan Bank, and other bankers have obviously taken the old man's observation to heart. But this time they are applying the principle to individual states, playing them off one against the other, forcing them, especially in the Northeast, to prey on each other for whatever dwindling amounts of private capital funds are thrown out to them. "We are trying to overcome this problem," says Walter Kicinski of Governor Carey's office in Albany. "Clearly, we have a problem in trying to get together in the face of this counterproductive competition." Kicinski contends that the individual states "are sensitive to the subject of stealing from each other," but sensitivity alone doesn't alter the facts.[15] For example, in Boston a coalition of industry, labor, and government, called Jobs for Massachusetts, has developed a hit-list of twenty-four major corporations headquartered in New York that it is attempting to lure away. In New Jersey, Commissioner of Labor and Industry Joseph Hoffman says: "What the South has been doing to New Jersey for fifteen years, I'm now doing to New York. It's cut-throat, regrettably, but it's every state for itself."[16] In state after state, all hard-hit economically and desperate for new capital and jobs, the story is the same. In the end, every state in the region is a loser and the only big winner is the investment community itself as it extorts concessions in the form of reduced taxes, cheaper labor, more lenient environmental and zoning laws, and subsidies such as low-interest loans and free industrial park space—all in return for locating a few more businesses in the region.[17]

The research arm of the National League of Cities and the National Conference of Mayors—the Academy for Contemporary Problems—seems to be advocating just such concessions. In a report published in late 1977, the ACP agreed with business claims that a hostile climate has been created by labor and government. The solution, says the ACP, is for the North to be more cooperative and friendly with private enterprise—to emulate the southern states, in effect.[18]

As long as the northern coalitions continue to fashion public programs based on increased dependence on the private sector, the downward economic spiral will continue, either in the form of more loss of capital investment if the states do not go along with private-sector demands, or greater loss of their standard of living as the hard-earned gains that the states have won over the years are stripped away in order to accommodate the increasing demands of private capital.[19]

Chapter 8: A Catch-22

The problem facing both organized labor and the Graybelt is their relationship with private capital—a relationship which has become increasingly untenable over the past several years, and which is now at the breaking point.

"You've got to understand something fundamental about the American labor movement," says Jerry Wurf of AFSCME. "You have a labor movement that ideologically buys the system. That makes our labor movement different."[1] "Buying the system" has meant accepting a dependency relationship to private capital. Labor leaders sometimes prefer to characterize their role as that of a junior partner. Regardless of euphemisms bantered about the net effect of being a junior partner is the acceptance of the notion that what's good for GM is ultimately good for organized labor. In business schools like Harvard and Wharton they explain the advantage of this partnership in terms of the so-called trickle-down theory: the more private capital profits, the more is funneled down to the working man and woman in terms of wages and other benefits. The mainstream of organized labor has gone along with this theory over the years, although not without reservations, because the expanding economic dividends of private capital have always been large enough to assure labor that it would continue to get at least a share for itself. This doesn't mean that organized labor hasn't understood the schizophrenic role that such a relationship has placed it in.[2] In 1937, during a mass rally of Akron rubber workers, the great labor leader John L. Lewis asked: "What have Goodyear workers gotten out of the growth of the company?" "Partnership," he exclaimed. "Well, labor and capital may be partners in theory but they are enemies in fact." [3] It is this contradiction "of fighting capitalists, yet accepting capitalism," says Gil Green in his writings on American labor, that have "introduced elements of conservatism in all unions." [4] This built-in schizophrenia is what has kept American trade unions from aggressively developing the kind of truly adversary role that exists in most European labor movements. In failing to develop an independent ideological stance of its own, organized labor in America has remained a reactive movement, always more or less a captive but certainly never an equal partner of private capital.

The same pattern holds true in the relationship between private capital and governing institutions. Again it is private capital that makes the important decisions regarding economic growth, planning, and allocation of resources and jobs. Like organized labor, local and state governments have also become captive partners, accepting the notion that what's good for business is good for the community. Moriarty of the Congressional Coalition put his finger right on the problem when he remarked that "given the nature of the capitalist system, you have to count on them all the time to carry the major load." [5] The role of local and state governments in this partnership has always been to accommodate to the needs of private capital, and on occasion to act as a mediator between its abuses and excesses and the reactions of an angry public.

Herein lies the dilemma facing both the unions and the local and state governments of the Graybelt region. What happens to them when private capital no longer sees any advantage in continuing its so-called partnership with either group? Congressman Harrington summarized the nature of the problem. "Because the fundamental thrust of private capital is to seek the highest rate of return, it appears unlikely that the private sector will shift capital investments to areas of the country which face large economic problems, when higher, safer, and quicker returns are available elsewhere." [6] Very simply, the private-capital market is saying to organized labor and to the northern region where its membership is concentrated: "Sorry, the party is all over; we don't need either of you any more." [7]

The implications of this new reality have not yet completely sunk in. The elected officials in the northeast/midwest corridor still hope to win back private capital by sweetening the pot with enough public subsidies. While they might win back a few private-investment crumbs with this approach, a Congress increasingly dominated by Sunbelt politicians has no intention to allow its northern neighbors to launch a massive raid on federal funds to entice private capital back from the sunshine states. Organized labor, for its part, is pinning its hopes on organizing the unorganized, especially in the South, while the ranks of its already-organized membership in the North are fast depleting as private capital flees the region. The unions have not yet fully come to grips with the fact that with the rise of the multinationals and the extraordinary advances in technology, private capital can now shift locations faster than labor can organize. Even if the unions do organize the Sunbelt at a faster rate than they lose their membership in the North, there won't be a corporation in sight by the time they've completed their southern organizing drive—they will all have long departed to Brazil, Hong Kong, or some other more favorable location. [8]

The irony of it all is that much of the private sector which is now severing its bonds with organized labor and the Graybelt states belongs to the very power blocs it is deserting. For years, the unions and the northern industrial states have been literally chasing after their own funds in what amounts to one of the most macabre Catch-22s in contemporary economic history. The fact is, union moneys are being used to destroy union jobs and state moneys are being used to undermine state economies. This is a contradiction of such monumental proportions that it would be almost amusing were it not for the cruel results.

Private investment capital, that precious commodity which determines the economic fate of unions, regions, and the country as a whole, is no longer made up exclusively of the savings of wealthy capitalists like the Rockefellers, Morgans, or Duponts, or even of the savings of millions of individual investors in the marketplace. In just thirty years, a new source, the pension fund, has become the largest pool of private capital anywhere in the world. At $500 billion and growing by 10 percent a year, pension funds already own between 20 percent and 25 percent of the stock of companies on the New York and American Exchanges.[9] Nearly half of these funds, some $200 billion, represent the deferred savings of 19 million unionists and the public pension funds of the sixteen industrial states that make up the northern tier of the continental United States.[10] Because the Graybelt states and the unions have relinquished the day-to-day control over their share of the pension-fund pool to a handful of banks and insurance companies to use as they see fit, they have had to suffer the consequences of seeing their own moneys used against them by the investment community.[11] Now the gradual realization of this contradiction is beginning to hit home, especially as the unions and the northern states find themselves increasingly unable to maintain any kind of workable partnership, captive or otherwise, with those to whom they have entrusted their funds in the first place.

For these reasons, some labor leaders and northern politicians are, for the first time, talking actively about asserting direct control over their own pension funds and using them to form a competing capital market in this country; one that can be used to preserve and enlarge the membership base of organized labor and to rejuvenate the sagging economies of America's aging industrial corridor.[12] The confrontation that is likely to take place between the unions and northern states on the one hand, and the private-sector investment community on the other, for control of the massive financial power pension funds represent may well have a profound impact on the future shape and character of the American economic system. To understand better the full implications and likely consequences of such a contest, it is essential to take a close look at the history of pension-fund growth.

II

Claims and Counterclaims
over Pension Capital

Chapter 9: A New Form of Wealth

When most of us think of a pension fund, we think of the amount of money we earn each pay period that is put aside for us by our employer to be given back eventually in the form of retirement income when we reach sixty-five years of age or thereabouts.

When financial economists think of pension funds, they think of the most powerful pool of private capital that exists anywhere in the world.

While pension funds still provide the means of accumulating retirement income for millions of Americans, their initial purpose has, in just twenty years, been eclipsed by their new role as the financial linchpin of the American capitalist system. Not only have pension funds become the major source of new capital for the American economy, but they have also redefined the nature of ownership in this system. Before World War II, there was little disagreement over who owned the American economy. The retained earnings of individual corporations and the accumulated savings of a handful of wealthy entrepreneurs, augmented by the personal savings of millions of individual Americans and the revenue expenditures of the local, state, and federal governments, provided the capital funds which kept the system going and growing. Before World War II, America was largely a privately owned capitalist system. It no longer is.

Pension funds, the new source of capital, are neither privately owned nor publicly owned. These funds represent a new form of ownership which falls somewhere in the middle. While they legally represent the deferred wages of millions of American workers, *pension funds are not controlled directly by those who are their beneficiaries* (more on this in Chapter 14, which discusses who owns pension funds). Instead, they are held in trust and invested in the capital market on behalf of those beneficiaries. There are other differences as well between pension funds and other forms of property. For example, pension funds cannot be inherited. There are also more federal regulations regarding these funds than other forms of property. The pension fund thus falls into a unique new category. Being neither completely privately nor publicly owned, it is more than anything else a form of "social" capital. Because it falls into this new and still vaguely defined category, many contending forces are making claims over its control and use.[1]

The future battle for control of pension capital will, in the words of the late Senator Philip Hart, "be the central structural and policy problem of the American economy and society for years to come." [2] For the victors in this contest, the reward will amount to control over much of the future economic life of the nation. The statistics explain why.

Federal, private, state, and local pension funds are now worth over $500 billion.[3] That is more money than was spent on food, clothing, and shelter by all 215 million Americans last year. Pension funds are now larger than the combined GNP of the United Kingdom and France. They equal the total fiscal budget for all federal expenditures for the U.S. government in 1978. For a nation that is used to thinking of wealth in terms of private savings, it would probably shock most Americans to know that pension funds are now four times larger than the amount of all individual savings in the United States, and that's just the beginning.[4] Today, pension funds own 20 percent of all the financial securities in the country (corporate stocks and bonds, state and local government securities, and U.S. government and agency securities). Given the present growth rate, which is now around 10 percent a year, pension-fund assets will be worth over $1.3 trillion in just eight years.[5]

Most private pension funds come out of the earnings of America's corporations, and it is here where the real impact of this new form of social capital becomes strikingly evident. For example, America's one hundred largest industrial corporations owe their employees $38 billion in pensions while their combined profits for 1976 were only $32 billion. For specific companies, the figures are even more dramatic. UniRoyal's pension costs of $79.4 million were nearly four times its $20.1 million in profit in fiscal 1976. McDonnell Douglas's pension cost in the same year was $115.6 million, but its profits only amounted to $108.8 million.[6] For companies like Allis Chalmers, American Airlines, American Motors, Armco Steel, A & P, Grumman, LTV, Lockheed, Republic Steel, TWA, Northrup, and many others, the story is pretty much the same. All paid out more in pension costs than they had in profits during the same year. The overall averages, while not quite so stunning, are still more than impressive.[7] According to analyst Max Shapiro, writing in *Dun's*, corporate contributions to pension funds now equal 38 percent of profits and 41 percent of all cash expenditures by corporations.[8]

The concept of providing a retirement income for employees first began to gain support during the great period of industrial expansion following the Civil War. Employers, worried about the high costs of worker turnover, fixed their sights on the pension concept as a means of maintaining a captive employee pool. They reasoned that workers would be less inclined to move from job to job if they knew that it would mean losing an accumulated sum of money put away in a retirement fund earmarked for them. Then too, pension funds provided a convenient way to allow management to ease out older and less productive employees.

Early labor leaders saw the pension-fund concept as a clever management tool designed to increase the workers' dependence on the company and to alienate them further from the union. Samuel Gompers contended that organized labor should concentrate its efforts on increasing workers' salaries instead. If workers had more money, argued the labor leaders, they could provide for their own retirement years without needing any so-called pension assistance from their employers. Gompers's attitude toward pensions prevailed among labor leaders well into the twentieth century. Still, between 1900 and 1929, some corporations did manage to set up some rather poorly financed and generally unreliable pension plans for their workers. A few unions also set up plans for their own membership. Still, without organized labor pushing for pensions in their bargaining demands, the notion remained largely experimental.[9] The Depression radically changed public opinion and labor views concerning the need for retirement benefits. With the savings of millions of Americans virtually wiped out overnight, labor leaders and public officials could no longer continue to harbor the view that workers could provide for their own retirement needs. The desperate plight of the aged became so acute that the Roosevelt Administration finally adopted a federal retirement income plan in 1935. The Social Security Act, however, only provided a minimum income, one far too small to adequately cover the financial needs of senior citizens.[10]

World War II provided an impetus for both unions and management to negotiate an increase in pension plans for American workers. With a government-imposed ceiling on salaries and wages and the high personal and corporate taxes being levied by the IRS, pension plans became the ideal collective bargaining focus for labor. Because the IRS exempted pension funds from federal taxation, it seemed to make good practical sense to establish such plans, especially since wage controls effectively prohibited any collective bargaining in that area.[11]

Although labor's views regarding pensions changed considerably after the early days of the Depression, most union leaders still regarded the entire mechanism with a degree of skepticism. In fact, many of them hoped that by pressing the corporations for greater contributions to retirement funds, they would eventually be able to convince both the business community and the politicians of the desirability of adequately funding social security so that private pension funds could be dispensed with altogether. That, of course, never happened and pension funds continued to multiply in number until today their combined assets represent the most formidable pool of money that exists in the country.[12]

In fact, pension-fund growth has been so phenomenal that workers' assets are now worth more than the assets of many of the companies they work for. Even Karl Marx, for whom the dialectics of economic life offered few surprises, would no doubt be taken aback to learn that in America today, the stockholders' equity of corporations like GE, Western Electric, Rockwell, United Technologies, General Dynamics, and Boeing is actually worth less than the pension-fund assets of the employees that work for them. In fact, in nine of the top one hundred industrial firms, workers' pension funds are equal to or surpass the value of the companies' equities; in twenty-two of the firms, the pension funds are worth at least half of the stockholder equity, and in twenty of the companies such funds equal approximately one-fourth of the entire assets of the companies.[13]

Pension funds fall into two broad categories: public and private. The public funds, which presently account for a bit less than half of the $500 billion in total pension-fund assets, cover public employees and are paid for and administered by the local, state, and federal government.[14] Over 19 percent of the American work force is now publicly employed, and most of them are covered by some kind of public pension fund.[15]

Approximately 46 percent of all full-time employees in the private sector are covered by private pension plans. Not unexpectedly, more men are covered under these private plans than women and more whites than blacks. Moreover, nonparticipants tend to be concentrated in low-paying and marginal industries.[16] According to pension expert Robert Tilove, the major reason why over half of all American workers are not covered is the absence of a union to bargain on their behalf for adoption of a fund.[17] Unions have been the most important single factor over the last thirty-five years in securing private pension plans for American workers. As will be discussed later, this fact is becoming central to the "claims" being raised by the unions for greater control over pension funds.

While there are around 500,000 private pension plans, over two-thirds of them cover ten or fewer employees.[18] In contrast, the 350 largest plans accounted for more than two-thirds of the assets of all the private plans, or about $120 billion, in 1976. The twenty-five largest plans alone accounted for nearly 25 percent of all private funds, and each have assets exceeding $1 billion.[19] According to the Bureau of Labor Statistics, over 20 percent of all American workers in the private sector are covered under the seventeen largest plans.[20] In 1976, the companies with the most pension-fund assets were General Motors, with $5.2 billion; General Electric, with $4.9 billion; United States Steel, with $3.3 billion; Ford Motors, with $3.3 billion; and Western Electric, with $3.1 billion.[21]

There are two basic kinds of collectively bargained pension funds; the single-employer and the multi-employer plans. Single-employer funds are more common in heavily concentrated industries with a few dominant employers, like steel, auto, rubber, and they are controlled solely by the company. Multi-employer plans are usually found in more competitive industries with many smaller employers (construction, needle trades, coal, trucking), and are jointly controlled by union and management trustees. The largest multi-employer plans are administered nationwide, but many are run on a regional or local level. In the late 40s and early 50s, the large industrial unions such as the UAW and the United Steel Workers demanded joint administration of the funds they were in the process of negotiating, but the giant steel and auto corporations resisted and the unions settled for single-employer plans.[22] Over half of all the workers in private retirement plans are covered under collective-bargaining agreements between unions and management and a little less than half of these negotiated plans are multi-employer based.[23]

As for the contribution formulas, private plans are either noncontributory, that is, solely financed by the employer; or contributory, where the employees also contribute to the fund. Of course, in those industries that are highly organized, the unions generally bargain for noncontributory plans. The Bureau of Labor Statistics estimated that as of 1970, over 79 percent of all private plans were noncontributory.[24]

Pension funds are power, and that power is felt most in the stock market, where almost half of the $400 billion in private, state, and local funds are currently invested in the stocks of America's giant corporations.[25] As mentioned earlier, it is estimated that social capital now owns anywhere from 20 percent to 25 percent of the companies on the New York and American stock exchanges. These companies, in turn, make the critical economic decisions that affect the security and well-being of the American people. Pension-fund capital, the worker's own money, is now a new owner of America's giant corporations. This fact, virtually ignored by American unions and local and state governments for over two decades, is now raising more than just a few eyebrows; especially since over half of the $400 billion in non-Federal pension funds now represents the combined deferred savings of 19 million trade unionists and the public pension funds of the sixteen states that make up the northeast/midwest industrial corridor.[26]

The realization of this new situation is posing some embarrassing questions. Unions are beginning to ask why their pension funds are being invested in companies that often undermine union jobs. Northern politicians are asking why their public-employee pension funds are being invested out of state, thus subverting their own regional economies. With these questions are coming the first rumblings of indignation as well. In northern statehouses and in union offices there is talk going on about counterclaims over this new form of social capital; counterclaims that threaten to explode into an all-out battle for control over pension-fund assets.

Organized labor and northern state governments find themselves increasingly abandoned by industry and the private capital markets. Unable to secure adequate financial help in Washington to cushion their economic decline, members of both blocs are starting to see merit in pressing what they consider to be justified claims for control of the billions of dollars in pension-fund capital.

On the other hand, the private investment sector, which is experiencing a long-range decline in earnings and an expanding capital shortage, is equally adamant in its claims over control of pension-fund assets. For the investment community, losing control over this source of capital funds would, in effect, be tantamount to losing control over much of the economy.

This, then, is the struggle that is about to unfold. It is a struggle for power over an economy in transition, one that is moving from a center once based on private ownership of capital to one increasingly based on social ownership. The investment community has for some years now already been following a carefully orchestrated campaign to institutionalize this new form of social ownership in private hands. The emerging counterclaims of organized labor and northern state governments, though still unformed either strategically or ideologically, are paving the way toward a very different alternative, one which involves the increasing socialization of this new capital in the form of labor and public control over production and economic planning.

The battle over control of pension-fund capital is a battle between these two forces and these two emerging perspectives.

Chapter 10: Propping Up the American Economy

Relatively few corporations, state governments, or unions manage their employee pension funds in-house. Most give over investment responsibility to bank trust departments, insurance companies, and independent asset managers. Of the three, banks manage by far the largest number of accounts, about half of these tax-exempt assets. Independents account for 21 percent of the pension-fund business and insurance companies, the remaining 29 percent or so.[1]

Control over pension funds means control over capital allocation and economic planning, and that control is now concentrated in a handful of financial institutions. At the end of 1975, the one hundred largest banks controlled over $145.6 billion in pension funds and the top ten controlled some $80 billion. Banker's Trust and Morgan Guarantee each control nearly $15 billion of these funds.[2] What is even more disturbing is the number of people who are ultimately responsible for making the all-important decisions on how and where to invest these funds. The general public has never heard of Harrison Smith, Willard Wheeler, or Al Thompson, but, as investment managers of Morgan, Manufacturers Hanover Trust, and Citicorp, they each control as much investment money as the Dupont, Rockefeller, Morgan, and Ford families. In fact, the average *individual* portfolio manager alone controls some $112 million.[3]

This control over pension-fund assets and investments has provided the American financial community with a captive financial pool which is increasingly being relied on to prop up an economic system that has all but run out of steam. The story of how the private investment fraternity has used and manipulated this new form of social capital in

order to subsidize an equity market that might otherwise
have long since collapsed is one of the most important chapters in contemporary American economic history.[4] Yet, interestingly enough, a computer index search at the Library
of Congress turned up not one single article from a major
U.S. daily newspaper or popular magazine on the subject.
But from sources inside the investment community and from
investment trade journals, the following story emerges.

To begin with, it is no secret that American economic
growth has steadily declined over the years. The real economic growth (adjusted for inflation) of the United States
between 1960 and 1970 averaged about 4 percent. This
placed it behind seventeen other nations, including virtually
all the countries in Western Europe. The declining growth
rate is reflected in the figures on capital investment. Between
1970 and 1974, the United States had the worst record of
capital investment of any of the seven major industrial nations of the capitalist world, with only 14.6 percent of its
GNP being put back into new capital formation.[5]

Traditionally, retained corporate earnings have been the
largest single source of savings for new capital investment.
However, over the past ten years or so, corporate earnings
have been whittled away by the loss of markets to foreign
competition, the increasing costs of energy, the rapidly diminishing supply of natural resources, the escalating costs of
maintaining and renewing plants, equipment, and facilities,
and a host of other all-too-familiar factors. As a result, it has
been more difficult to get new capital investment out of the
retained earnings of America's giant corporations. Increasingly, new capital has had to come from external sources.
According to the American Bankers' Association, in 1970 29
percent of new capital investment was generated externally,
but by 1974, the figure had climbed to 40 percent and within
a year or two it will be over 50 percent.[6] The New York
Stock Exchange estimates a somewhat lower figure, but it is
still clear that corporations will be increasingly dependent
on outside sources for their new capital needs.[7] External in-

vestment depends on the ability to induce would-be investors to buy stocks or bonds or lend money. To do that requires that the return on investment be attractive enough to convince people to take money from their savings; at least that's how the traditional market principle is supposed to function.

But the sorry fact is that the inducements to invest just are not there. The reason is that the rate of return on investment is simply not high enough and is getting worse over the long term. According to a detailed study done by economist William D. Nordhaus of Yale University, "the genuine rate of return on corporate investment did indeed decline substantially between 1948 and 1973," and there is no indication that the trend will reverse itself.[8] The figures are even worse for the last twelve years. According to a *Time* magazine "Special Report," the purchasing power of money invested in corporate stocks has declined drastically since 1965.[9] It's no wonder, then, that between 1970 and 1975 the number of Americans investing in the stock market declined by 5.7 million, or a whopping 18 percent.[10]

With equity financing becoming increasingly difficult, corporations have had to depend more and more on borrowing. It is ironic that the very business community that is forever berating the federal government for debt financing has itself turned to debt financing to stay afloat. In the old days, the general rule of thumb was that a healthy company would maintain a ratio of equity to debt financing that was weighted four to five times in favor of equity money. By 1976, major American companies were only able to "count on barely two dollars in equity capital to a dollar of debt." [11] Still, one way or another, businesses will have to generate new equity financing from somewhere. The New York Stock Exchange estimates that American companies will need to raise over $250 billion in new equity between now and 1985 alone. But they then add that given the poor trends in investment climate, top corporations will fall well short of their needs.[12]

Of late, the business and financial community has been

issuing dire warnings that the economy is going to be in big trouble if it is unable to attract new capital investment over the next few years. Chase Manhattan Bank, for one, has been running full-page ads in newspapers across the country forecasting a capital shortfall of $400 million a day and double-digit unemployment unless ways are found to attract more capital investment to industry. Chase's solution to the crisis is an old and familiar one: the federal government should reduce taxes, especially on corporations and wealthy individuals, cut spending on expensive social programs, and help underwrite new capital ventures with the private sector. This, the nation's third-largest bank contends, will help free more savings and encourage people to invest. How much this will aid the private sector is questionable, since the corporations are now paying only 13.8 percent of all of the taxes generated by the federal government, and Washington is already pumping $50 billion in grants, contracts, and subsidies into propping up the sagging private sector.[13]

Yet the market could be worse—in fact, a whole lot worse—and here's where the real story lies. Without the automatic infusion of tens of billions of dollars of new pension funds into the equity market over the last decade, the New York and American stock exchanges would be only a shadow of their present selves. The rub is that these pension funds are not going into the exchanges because that's necessarily where the best return on investment is. Rather, they are being funneled into the market to fill the vacuum left as millions of individual investors make their exodus. Moreover, with corporate earnings less and less able to finance new capital, even greater pressure is being put on investing pension funds in the exchanges in order to provide more equity financing.

Between 1964 and 1974, institutional investors used pension funds to purchase over $80 billion in corporate stocks.[14] Writing in the *New York Review of Books*, Jason Epstein points out that at the end of that same period, the Dow Jones Industrial Average was no higher than at the beginning. In the interim, disastrous rates of return, coupled with inflation, ate up literally tens of billions of dollars of those pension-fund investments (a detailed look at this entire financial debacle will be examined in a later section). The only logical conclusion that can be drawn, contends Epstein, is that employee pension funds were used "to prop up the market while much of the smart money got out more or less intact." [15] The investment community has even more ambitious plans for pension-fund assets in the future. Remember the $250 billion in new equity financing that the New York Stock Exchange said would have to be raised between now and 1985? According to the exchange, private and public pension funds will provide over half of the money needed.[16]

The point to be made here is that smart individual investors are not about to continue to throw good money after bad, no matter how much they want to help out their favorite companies on the exchanges. In fact, that's exactly why millions of Americans have been leaving the market. But with pension funds or social capital, there's no one to say: "Hey, you can't invest my money in the top 500 industrials because I'll get a lousy return or I'd get a better return somewhere else." With pension capital the individual owners have been effectively divorced from control over their own funds. The funds are a captive pool, which is why the banks have been able to pour them down the drain on the New York Stock Exchange. For the banks and the business community, these pension funds are made to order, providing them with a constant flow of guaranteed dollars which can be used to insulate and subsidize their deteriorating economic investments. Here is what *Pensions & Investments* magazine has to say about the value of having control over this new captive pool of social capital:

Individual corporations are going to the capital markets to raise new equity in amounts that are intriguingly similar to the capital they must contribute each year to their pension funds.

The obvious reaction is that pension funds have become

an onerous burden, and if the corporation did not have to
contribute, it could retain the money in its capital base and
not have to go to the bond or equity markets.

But it is interesting to consider the situation if there were
no private pension system. Onerous though pension contributions might be, corporations could be worse off.

First, if there were no private pension system, corporations certainly would pay higher taxes since their pension
contributions significantly reduce their taxable incomes.

They would thus turn over to the government money
that would otherwise be saved and invested through the
pension fund in the economy.

Few government programs lead to investment in capital
goods which increase the productive capacity of the economy, and most of the additional taxes would be spent on
current consumption.

Second, part of the money not paid in contributions
would accrue to the employees in the form of higher wages.
Part of these wages would be saved, but part would be spent
on current consumption.

Third, part of the money would be paid out in increased
dividends to shareholders who would spend some and save
some.

Finally, part would be retained in the company and be
added to its capital as retained earnings.

In sum, current consumption would be increased over
current levels, while savings and investment would be de-
creased—to the general detriment of the economy in the
long run.[17]

Forced savings, then, says *Pensions & Investments,* is
what makes pension funds such a plus; that, along with the
virtual guarantee that the individual beneficiary will have
no say in how the funds are used. In a sense, this new form
of social capital is even better than taxes as a source of revenue. With taxes there is some accountability built into the
system itself. In the final analysis, the private exploitation
of pension capital represents "investment without representation."[18]

One business insider, who himself controls a billion-dollar
pension fund and understandably wishes to remain anony-

mous, made the following observation about the captive use of pension capital to prop up the existing system.

I realize the system I'm operating in is no longer a capitalist system in terms of the way people believe it to be. It's a farce. . . . I don't think pension assets should be used to prove that capitalism still exists. Why put assets into a system that's really dead? [19]

Why indeed! Just consider the sheer magnitude of what has taken place in the American economy. Out of nowhere springs a new form of wealth—pension funds. It multiplies at such an incredible speed that it soon becomes the chief source of capital in America. Although it represents the deferred wages of millions upon millions of American workers, they remain virtually unaware that it is being used by a handful of banks and insurance companies to keep America's major corporations afloat. The manner in which the financial community has succeeded in gaining control over this new form of social capital remains one of the great untold stories of contemporary economic history.

Chapter 11: Setting the Precedent

It was not a coup d'état in the traditional sense. There was no seizure of key military and commercial installations, no tanks rumbling down the major boulevards, no bloodletting in the streets, no summary executions; in fact, there was no visible indication at all, on that thirteenth day of May 1946, that anything particularly unusual was taking place in official Washington, let alone anything so extraordinary as a coup in the making. For romantics, May 13, 1946 was not a day to remember. But for students interested in the dialectical subtleties of history that shape the great transformations of power, May 13, 1946 must certainly be recognized as a true tour de force. On that day, members of the U.S. Senate sparred in the opening skirmish of a legislative battle to decide who should control an emerging new form of wealth in America—pension capital. The debate that unfolded that spring day in the Senate was at best only half conscious, certainly bumbling and unfocused and somewhat uninspired. Such an inauspicious beginning to mark such a monumental turning point in history could probably only have taken place within an American setting, where the great arbiters of power pride themselves on being unversed in the ideology of social movements, but well trained in the pragmatic necessities of the moment.

The domestic calm of the war years had been shattered. Shortly after the celebrations of victory came the inevitable internal turmoil and disintegration that follow all long periods of forced wartime unity. The wage and price controls of World War II were lifted. Prices skyrocketed overnight. Unions reacted with new demands. Corporations resisted and strikes began to sweep through the nation. At the same time, Republicans in Congress were anxious to exert new controls over organized labor in order to restore what they perceived to be the declining influence of the American business community during the previous thirteen years of New Deal politics. A wave of labor disruptions and the death of President Roosevelt provided the opportunity and a crippling nationwide miners' strike led by John L. Lewis in 1946 provided the lightning rod to launch an all-out offensive.[1] That offensive came in two legislative installments; first, in the form of the Case Bill, presented to and passed by Congress in 1946, but vetoed by President Truman; and second, in the form of the Taft-Hartley Bill, ramrodded through Congress and passed into law over a veto by Truman the following year. The Taft-Hartley legislation, by intent, seriously weakened many of the rights organized labor had won nearly ten years earlier with the passage of the landmark National Labor Relations Act. Most important, there were two provisions contained within this new act which, while not of overriding concern at the time, nonetheless provided the opening wedge for wresting the future control of hundreds of billions of dollars of pension capital out of the hands of the unions and into the waiting embrace of America's financial community. It all began rather haphazardly as the President Pro-tem of the Senate recognized Senator Byrd of Virginia, on that May 13, 1946, to address the question of an amendment to the Case Bill.[2]

At issue was a bargaining demand by John L. Lewis that would require employers to contribute 10¢ for every ton of coal mined by their workers to a union health and welfare fund. The fund, in turn, was to be administered solely by the union on behalf of its membership. Senator Harry Byrd and his fellow Dixiecrats and Republicans argued that such demands, if allowed to go unchallenged, would set a dangerous precedent for the country. First, he argued, it would amount to wholesale seizure by labor of a large portion of the productive wealth of industry. "If such a privilege were extended to all contracts made between employers and em-

ployees throughout America," said Byrd, "it would result in
payments totaling at least $4 billion a year and perhaps
more."[3]

What Byrd was most concerned about was the control
of those large sums of money ($5 billion, at the time) in
labor's hands. "I am endeavoring to strike at the attempt of
representatives of labor to use such payments in establishing
funds over which no one but the labor representative would
have any control. I assert that if such a condition were allowed to take place, labor unions would become so powerful
that no organized government would be able to deal with
them." Here, for the first time, was a public discussion of the
enormous financial power that could be derived from control
over pension and welfare funds. To make sure this new form
of social capital didn't get into the wrong hands, which for
Byrd meant labor's hands, Republicans and Dixiecrats joined
together to propose an amendment to the Case Bill making
it unlawful for an employer to pay money or other things of
value to any representative (the union) of his employees.
Conversely, the amendment also made it illegal for any representative of the employees to demand, receive, or accept
from the employer any money or other things of value. The
only exception to this general rule was the transfer of union
dues from the employer to the union.[4]

In a prophetic aside, Senator Byrd concluded that if
John L. Lewis were to get his way and a precedent for labor
control over these funds was to be firmly established, it
would mean a "complete destruction of the private enterprise system of the U.S."[5]

The Case Bill, amendment and all, passed both Houses
in 1946, but Congress was unable to override a presidental
veto by Truman.[6] A year later to the month, however, the
debate tumbled onto the Senate floor once again, this time
during consideration of the Taft-Hartley Bill. Robert Taft,
or Mr. Republican, as he was affectionately known, included
a provision in his antilabor bill that would insure that unions
did not gain exclusive control over pension funds. The

amendment called for a jointly trusteed board in all union-bargained pension plans with 50 percent of the representatives coming from the employer and 50 percent from the union. Taft outlined his reasoning for the provision:

Certainly unless we impose some restrictions, we shall find that the welfare fund will become merely a war chest for the particular union. . . . [In labor's hands] the whole thing could become a great weapon of power.[7]

Taft said, at the time, that he was concerned that the fund not become a "racket" for organized labor but that it be protected so that the beneficiary could receive the maximum returns for his retirement income. Montana's Senator James Murray challenged Taft's assumption about crooked dealings and pointed out that with the many funds already exclusively administered by unions, there had been no evidence of widespread mismanagement. Senator Claude Pepper of Florida took labor's argument a step further, suggesting that Taft and his business friends, when they fretted over possible union abuses of the funds, were really fretting over the possibility that they might lose control of the potential pool of capital that pension funds represented.[8] Pepper was right, but despite the fact, or probably because of it, the vote went against labor. The provision of the bill was sustained and the bill itself was passed, this time over President Truman's veto.

Section 302 of the Taft-Hartley Act (regarding the regulation of pension funds) set the first major legislative precedent for the institutionalized control of pension capital by the private financial community. First, the act took exclusive control of these funds out of the hands of the unions by requiring that management representatives comprise 50 percent of the board of trustees of jointly administered pension plans. (On other corporate plans covering union workers, labor was to have no representation at all on the board of trustees administering the fund.)[9] Secondly, by implying that the funds should be invested solely with the idea of

producing the maximum short-run return on investment for
the beneficiaries, the Taft-Hartley Act effectively narrowed
the ways that pension capital could be used, so that it would
conform to the traditional objectives of a private capital
market.[10]

For the business community, this was just the opening
wedge. Subsequent legislation in 1958 (the Welfare & Pension Reform Act) and in 1974 (the Employee Retirement
Income Security Act—ERISA) further strengthened its control over the use of pension capital by putting more restrictions on labor's involvement with the funds and by further
refining the terms of investment to mesh with the needs of
a private capital system.[11] New terms like the "prudent man
rule" were introduced into these later legislative enactments,
in order to insure that control over these billions of dollars
would continue to remain in private banking hands.[12] Says
William Winpisinger of the Machinists Union:

> The whole question of prudence was, in my mind, a façade
> behind which the business community hid in backing the
> passage of the law. They wanted to make damn certain they
> got controls guaranteeing that we [the unions] couldn't get
> together and regiment the money in any certain way. I felt
> all along that this was the capitalist motivation for Taft-
> Hartley and ERISA.[13]

In fact, the prudent man rule laid down in the ERISA
legislation is really no more than a convenient legalism to
justify the continued infusion of pension-fund moneys into
Fortune 500 investments. According to the prudent man
rule, pension investments must be made in such a way as to
minimize risk and maximize returns. The banking community has been able to convince its friends in Congress and in
the courts that investments in the stocks and bonds of America's giant multinationals are the best application of the
prudent man principle, even though the financial facts of the
past ten years do not effectively support these claims. According to Joe Swire, who teaches pension courses at the
AFL-CIO Labor Study Center, "bank investment people

and insurance people are losing hundreds of millions of dollars in the market with our pension funds ... and when you talk to these investment managers, they say they want to maximize yield and minimize risks." The results are the opposite, argues Swire. "They're getting maximum risk from the investments with a minimum yield." [14]

Mr. Swire's admonitions aside, the financial community has been successful in using the legislative restrictions imposed by the Taft-Hartley Act, the Pension and Welfare Reform Act, and ERISA to control the vast pool of pension-fund capital for nearly thirty years. The history of that control is a history of manipulation, self-dealing, and mismanagement that makes a mockery of the very principles that the legislation was allegedly designed to protect.

Chapter 12: A Corporate "Asset"

Raise the question of corruption and self-dealing with pension funds and the average person on the street is likely to conjure up immediately the image of a bunch of tough Teamster types sitting around a real-estate office in Vegas divvying up funds for shady, fly-by-night ventures. In fact, the Teamsters' Central States, Southeast and Southwest Pension Fund has been found guilty of just such activity. Years of investigations by the federal government have disclosed an entire laundry list of illegal or questionable investment practices by the Teamster Fund, including the bankrolling of underworld business dealings in Las Vegas and across the country. In March of 1977, the Labor Department finally succeeded in forcing the resignation of the fund's chief trustees, including Frank Fitzsimmons, president of the Teamsters' International. The Teamsters' is the most blatant example of union corruption and self-dealing but there have been similar cases of pension-fund abuses within other unions as well.[1]

While the instances of union abuse of pension funds have achieved tremendous notoriety, the countless examples of corporate and banking abuses have gone virtually undetected over the years. In fact, the record shows that while union mismanagement of funds has been usually the result of either the ignorance or corruption of particular individuals, corporate and banking abuses have been more the result of standard operating procedures that have become an accepted part of day-to-day management of pension assets. According to Michael Gordon, former minority counsel to the Senate General Subcommittee on Labor and Pensions, the instances of labor misuse of pension funds are generally more obvious and dramatic because they involve a single hand in the till. Corporate abuse, while equally improper, is less easily detected or publicized, says Gordon, because it involves a much more sophisticated manipulation of pension moneys.[2]

Most corporate pension funds are turned over to banks or insurance companies to invest. Some, however, like U.S. Steel, du Pont, W. R. Grace, and Wells Fargo, are managed in-house. Others combine internal management of a portion of the funds with external management of the rest.[3] The opportunity for self-dealing and manipulation of fund assets by in-house managers is considerable. A detailed study conducted by the 20th Century Fund and published in 1975 catalogues the numerous ways in-house funds have been used to advance the interest of the company or its top executives at the expense of the fund beneficiaries.

According to the study, one of the most obvious abuses occurs when in-house pension managers invest the funds in the common stock of the sponsoring company. This often takes place when the company is "engaged in an acquisition program based on exchange of shares and needs a high stock price in order to make favorable deals." Though less frequent, companies will occasionally use their own pension funds to invest in companies targeted for takeovers.[4] The Genesco Company case is a typical example of how funds are manipulated during acquisition periods. In the early 1960s, the trustees of Genesco's pension fund (who were also officers of the corporation) began buying large amounts of Genesco stock—so large, in fact, that in the last quarter of 1961, the fund purchases amounted to 41.6 percent of all the Genesco stock traded on the exchange, and in the second and third quarters of 1961 they represent 75.2 and 78.1 percent of all stock traded. Eventually, nearly one-third of Genesco's pension fund consisted of Genesco stock. Of course, these large purchases resulted in the value of Genesco stock going up. Not coincidentally, the company began pursuing an ambitious acquisition campaign during the same period.

Between 1961 and 1965 Genesco exchanged over one million shares of its own stock for the stock of twelve other companies, thereby acquiring either control or a minority interest. The 20th Century Fund report concluded that "if the buying programs of the two [pension] funds had not maintained Genesco's stock price, this cornucopia of acquisitions could not have been accumulated on such favorable terms, if at all." Under the existing laws, Genesco was technically not commiting a crime, even though its practices were clearly unethical. Not surprisingly, Genesco stock eventually plummeted from a high of 60 in 1965 to a low of 6 in 1974, thus seriously undermining the value of the company's pension funds which owned so much of the company's own stock. Although under the new provisions of ERISA, companies are only permitted to invest up to 10 percent of their in-house funds in company stock, it is still more than enough to allow businesses to continue to self-deal in the same manner that Genesco did.[5]

Genesco is just one example of the countless cases of corporate self-dealing that go on every day with in-house pension funds. In April 1970, Secretary of Labor George Schultz testified before a House committee on the kinds of abuses his department had uncovered with in-house management of pension-fund plans. Schultz recounted one case where pension-fund trustees, again company officers, purchased shares of company stock for the fund, while unloading their own personal holdings. The outcome was "a resulting depreciation of fund assets estimated at over $4.5 million." In another instance, said Schultz, company trustees simply "borrowed" two-thirds of the fund's assets to "finance private business of their own."[6]

Even these kinds of abuses, however, start to look like playground antics when compared to the use of pension funds as a tool for misrepresenting corporate profit-and-earnings statements. Here is where the corporations have really made their score. For example, every company uses

actuarial assumptions to estimate the rate of return they can
expect on investments. The rate of return a firm makes on its
pension investments is directly related to the amount of
money the company will have to pay into the pension-fund
account. In other words, if the company makes money from
its pension-fund investments, it can use that money instead
of its corporate earnings to fulfill its contribution requirements to the pension fund plan. It is estimated that for every
1 percent rise in the rate of return on its pension investment, a business will have to pay approximately 20 percent
less out of pretax corporate earnings into the fund. And
here's where the scam comes in. Companies use actuarial
assumptions to estimate what they hope their returns on
pension-fund investments will be. By arbitrarily raising return assumptions, they are able, on paper, to show an amount
of future returns that they may or may not see. Still, this
accounting procedure allows them to pay less of their corporate earnings into the pension-fund account. "Some companies treat an actuary as though he were a legalized
bookie," says James Curtis, president of a large actuarial
firm. "They just want us to get figures together that will help
their profit picture." [7]

Take the case of U.S. Steel. In 1971, the company reported a net income of $154 million, up $7 million from the
previous year. In reality, U.S. Steel suffered a severe decline
in earnings during fiscal 1971, but by the manipulation of
its actuarial assumption, it was able to hide the fact from the
rest of the business community, its stockholders, and the general public. What U.S. Steel did was merely to increase its
actuarial assumption on the rate of return to the fund from
5 to 6 percent, thus decreasing its pension costs from $104
million in 1970 to $62 million in 1971. This sleight of hand
left $42 million in its retained-earnings account, money
which should have been transferred to its pension fund.
Thus U.S. Steel came out with instant profit, and the company officers could relax at the annual board meeting, all

thanks to the magic of modern-day accounting methods and the ability to manipulate pension-fund actuarial assumptions.[8]

Lest U.S. Steel be unfairly singled out, it should be noted that between 1968 and 1972, according to a Chase Manhattan Bank study, over 70 percent of a sample of 465 firms revised their interest assumptions or expected rates of returns on investments of pension funds. All of this is more than just a little bizarre when one stops to consider that the Dow Jones Industrial Average remained virtually unchanged during the same period. By hyping the assumption rate, or hoped-for returns on investment, beyond what the company knows they can really expect to receive, these firms end up paying less into the pension kitty (out of earnings) in the short run, but in the long run they end up with a pension fund that is increasingly underfunded.[9]

Earnings aren't the only item the corporations manipulate with actuarial assumptions. Taxes also come into play. It seems that during high profit periods, like the first half of the 1960s, companies lower their actuarial assumption below what they accurately reflect in the marketplace so they can pump more corporate earnings into the pension funds in order to avoid paying taxes on those moneys. This practice became so widespread in the 1960s that the IRS had to step in and pressure companies to raise their assumption rates.[10]

Under the provisions of ERISA, actuaries must now certify pension-plan assumptions and funding methods, and sponsoring corporations must report all this to the Department of Labor, including explanations of changes in the rate of return percentages. Still, without the power to obtain other necessary financial information from the companies, it remains difficult, if not impossible, to prove that a particular firm is purposely hyping (as they say in the investment community) its assumptions. And even with ERISA, writes A. F. Ehrbar in *Fortune* magazine, "the accounting and actuarial treatment of pension liabilities is a masterpiece of obfusca-

tion. There is so much latitude in the way pension calculations are performed that companies can come up with virtually any level of contributions and liabilities they choose." [11]

The corporations, then, have come to use their pension
funds more as an adjunct to their profit-and-earnings practices and less as a deferred wage cost in which their sole
responsibility is to advance the financial interest of the pension fund itself. In fact, corporations often refer to the concept of a "profit center" when talking about their pension
funds. According to the 20th Century Fund study, a 1973
survey of major American companies showed that a majority
of the top executives recognized "to a high degree" or "to a
very high degree" the importance of pension-fund investment to corporate profits. The profit center notion rests on the
understanding that if the corporate pension fund improves
its rate of return on investment, then less money out of earnings need be paid in, thus improving the profit picture of the
company. Of course, as far as the beneficiary is concerned,
increased rates of return do not increase what he or she will
receive in benefits. However, if the rates of return plummet
and the fund becomes shaky or insolvent, the beneficiary
could lose his or her benefits altogether. For this reason, the
investment policies of companies anxious to use pension
funds as a profit center can prove to be dangerous for the
beneficiary, especially when the company trustees invest in
riskier and riskier ventures, hoping to improve their profit
performance by getting higher returns. [12]

The hyping of actuarial assumptions, the leveraging of
profit centers and poor returns overall, have resulted in tens
of billions of dollars of unfunded liabilities in major corporate pension-plan accounts. According to a 1977 study conducted by Investors' Management Sciences, Inc., a subsidiary
of Standard & Poor's Corporation, some 1,500 of America's
largest corporations currently have unfunded prior-service
liabilities of $48 billion and unfunded vested benefits total-
ling nearly $23 billion. Unfunded prior-service liabilities are
the total funds a company would have to pay out to its bene-

ficiaries in the future to meet all of its funding obligations. Unfunded vested benefits are the total funds a company would have to pay out now if it terminated its pension plan. Seventy-four giant companies alone account for $36 billion of all the prior-service liabilities and some seventy-seven firms account for $18 billion of the unfunded vested benefits. Even more frightening is the speed with which these unfunded liabilities are growing; unfunded prior-service liabilities are up 62 percent in just two years and unfunded vested benefits are up 48 percent in the same twenty-four-month period for those companies.[13]

The unfunded liabilities of major U.S. corporations are so substantial that it would take Chrysler nearly thirty years to pay off what it owes on its fund, even if it gave over its entire pretax earnings every single year from now until then. Based on current average earning levels and no increases in benefits, it would take the entire earnings of UniRoyal for twelve years to pay up on its fund liabilities and for companies like American Motors, Pan American, and United Brands, all of which had a pretax earnings deficit as of 1977, it would take even longer to pay what they owe. In many large corporations today, unfunded liabilities represent one-fourth to one-third of the net worth of the company. In some of the giants like American Motors, the unfunded liabilities are almost 60 percent of the net worth of the firm.[14] Since ERISA requires companies to pay off a portion of their liabilities each year over a thirty- to forty-year period, the costs of pension contributions are going to increase dramatically over the next decade. With current pension contributions already increasing by 20 to 25 percent per year and ERISA requiring many companies to upgrade benefits and funding still further, some experts in the field estimate that U.S. corporations will be contributing nearly $81 billion a year to fund pension benefits by 1983, compared to $25 billion in 1975.[15]

For America's corporate giants as well as for millions of pension beneficiaries, these statistics are a grim forewarning of what lies just ahead. Dramatic increases in pension funding obligations under ERISA will mean more corporate cash will have to be paid out, cash which would otherwise be available for earnings. A decline in corporate earnings, in turn, means a decline in both dividends and in the value of blue-chip equities on the exchange. All of this means a further drop in the returns for pension funds invested heavily in those same stocks. As returns for pension-fund investments decrease, even more corporate earnings will have to be paid out and the cycle repeats itself over and over again in a downward spiral.[16] Add to this the prospect of a major recession (which would significantly lower corporate profits, force some companies out of business, and reduce the prices of most stocks—thus swelling unfunded liabilities further), and the result is a formula for economic disaster.

For those corporations that collapse first under the weight of this downward spiral, fund beneficiaries will *probably* not suffer too much. ERISA created the Pension Benefit Guarantee Corporation (PBGC) to insure the pensions of participants in defined benefit plans (but not for defined contribution or profit-sharing plans).[17] Under this provision, an individual company is responsible for paying its unfunded liabilities with up to 30 percent of its net assets if the company goes out of business and/or terminates its pension plan. Where unfunded liabilities equal or exceed this 30 percent limit, the PBGC pays off the difference to the beneficiaries. This insurance will, in theory, be paid for by all pension participants through a yearly premium assessment—in effect the strong plans insure the weak ones. But if many plans with large unfunded liabilities terminate, the PBGC will have to raise premiums drastically from the present $2.65 per participant to $25 or even $50 a head. This move in itself could precipitate a sort of pension dominoes, forcing other weak pension plans to terminate.[18]

In late 1977, this specter spurred Congress to postpone termination insurance coverage for multi-employer plans for eighteen months—from January 1, 1978 to July 1, 1979

(single-employer and multi-employer plans are covered under separate PBGC programs). The fear was that the imminent termination of several such plans in declining or dying
industries would saddle the PBGC with hundreds of millions
or even billions of dollars in liabilities. Also, many were concerned that some companies would prefer paying the 30 percent net asset liability to meeting much larger unfunded
pension obligations. This fear was heightened because, at
that time, the United Mine Workers' 1950 fund—with over
80,000 beneficiaries and at least $2 billion in unfunded lia-
bilities, was perilously close to insolvency. Contributions to
the fund were based on production, and since an extended
strike was a certainty, the fund would run completely out of
money within a month of the strike. The coal operators were
clearly using this situation as a weapon against the union,
and some companies were known to favor dumping the plan
into the lap of the PBGC. So Congress has postponed insurance for millions of pension participants while it attempts to
rework the whole area of benefit insurance.[19]

As if this is not bad enough, ERISA requires the PBGC
to offer insurance even on the 30 percent net-worth liability.
The American Bankers' Association insisted on this provision,
fearing that PBGC claims on a bankrupt company's assets
would supersede any bank claims. Thus, companies won't
be required to pay back anything at all if they go out of
business or simply terminate their plans. This would make
it even more attractive for them to dump their pension funds.
Not surprisingly, the PBGC couldn't find any private in-
surers to underwrite this "contingent employer liability insurance." As Lloyds of London noted, underwriting unfunded
pension liabilities amounts to "insuring the profitability of
the American economy." [20] If the economy experiences a
mini-depression equal to or worse than the kind it went
through in 1975, scores of America's giants could topple under the combined weight of depression and pension obligations. In such a case, it is doubtful that the federal government could continue to honor its obligation to guarantee the

benefits of the millions of workers affected. What's more likely to happen is a complete restructuring of the entire concept of private pensions, probably in the direction of their being phased out altogether or absorbed into the social security system (more on this in Chapter 19).[21]

In their self-dealing practices, then, corporations have not only jeopardized the pension funds and their beneficiaries, but also the long-run financial health of the firms themselves. But since most of the actual control over pension investments resides with the banks (and insurance companies), it is there that the worst abuses are being perpetrated.

Chapter 13: A Boon for the Banks

Everyone has probably had the experience at one time or another of being accosted by either a right-wing or left-wing ideologue ranting and raving that a handful of New York bankers control America. While one is generally left with the impression that the given party is a bit paranoid, there still exists that lingering doubt that suggests there might, in fact, be some kernel of truth in the statement. With the emergence of pension-fund capital and its takeover by America's largest banks, that assertion has become a reality, the proportions of which are not yet fully appreciated by the general public.

As mentioned earlier, the one hundred largest banks already control over $145 billion in pension assets, with the top ten banks controlling nearly $80 billion between them. The banks invest a majority of these funds in the equity and debt financing of America's largest companies. With this kind of financial clout the big banks are able to exert a tremendous degree of control over corporate America.[1] Insurance companies exert power as well since they manage over $80 billion in pension-fund assets.[2]

Bank control over the corporations is secured by various means, some direct and some indirect. First, there is the direct control exercised by virtue of the fact that banks, for the most part, have sole voting rights for the stock they purchase with pension-fund assets. This is of no small consequence in light of the fact that many banks hold sizable portions of major corporate portfolios. A general rule of thumb used by financial experts to measure influence or control is the 5 percent threshold. That is, if a bank owns 5 percent or more of a large company's stock, it usually gains substantial influence and, in some cases, even control of the firm. Several years ago a study done for the House Banking and Currency Committee showed 176 separate instances involving 147 giant corporations in which just forty-nine banks held 5 percent or more of the common stock of the company.[3]

Often bank control over a corporation is exercised by subtle, indirect means. For example, one of the most powerful levers a large institutional holder of stock has is the simple decision to sell its portfolio if it becomes disenchanted with specific policy initiatives of the management. When a large investor pulls out, it often signals to the rest of the financial community that it is unhappy with the direction in which the company is headed. This can and often does have a deflating effect on the value of the stock. For this reason, top corporate executives are usually careful to run all new plans and proposals by the large bank holders well in advance, and generally will not even entertain the prospect of going ahead without their prior consent.[4]

Bank control over corporate policies is also exercised through their role as creditors. With corporations relying more and more on external debt financing from banks, they find themselves increasingly tied to a web of restrictions and conditions. According to the House Banking and Currency Committee, those bank strings can include "limitations on the payment of dividends, requiring the maintenance of a specific amount of working capital, limitations on the amount of investment made outside the corporation, restrictions on the sale of certain percentages of assets without consent of the creditor and restrictions on incurring further debt." [5]

When it comes to influence, there's nothing like having your own man or woman on the board of directors. In fact, the extent of interlocking directorships between banks and major corporations should convince even the dyed-in-the-wool skeptic that the financial community is truly in the driver's seat. The same banking committee study showed banks holding a total of 768 interlocking directorships with 286 of the 500 largest industrial corporations, for an average of three directors per company. The same interlocking relationship existed between banks and the fifty largest merchandising, transportation, utility, and life-insurance companies as well. Again, forty-nine banks were found to have seventy-three interlocking directorships with twenty-seven of the fifty largest transportation companies; eighty-six interlocking directorships with twenty-two of the fifty largest utilities; and 146 interlocks with twenty-nine of the fifty largest life-insurance companies.[6]

A case in point illustrates what real control by the banks begins to look like when pension funds, large equity holdings, major creditor leverage, and key interlocks are welded together. Pan American Airways is typical. "The Chase Manhattan Bank (at one time) held 6.7 percent of Pan Am's common stock, had an $8.5 million loan outstanding, and was a pension fund trustee; the First National City Bank had a director interlock, managed two Pan Am pension funds, and had a $7 million loan outstanding; Morgan had a loan to Pan Am of $20.5 million." In addition, all three banks had interlocking relationships with major insurance companies that were lending money to Pan Am.[7]

It is this kind of control exercised by banks over corporate America that led the distinguished economic historian Adolf Berle to remark that he foresaw "a permanently concentrated group of officials building a paramount and virtually unchallenged power position over the American industrial economy."[8] The exercise of this virtually unchallenged power brings banks into constant conflict with their role as protectors of pension-fund assets. The bankers, of course, are always protesting that they know of no instances of conflicts of interest that have placed their pension-fund accounts in jeopardy. The fact is that there is no way they could avoid conflicts of interest—unless their primary objective is not to make money for the bank.

Let's take an example. Chase Manhattan jointly manages a $423 million pension fund for Firestone. Former Chase president Willard Butcher sits on the Firestone board. Fire-

stone is a commercial customer of Chase and the bank trust
department holds 950,000 shares in Firestone. Can Mr.
Butcher really look the American public square in the eyes
and claim, without qualification, that there is no possibility
of a conflict of interest occurring here? [9] Quite the contrary.
These meticulously woven interlocks are not just the result
of coincidence or happenstance. They represent the *sine qua
non* of bank culture. They are what makes a bank a bank. So
what might be regarded as a conflict of interest by outsiders
is really an opportunity of interest to a banker.

It is important to remember that all of these interlocks
(as in the Chase example) exist for the bank to make money.
Because it is not a charitable institution, when a bank says
that its objective is to maximize the return on investment of
its pension-fund assets, what it really means is to maximize
in accordance with its larger overriding objective of making
money for the bank itself. How could it be otherwise? Major
banks are controlling tens of billions of dollars of pension
funds. These moneys are increasingly providing these institutions with the primary instrument through which they
carry on their overall business dealings. The pension fund
has become indispensable to their operations and their success. Therefore it is absurd to continue to harbor the myth
that their sole and exclusive interest is the welfare and benefit of the fund itself. *The fact is that the banks are not the
instrument serving the fund. Rather, the fund is the instrument serving the banks.*[10]

The 20th Century Fund's detailed study of bank trust
departments recounts the many ways banks use their pension assets to foster other bank objectives. In many cases this
kind of exploitation seriously undermines the interest of the
fund itself. For example, banks will often accommodate their
own bank customers by investing bank pension assets in
these firms even when they might be getting a better return
somewhere else. A study of one major bank revealed that
over 30 percent of the number of stocks in some fourteen
portfolios in its trust department were issues of customers of

the bank. In addition, 29 percent of its bond holdings were bonds of bank customers. Another bank, Continental Illinois, reported a few years ago that of the fifty companies in which it holds its largest equity investments, "75 percent are commercial borrowing customers and 37 percent have outstanding loans or lines of credit in excess of $5 million each." [11]

The author of the 20th Century report on bank trust departments, Edward Herman, professor of economics at the Wharton School of Finance, says that bank trust departments assist their commercial customers in a variety of other ways as well, "by buying or not selling their securities in declining markets, by purchasing or financing in support of acquisition efforts, by refusing to sell to outsiders in takeover bids threatening customer managements, and by supporting customer management groups in proxy contests." [12]

It is not uncommon, says Professor Herman, for bank trust departments to maintain their holdings in a commercial customer's firm even though it would mean a loss for the pension funds. In one case, where an officer of the bank was also a director of a customer company, the pension-fund managers "were prevented from unloading a part of their holdings because of the 'explaining' that the officer would have to do as a director of the customer." The fund lost in this instance, but the bank gained by staying on the good side of a major commercial customer, and, of course, the bank director who sat on the customer's board came out smelling like a rose.[13]

Trade-offs are also considered a common part of the financial ballgame when it comes to getting bank directors on boards of other companies. A typical case involved the purchase of a large amount of bonds in a customer company by a trust department of a major bank. While the company was not listed on the trust department's approved list of investments, the bond specialist of the bank said that the purchase of the bonds "was expected of the bank" as a *quid pro quo* for securing an interlocking board directorship.[14] Then too, companies will often hand over their pension funds to the bank where they do their commercial business in the hope that it will improve their chances of obtaining better terms for their borrowing requirements or other financial needs.[15]

The effect that these types of bank manipulations have on pension funds is reflected in the three following cases, all of which illustrate, in one way or another, the inherent conflicts of interest that permeate bank involvement in the pension field.

In 1974, the U.S. Steel/Carnegie pension fund brought suit against Citibank of New York. The suit charged Citibank with investing over $3 million of the U.S. Steel fund in debentures made to the Topper Corporation, knowing at the time that the company was in serious financial trouble. According to the suit, the bank did not warn the pension fund of this fact because it had major loans outstanding with Topper and needed to secure the placement of pension-fund loans with the company in order to protect the bank's position as a major creditor. Eighty days later, the Topper company filed for bankruptcy and the proceeds from the sale of the debentures went to the bank and were used to reduce Topper's debt under a previous financing agreement between Citibank and Topper. While the bank argued that it had separated its trust department loyalties from its commercial department loyalties, the pension fund maintained that such claims were ridiculous. They argued that the bank was well aware of the deteriorating financial picture of Topper but went ahead with the debenture investment anyway, in order to protect and shore up its own claims against the company.[16]

A similar case was brought against Continental Illinois Bank in 1973 by the Airline Pilots Association pension fund. Continental had invested the ALPA's funds in the equities of several companies, including TWA, Lums, U.S. Freight, and Management Assistance, Inc., with whom the bank also served as a major creditor. In each case, the bank either continued to hold on to the securities even after the stocks plum-

meted or only sold them well after they should have. The
suit alleged that the bank did so because it was a major creditor and was more concerned with protecting its outstanding
loans than in protecting the interests of the pension fund.[17]

Probably the best-known and most controversial example
of alleged conflict of interest arose over the Penn Central
stock held by trust departments of major banks including
Chase and Morgan. Questions arose as to why these banks
waited so long to unload these stocks when they knew, because of their inside information as creditors, that the railroad giant was on the verge of collapse. According to the
findings of Professor Herman in the 20th Century Fund
study, there is reason to consider the possibility that bank
management held on to the deteriorating stocks so as not to
"disaffect the management" and "risk losing substantial
(commercial) deposits"; and because they were large creditors and did not want to risk a stock pullout for fear that the
company would go under. So in the end it was the pension
fund that suffered, once again, in order to protect the other
interests of the banks involved.[18]

It may be a little unfair to single out individual examples
of self-dealing and conflict of interest in bank use of pension
fund assets; unfair in the sense that it conveys the impression that at particular moments in time certain wrongdoers
have committed specific offenses for which only they are to
blame. In fact, they are only guilty of wrongdoing to the extent that they are faithfully pursuing policies and practices
which are themselves the source of the conflicts. The point
is this: private banks simply cannot look out for their own
profit interests first and at the same time be asked to look
out for the pension funds' profit interest first. This inherent
conflict between the bank's interest and the pension fund's
interest manifests itself on two levels. First, there is an inevitable and direct conflict involved when banks use pension-fund assets in ways that jeopardize the funds themselves. Second, there is an indirect and long-range conflict
involved when banks invest these pension funds in ways that

undermine both the job security of the beneficiaries and the economic security of the communities in which they live. Private control of pension capital gives the financial community (and the corporate community) a double-edged sword. It can profit by and at the expense of other people's moneys in the short run, while further consolidating its power over both the pension capital pool and its beneficiaries by continuing to control the long-range economic planning decisions as well. Thus the financial community enjoys two captive relationships: one over the pension capital itself and the other over the people and communities that pension capital belongs to.[19]

Leaving aside the question of conflict of interest, the private financial community still claims that it is best suited to exercise control over this enormous pool of pension capital because of its "expert" ability to maximize returns on investments. Here again the facts belie the claims. As was already touched on in Chapter 11, returns on capital have declined over the past twenty-eight years. What is less well known but even more shocking is that pension-fund investments in the market have done even worse than the market itself. The record of bank investments of pension funds is so poor that one is forced to conclude that either the investment community is virtually incompetent or the system in which it is investing is on its deathbed, or both. In either case, it raises some fundamental questions about who should control pension capital investments in the future and for what ends that capital should be used.

In a world where modern education has been largely reduced to the taking in and storing of visual images, there could be no better introduction into the world of finance than a close-up look at the floor of the New York Stock Exchange during a normal workday session. The shouting, the handwaving, the pushing and shoving and general air of chaos and confusion are, at first glance, likely to be unsettling for the onlooker who, after all, would probably like to think that there exists some grand internal logic in the overall functioning of the system. If it all looks a bit too much like a scene from a Las Vegas gambling casino, then a lesson has indeed been learned.

Like the professional gambler, the professional pension investor is playing against the odds all the time, hoping to beat the house. And like many professional gamblers, he or she is playing with other people's money, mainly tens of billions of dollars of pension funds. Of course professional pension investors, like their gambling counterparts, are always assuring those who have entrusted them with their funds that they have their own fool-proof system that can't miss. Like most gamblers in Vegas, their performance has proven them wrong time and time again.

In the ten-year period from December 31, 1966, to December 31, 1976, the annual return on investment for pension fund equity was 33 percent below the average annual return of the Standard & Poors 500 index stocks. (The S&P is a representative cross-section of all stocks listed on the New York Stock Exchange.) During that time, the S&P average annual rate of return was 6.6 percent, while banks averaged only a 4.4% return and insurance companies only a 4% return between 1966 and 1976. For the period of 1972–76, the figures are even more embarrassing. While the S&P index return averaged about 4.9 percent for the five years, bank equity returns were averaging .8 percent and insurance companies only 1 percent.[20] In fact, between 1962 and 1975, 87 percent of all the money managers in the country performed below the S&P index.[21]

The effect of these low returns on pension funds has been devastating, especially with inflation hovering at 8 to 10 percent a year. In the 1974 bear market, for example, over $21 billion worth of pension funds were wiped out by equity losses.[22] The assets of some pension funds decreased by 30 to 40 percent during 1973 and 1974.[23] In the first quarter of 1977 the figures on returns on investment showed that only two of the 162 pooled equity funds surveyed achieved a positive rate of return at all.²⁴ Not only are major banks using their pension-fund assets to prop up a market exchange that is continuing to stagnate, but even then their losses are compounded by their investments doing worse than the market itself.²⁵

It is not surprising, then, that in recent years there has been a movement afoot to replace these so-called money experts altogether with computers, the notion being that a well-programmed machine can do better in the market than an $80,000-a-year investment analyst.²⁶ Market indexing is becoming increasingly popular in light of the embarrassing performance of professional money managers. The theory behind computer market indexing is called the "random walk." It asserts that future price changes in the market value of particular stocks are random, and therefore it is impossible to predict stock performance based on available current knowledge. What this means is that all of the money banks invest in market research and high-paid analysts is mostly a futile exercise. Proponents of market indexing have demonstrated that a well-programmed computer can beat the pros almost every time.²⁷

The indexing theory works something like this: a computer is programmed with a portfolio that has "the overall risk characteristics and industry diversification of the S&P in much the same way that pollsters find a representative cross section of people to interview." ²⁸ Thus, performance is intended to mirror the market and not designed to try to beat it. Indexing is growing dramatically, and Michael Clowes, editor of *Pensions & Investments* magazine, expects that it will soon be used to invest over 30 percent of the nation's private pension assets.²⁹

Needless to say, many of the so-called experts are less than happy with computer market indexing, especially since it threatens to replace their own jobs. And there is the ego aspect as well. A. F. Ehrbar, writing in *Fortune* magazine, says: "There is the natural tendency of managers to find uncongenial the notion that they've spent their whole professional lives trying to do something that's impossible, i.e., beat the market." [30]

Herein lies the final irony. Not only are the investment bankers failing to look out for the interest of their pension-fund beneficiaries first; not only are they using these funds to protect their own financial interest and to protect a capital market that is sick and unstable; not only are they continuing to underperform in this already weakened market structure year in and year out with disastrous rates of return on investments; but to top it all, a well-programmed computer could do a better job of maximizing returns on investments than they can.[31] Still they continue their practices with impunity because those who are the victims of these unconscionable injustices have remained ignorant of the crimes being perpetrated against them. Two hundred years ago a great American radical, Thomas Paine, observed the nature of such injustices. His words should be passed on to every American worker whose deferred wages are being placed in a pension fund account.

While men could be persuaded that they had no rights, or that rights appertained only to a certain class of men, it was not difficult to govern them authoritatively. The ignorance in which they were held and the superstitions in which they were instructed, furnished the means of doing it. But when the ignorance is gone and the superstition with it, when they perceive the imposition that has been acted upon them and when they reflect that the [workers] are the primary means of all the wealth that exists in the world, beyond what nature spontaneously produces ... it is no longer possible to govern them as before. The fraud, once detected, cannot be retracted. To attempt it is to provoke derision or invite destruction.[32]

It is time to strip that ignorance and that superstition away once again. The rights of American workers are being trampled upon. Obviously the first step in reclaiming those rights is to understand the fraud that has been perpetrated against them.

Chapter 14: Who Are the Real Owners?

The Individual Beneficiary

Most workers covered under pension plans might be surprised to learn that on the average, their individual little fund is worth more than $8,000. In fact, pension funds are now the largest single asset most working Americans own.[1] But before people start laying plans for their pool and retirement cottage in Florida, says Ralph Nader, they should take a close look at the fine print in those pension agreements they're covered under. When they do, they'll find that there is a good chance they'll never collect a single dime of their own fund. Why? It could be because they've changed jobs or unions, or were laid off somewhere down the line for a small period, or were disabled on the job, or the company went out of business or was merged into a larger conglomerate or the plan was terminated or whatever.[2]

Horror stories surrounding pension abuses abound: the welder in Detroit who found himself mysteriously laid off after nine years and eleven months, just weeks before he was to qualify for his pension; the textile worker in Georgia who was seriously injured on the job and became permanently disabled after years of faithful service, only to find that the only compensation waiting for her while she was convalescing was a get-well card signed by her fellow workers; the salesclerk in New York City who was laid off one winter for a few short weeks immediately following the Christmas rush season, only to learn, several years later when he reached sixty-five years of age, that as a result of that layoff, he had forfeited any rights to a retirement income.[3]

Sometimes the victims of a pension hustle are picked off one by one. At other times they are rounded up and disposed of in mass as when the Studebaker Packard Corporation refused to honor its pension obligations to over 3,300 workers who were fully qualified to receive a retirement income from the company.[4]

For the millions of American workers who fall victim to these corporate practices, the cruelty of being left high and dry in the last few years of life is an unpardonable sin by any standard. But for the companies who mete out this punishment, there is certainly nothing personal in it. Nor are their actions in any way meant to be arbitrary. In fact, quite the opposite. There is not a corporate pension plan in the entire country that is set up to pay off all, or even a majority, of the employees for whom contributions are set aside each pay period. Like insurance companies, pension plans work under the principle that, while everyone takes part, only a few will be able to benefit; and that's exactly why nearly one out of two workers covered under pension funds will be left in the lurch. It's designed that way, contributions to the funds being based strictly on the same kind of actuarial assumptions used by insurance companies.[5]

Nader and Blackwell, in their book, *You and Your Pension,* illustrate how the whole thing works.

Assume that one hundred employees enter the plan simultaneously at the age of thirty. The actuary estimates that a certain number will not survive until retirement (the mortality rate), a certain number of others will leave the plan before meeting the conditions to qualify for a pension (the withdrawal rate), and a certain number from those who remain will become disabled before qualifying for a benefit (the disability rate). If this leaves only fifty of the original one hundred who are expected to receive a benefit, the amount of contributions needed to pay benefits to those who will get them is only half as much as if all one hundred were expected to receive pensions. However, those contributions are usually estimated as a percent of the payroll going to all one hundred employees, even though half are not expected to receive a pension.[6]

In 1974, public clamor over pension-fund abuses of the kind mentioned here led to the passage of the Employee

Retirement Income Security Act. The legislation did reduce a few of the abuses, by strengthening funding requirements and making administrators and trustees personally liable for breaches of their fiduciary responsibility. It also provided for a government-backed guarantee of pension benefits, but, as we have seen, this promise is quite tenuous at best. Moreover, ERISA still fails to deal with the most important abuse perpetrated by the funds: vesting. Under the new act, a company must vest (or qualify) an employee for some part of his retirement income after ten years of service.[7] This kind of so-called reform led one expert in the field, Professor Merton Bernstein, to caustically remark that "unless Congress can do better ... on vesting, the reform bill will constitute as big a fraud as the plans it purports to improve."[8] Mr. Bernstein has obviously seen the Department of Labor figures on worker mobility. Over one-half of the work force covered by pension funds changes jobs well before the ten-year vesting standard imposed by ERISA. Because there is no legal mechanism by which workers can transfer their accumulated employment time to other jobs, they lose all the deferred wages that have been set aside for them.[9] To collect a full pension is even more difficult. A worker usually needs to accumulate twenty-five years or more of credit with the same employer to receive the maximum pension.[10]

Of course, under normal circumstances, if millions of Americans were cheated out of some $8,000 owed to them, there would be hell to pay. But with pension funds, we're not talking about the everyday run-of-the-mill cash asset. Pensions are different, as already mentioned, but the question is: exactly how different are they?

Separating Ownership from Control

Question: Since pension funds now own about 25 percent of all the companies on the New York and American stock exchanges, do the beneficiaries of these funds, the workers, own American industry?

An official of the American Bankers Association: The beneficiaries of pension funds do not own American industry.
When you look at the definition of ownership as controlling,
which is, as far as I'm concerned, the only real instance of
ownership, certainly they (the workers) can't own it.

Question: OK. Then who does own the securities held by
pension funds?

ABA official: If you define ownership as control, I don't
know. I don't think anyone is controlling these companies.

Question: Does this signal some sort of transformation of
the economic system?

ABA official: I'm not an economist. I don't know. Maybe it
does. Now certainly it is clear to a noneconomist like me
that it is a change. But what it means, I don't know.[11]

Four hundred billion dollars in private, state, and local
pension funds, the largest private pool of capital in the world,
and an ABA official says he really doesn't know who owns it
or, for that matter, who controls it! What then are the facts
about pension funds? Who does own them? And what are
the implications that flow from this new form of economic
power? [12]

Legal precedent has firmly established the principle that
pension money belongs to the workers and must be considered as part of their wages.

In 1948, a question arose during negotiations between
the Inland Steel Company and the United Steel Workers as
to whether the Taft-Hartley Act compelled an employer to
bargain with the unions in the matter of pensions. The
NLRB ruled that the company was obliged to bargain on
pensions on the grounds that they were part of the overall
wage package as defined in the Taft-Hartley Act. On appeal
to the courts, Inland lost once again. The court's ruling in
part said that "while the company has demonstrated a rea-
sonable argument . . . we think the better and more logical
argument is on the other side." Other court rulings since

then have upheld the notion that pension funds are a form of wages.[13]

Congress has also continued to uphold the concept that pensions are part of wages. In preparing the Welfare and Pension Disclosure Act, for example, the Senate Subcommittee on Welfare and Pensions concluded:

These employer-employee plans ... under existing law proceed on the basis that the contributions to them by management are in the nature of employee's compensation for employment or, stated another way ... that the cost of an employee's service is greater than the amount paid him as wages.[14]

Early on, the IRS recognized the principle of deferred wages in its statutes governing taxation of these funds. While contributions by employers to the fund are tax-deductible, because of their "social" value, the benefits of the funds are taxable to the retiree once he receives them; that is, they are treated for tax purposes as deferred income.[15]

The money, then, does belong to the workers, but in name only. What makes pension funds different from the normal kind of asset is that the true owners do not and are not allowed to exercise control over that which belongs to them. The funds are entrusted to other parties on their behalf. With nonnegotiated funds, the corporations appoint their own trustees to oversee the pensions. With collectively bargained funds, over half are controlled exclusively by management and approximately 40 percent are controlled jointly by management and union representatives.[16] In every case, however, almost all trusted funds are handed over to a third party, usually a bank, sometimes an insurance company or independent asset manager, to invest on behalf of the beneficiaries. Thus the real control over the use of the fund is not in the hands of the employer, the union that negotiated the fund for the employees, or the individual employees themselves. In the final analysis, then, all three parties lose effective control over these tremendous assets. Their loss is the bankers' gain, and to some lesser extent the insurance companies'. Even here we're not talking about banks or insurance companies *en masse*, but about some twenty-five institutional giants in both fields that controlled, in 1976, over $120 billion or one-third of all private, state, and local pension-fund assets in the entire country.[17]

What has happened in just thirty years is nothing less than spectacular. To summarize: a new form of wealth emerged with the creation and wide application of the pension plan. Because it was a form of forced savings, the beneficiary, the American worker, was separated from control over its use and the captive funds began to accumulate at a pace that soon outstripped all other privately derived wealth in the nation. This new-found wealth was put at the disposal of a handful of financial institutions who, in turn, used it to consolidate their control over the major economic decisions that affect the country.[18]

For their part, in their predictable understated manner, the bankers have taken all this in stride, even with a touch of self-effacement and humility, protesting all along that they neither sought nor covet the responsibility which has become theirs to shoulder. After all, they're just looking out for the interests of America's future retirees, doggedly pursuing those time-honored market principles of maximum return on investment so that John and Mary Doe can have a little nest-egg to fall back on when they approach the autumn of their lives. Says a vice president of a major New York bank, as far as investing pension funds go: "We're doing absolutely nothing in our own interests as far as I can see." [19]

Others disagree and are beginning to press their own claims for control over these funds. While the claims of union and state governments have already been touched on and will be addressed in much greater detail later on, another development has occurred which is worth more than a passing mention. A law suit of potential historic proportions is now in the federal courts. It deals with the potential claims by the individual beneficiary for control over his own pension funds. The developments in this case are being carefully monitored by the banking community, the unions, and the federal government.

Chapter 15: No Investment without Representation

John B. Daniel was a member of Teamster Local #705 in Chicago for over twenty-two years. Because of failing eyesight, he was forced to retire in 1973. When Mr. Daniel applied for his pension, he was shocked to learn that he did not qualify for a pension income, despite the fact that he had worked well over the twenty-year minimum required by the fund. It seems that Mr. Daniel had been laid off for three and a half months some thirteen years earlier and because of that fact, he had violated a clause in the pension agreement which stipulated that to receive full benefits, he had to work twenty consecutive years. Mr. Daniel took his case to court, which is not unusual. However, in his case, Daniel charged the union and the fund with violation of the antifraud provisions of the federal securities laws. Daniel argued:

A pension should be considered an investment security, one purchased by employers on behalf of union members who have factored the fund into their decisions about where to earn a living. Accordingly, the worker is partly making an investment decision when he takes a job and this investment ought to fall under the securities laws.[1]

Since the antifraud provisions of the securities laws require the full disclosure of the facts concerning any investment (including potential risks), Daniel argued that by failing to inform him of what constitutes a "break in service" in his pension plan, the fund had committed a violation of securities law.

In March 1976, Chicago Federal District Judge Alfred Y. Kirkland ruled in favor of Daniel's claim that his pension was a security that had been sold to him and therefore subject to the securities laws.[2] This was the first time a court had confirmed that an interest in a pension fund is an investment. This decision was upheld by the 7th Circuit Court of Appeals on August 20, 1977:

Because employee pension plans are now the major, if not sole form of investment for most American workers to provide for their old age and because of the now crucial role that such plans play in today's capital markets, they are just the sort of investment vehicle that the securities acts were passed to regulate.[3]

In his ruling, Judge Kirkland rejected the union's and fund's claim that a pension fund is involuntary and not contributory, and therefore does not constitute a "sale" of "securities." On the question of whether a pension fund is contributory or not, Judge Kirkland concluded that there was a disposition for value. That is, a proportion of the employees' overall wages was contributed to the fund. This part of the ruling concurs with other statutes and court cases affirming that pensions are part of wages. As to the question of voluntary vs. involuntary, the judge pointed out that since the rank-and-file union members must vote for ratification of whatever pension package the union negotiates, they certainly are making a voluntary decision about what should go into the final agreement of the fund itself. Having found that Daniel had been sold a security, Kirkland concluded that the antifraud provisions of the securities laws applied, requiring disclosure of material facts affecting the chances of collecting a pension. Kirkland commented that he was persuaded that "few members would ever vote for an allocation to a pension increase in lieu of a greater salary increase if they know at the time of the vote that they would have an 8 percent chance or smaller of ever realizing any benefit from the increased pension allocation." [4]

The decision was a bombshell and the shock waves are still reverberating up and down Wall Street and in union offices across the country. There are several reasons for this.

First, future pension contracts will have to clearly spell out the conditions under which individual beneficiaries might or might not receive their pensions. As beneficiaries become aware that they have been short-changed by the small print in their existing contracts, they will demand protection for their retirement benefits. This, in turn, will increase the expenses that must be paid by the funds. Further, by declaring that a pension fund is a security, the courts have opened up the very real possibility that the Securities and Exchange Commission will enter the field of pension regulation—thus adding another government agency to an already confused regulatory situation (at present, the Labor Department, the Internal Revenue Service and the Pension Benefit Guarantee Corporation are involved).

Needless to say, the dynamics of the *Daniel* case and Judge Kirkland's ruling have not gone unnoticed by the parties who stand to lose the most. Industry and labor groups have filed friends-of-the-court briefs protesting the decision, on behalf of the defendants, the Teamsters' Union and its Central States pension fund.

Joining in the melee over the *Daniel* case are two federal agencies, one siding with the plaintiff, the other with the defendant. The Labor Department, which has lined up with the Teamsters, argues that if Daniel wins and is paid off by the union, the precedent it sets for tens of millions of other workers would be, as the department put it, "catastrophic." According to this view, malpractice suits that pose a serious financial problem for the medical community will look like kid stuff if millions of deprived retirees begin bringing similar cases into court, demanding billions of dollars in pension funds they never received. It could well end in breaking the bank and tumbling the economic system itself.[5]

On the other side, favoring the court's ruling, is the Securities and Exchange Commission. In support of its contention that a pension is a security, the SEC concurs with the court's finding that workers now wear two hats when they make a decision about taking or not taking a job: the first is the employment decision itself, and the second is an investment decision:

We recognize that an employee's decision to take or keep a job is not, by itself, an investment decision. But when that decision is materially influenced by the existence of a security—in this case, an interest in a pension fund—which he will purchase with his labor, he is making not only an employment decision but also an investment decision.[6]

By confirming that a pension fund is an investment for the participant, the court's decision leads inevitably to the next logical argument, *that the individual pension beneficiary should have a measure of control over that investment as well.* No wonder the American Bankers' Association has filed a brief asking the Supreme Court to reverse the *Daniel* decision.

If the *Daniel* decision is upheld by the Supreme Court, the consequences could ultimately be catastrophic for America's powerful banking elite: it would amount to the nightmare prospect of losing direct control over billions of dollars in pension capital. For instance, the Appeals Court noted that pension funds resemble mutual funds. But the individual mutual fund investor has the right to vote his or her share in the annual stockholders' meeting; in addition, an interest in a mutual fund can be sold or borrowed against. Similarly, for the millions of individual pension beneficiaries, the advantage of controlling a financial asset of this size during their working lifetime would be considerable. A pension fund could serve as collateral for home mortgages or for loans to put children through college or for any one of a number of other investments which are now beyond the means of the average worker, whose savings are inadequate to provide for economic needs.[7]

Imagine, if you will, the implications of a court ruling granting 50 million working and retired Americans the right to exercise control over some $400 billion in pension assets. At the very least, imagine the reaction of a worker who is told by the courts that he owns his interest in a pension fund, but he can't control it. As soon as workers begin to say "this is mine and I should have a say in how it is invested" the financial community will really start to worry.[8] All this mayhem because one truck driver has decided to assert his individual claim to part of this new pool of wealth, this social capital. Says Karen Ferguson of the Pension Rights Center: "The *Daniel* case is probably the most important pension case ever to have been decided." [9]

In many ways, the implications of the *Daniel* case are not unlike the case made by American colonists two hundred years ago when they said "no taxation without representation." The Royal Governors of the time, men like Governor Hutchinson of Massachusetts, argued that while the colonists did not enjoy direct representation in Parliament they were still in fact represented because their taxes were being used for the benefit of the empire; and revenues that benefited the empire ultimately benefited them as well, since they were subjects of the Crown (and therefore privy to all of the "privileges bestowed" by the Crown on freeborn Englishmen). Sam Adams and the Sons and Daughters of Liberty disagreed. To their mind, there was a difference between privileges bestowed and rights conferred. The authority to bestow privileges rested in the hands of a king and parliament whose interests might or might not correspond to the interests of American settlers. The colonists argued that this arrangement made them forever dependent on others over whom they exercised no real control. Sam Adams remarked that "there must always reside somewhere, some absolute, sovereign and indivisible power, but that power can never be delegated by a few, but must instead reside in the people," the thought being that authority can only really be of benefit to the people when it is conferred or delegated directly by them.[10] As a result, the Americans forged a new form of social contract based on the principle that all people are equal and have certain inalienable rights to life, liberty, and happiness, and of course the right to property. To protect these first three rights they founded a democratic form of republic in which they elected representatives to look out for their shared interests, making it clear all along that whatever authority they delegated to others was still conditional. That is, it could be transferred to other representatives or be taken back altogether. As to the right of property, it was assumed that while the government might play a limited role in its regulation, it was one of those rights that could best be managed in private hands. Thus the separation of rights into two categories, those delegated to elected representatives to look after on the people's behalf, or political rights; and those left directly with the sovereign individual to look after, or economic rights. The economic life of the nation, then, was to remain in private hands (though not without government regulations) and the political life of the nation was to reside in a delegated representative form of government.

As long as they remained in an agrarian economy, and property was broadly dispersed among the general population, all persons could continue to protect their own individual property and property rights without too much of a problem. But with the advent of the Industrial Revolution, a new form of economic power emerged, one that was to challenge and eventually destroy an economy based on the principle of individual ownership of productive property.

In 1800, 89 percent of the American people were self-employed as small farmers and craftsmen. By 1945, 92 percent of all Americans were working as wage-earners, propertyless in the sense of owning "productive property" from which they could make a living. The Industrial Revolution transformed the concept of productive property from land to capital. With that transformation, the once-propertied American farmers became the disenfranchised propertyless wage-earners of the industrial era. As capital became the dominant form of property, and as industrialization itself replaced agrarianism, the bulk of the American people found themselves, once again, the ruled rather than the rulers. Capital became concentrated, and with this new form of property came a new form of power. The rights to property, which the founders thought could best be served by being maintained in private hands, were still in private hands, but in the hands of a handful. The rights once enjoyed by the many had become the rights now enjoyed by a few. With that shift of power from the many to the few, a new governing authority emerged, one that the founders could not have anticipated but with which they would not have been unfamiliar. The new owners of productive property, the bankers and the investment community, once again turned rights into privileges, just as the Crown had earlier. Individual wage-earners became dependent on the benevolence of the ruling capitalists whose control over property was nearly absolute. The question of privileges bestowed vs. rights conferred again became an issue just as it had been earlier in the political sphere. With the dawn of the twentieth century, American workers began once again to assert their rights, but this time over the only property they still had left, their own labor. Unions were formed, and with the passage of the Wagner Act in 1935 workers had their own Magna Carta. But like its English model, it merely served to put the new economic rulers on notice and to secure only partially rights which were supposed to be absolute. They could do little more, because working people did not yet have the power to demand more—power now being control over capital.

The pension fund has now changed all this. The irony is that when pensions were first adopted, they were in the form of a privilege bestowed by the capitalists; they could be granted or taken away at a moment's notice, without recourse. But as unions began to assert the *right* of working people to have pensions, they became in fact a right and not just a privilege.[11] With that right has emerged a new source of economic power—a form of social capital, if you will— that belongs to millions of American workers. This new property has created a new propertied class, and this new propertied class is now at a critical crossroads, as were the colonists two hundred years ago when they faced the question of whether or not to challenge authority based on privileges bestowed with the concept of authority based on rights conferred.

American workers like John Daniel find their productive property being taken over and used by others without any right to representation or control. The bankers argue that workers are represented indirectly because whatever moneys are used on their behalf ultimately benefit them, both in providing for their retirement income and in keeping the economy strong. Thus, if the system benefits, the individuals within it ultimately benefit.

Many pension plan participants would probably argue as Sam Adams did, that there is a difference between privileges bestowed and rights conferred and that since the funds belong to them as a right, that they should have the power to determine how the funds should be used.

There is little doubt that the pension funds belong to the beneficiaries. Still, there is also little likelihood of each propertied owner exercising an atomistic control over how his or her own fund is invested. It is simply no longer practical in a complex industrial setting of the type America is today. With the industrialized age has come not only complexity, but economic interdependence. In this sense the economic sphere has increasingly taken on the characteristics of the political sphere. That is, economic planning decisions can no longer be made in private or alone because much of our economic interests are now shared in common, as are our economic needs. This condition of collective economic dependence necessitates the delegation of authority and the conferring of rights in the same kind of republican form that we have already implemented in the political realm. The simple fact is that 200 million Americans cannot all gather together in the open marketplace to make all the important economic decisions jointly. It would be as impractical as the exercise of direct town-hall democracy in the national government.

The question thus becomes to whom these new rights

over social capital or social property should be delegated. At present there exists no explicit economic compact delegating such authority. In its absence, the private capitalist sector continues to operate as if the authority were its to control and dispose of. Yet it is in no way accountable to those millions of workers whose money it controls. To be accountable, authority must be delegated by the beneficiaries. They must be able to elect their own representatives to manage the funds and be able to recall those representatives if they are unhappy with how their funds are being used. At all times, the beneficiaries must reserve the right to make overall policy concerning the disposition of their moneys. While there is no mechanism between the workers and their employers or the workers and the banks to allow for the democratic delegation of such authority, there is such a mechanism between the workers and their unions and government officials.

Unions are the only economic institution expressly set up by the workers to represent the workers. When workers vote to have a union represent their economic interest, they are making a direct decision to delegate authority. As their bargaining representative, the union is charged with the responsibility of carrying out the directives of its members. Workers elect their union spokespeople, and they have the right to vote them out as well. The workers also reserve the right to determine the conditions of their employment by exercising their power to ratify or overturn whatever agreements are made on their behalf between their union representatives and their employers.

In other words, the unions already exist as a mechanism to represent the economic interests of workers. In fact, the unions are the institution most responsible for setting up pension funds on behalf of their members. They also act as the workers' delegated authority in determining any changes in the plans themselves. It seems illogical, then, to confer all of this authority to the unions, while denying them the ultimate authority to represent how the funds are invested as well. To argue that the private business sector is more likely to better represent the workers' interest is absurd. The very reason workers have unions in the first place is to protect their collective economic interests against the competing interests of the private sector. Why should it be assumed that, in regard to investing workers' funds, the private business sector makes a grand exception to its normal *modus operandi* by placing its own self-interest second and the interest of the workers first? In fact, as the evidence more than suggests, the private business sector exploits the workers' money just as it exploits the workers' labor; even more so, because at least with regard to the exploitation of labor, the workers have given their unions the authority to mitigate such abuses by looking after their collective employment needs. Until union members grant their own labor representatives the same authority to look after their collective investment needs, the business sector will continue to exploit the funds for its own gain at the expense of millions of individual workers.

Some will argue that there is no way to insure that union representatives won't use pension funds for personal gain or in other ways that undermine the interests of the beneficiaries. They will complain that unions are no longer accountable to their members or subject to the democratic control of the rank and file. With respect to particular unions or specific union leaders there is truth to these allegations, just as there is truth to similar allegations about our republican form of government and public officials. But in both cases, the fault lies not with the concept behind the institutions but with the neglect which has allowed them to atrophy. Immediately after hearing the Declaration of Independence read for the first time from Independence Hall in Philadelphia in 1776, a woman turned to Ben Franklin and asked him what kind of government America would have. "A Republic, madam," replied Franklin, "that is, if we can keep it so." Like representative government, the fact that representative unions have not always performed as they should is really the fault of a membership that has not demanded complete accountability and full democratic participation. The mechanisms for accountability and democratic participation exist within the union structures. If workers want to insure that their moneys are being used by the unions to foster their interest, then they need only exercise the inherent authority which they retain in order to make the unions truly representative and accountable to them. This is just what the mineworkers did in 1975. A reform group, Miners for Democracy, launched a grass-roots movement to oust the corrupt and entrenched leadership of the UMW. Under Tony Boyle's regime, the UMW had, for years, been involved in illegal financial transactions including the rifling of the union's pension funds for personal gain. The insurgent Miners for Democracy were successful in convincing thousands of rank-and-file members to vote Boyle out of office. Their victory was a mandate for cleaning up the union and making it more responsive to the voice of the membership. The subsequent internal conflicts in the UMW have been used by some to call for *less* democracy in unions, claiming that the average unionist is incapable of tending to the affairs of such a large and complex organization. Actually, the mineworkers' experience only highlights the difficulty of restoring a democratic and orderly process to an institution long governed autocratically.

The democratization of many unions will not come overnight. Years of bureaucratic domination have built up a community of interest between management and many labor leaders, who often come to identify more with employers than with their own rank-and-file constituency. As a result, some union leaders will probably oppose democratic employee or union control of pension investments. In many unions a push for alternative uses of pension assets will need to be accompanied by a push for major structural reform as well. For example, one emerging reform group, the Teamsters for a Democratic Union, is calling for rank-and-file control of the giant Teamsters' pension funds as part of their proposals for cleaning up the union.[12]

The only alternative to building a responsive and accountable union leadership that can represent these investment funds is for the workers to continue placing their faith and their money with the business community, whose inherent interest runs counter to theirs and whose authority is neither conferred nor delegated by them. Thus, they would have to continue to depend on paternal benevolence and bestowed privileges at the expense of their inherent economic right to control their own moneys. Given these two choices, and considering the dire consequences that continued control over these funds by the financial community would mean to the economic security of union workers, it is likely that unionists will begin to push for extended union control over jointly managed pension-fund assets. Their own survival depends on it. Moreover, unions who have allowed corporations to exercise exclusive control over their members' pension funds will likely begin to push for union representation on boards of trustees.[13] As to those millions of workers who are covered under pension plans but not represented by unions, their best hope of gaining a measure of sovereign control over their own funds also rests in their establishing union shops.

In considering whether state and local governments should be entrusted with the authority to invest public pension funds, many of the same arguments apply. These political bodies retain the democratic mechanisms through which workers and the general public can exercise their economic rights over how these funds are invested. If those democratic mechanisms are used vigilantly and judiciously by the people, their right to decide how their own capital is used will be guaranteed.

"To advocate unions or the state governments using pension funds to benefit society in general is to advocate a form of social revolution," argues Jean Lindberg, vice chairman of the Chase Investors' Management Corporation.[14] Mr. Lindberg is right. The real question underlying the use of social capital is a fundamental one: should a handful of private business interests be allowed the right to control the use of pension funds and therefore continue to make most of the major economic planning decisions for the country? Or should the economic and political representatives of the people whose funds are being used, the unions and local and state governments, be delegated the authority to exercise control over these moneys and the economic planning decisions that go along with that control?

That question is now beginning to be raised by labor leaders and public officials throughout the northern states.

Chapter 16: Vying for Economic Power

The damn pensions are our members' money... they own that money. I can't understand why, when we own something, we can't go get it and do whatever we please. Especially if it's subverting our interest. And when I have money in a bank and that money belongs to my members, and we make a decision that we don't like the way the bank is doing business, there is no reason why we should have to leave the money with that bank. It makes no sense.[1]

The frustration expressed by Ray Rogers, a young organizer for the Amalgamated Clothing and Textile Workers' Union (ACTWU), is spreading throughout the trade union community. While still not the number one priority on labor's list, there is serious discussion about how pension funds are now being used by the investment community and how they could be used if they were in the hands of the unions.

In extensive interviews conducted in 1977 with over fifty labor officials from local union organizers to presidents of large international unions, two themes continued to rear their heads in every conversation. First, there is a growing recognition of the new relationship that has developed between labor and capital assets. Lawrence Smedley, of the AFL-CIO Social Security Department, says: "The traditional adversary relationship between capital and labor needs to be reexamined, since labor now owns capital."[2] Second, there is a growing interest in beginning to assert control over these funds as a means of preserving and rebuilding the once-powerful trade union movement. I. Philip Sipser, an attorney who represents over a dozen union pension funds, says flat-out that "if we're going to have the responsibility for handling that money, let's use it as a weapon, a social weapon for us."[3] William Winpisinger, president of the giant

International Association of Machinists (IAM), couldn't agree more. If the banks continue to use union funds to undermine union interests, says Winpisinger, then "I'm going to tell them to get packing and we'll find another institution to take the $70 or $80 million [of our funds] they've got. That's talking turkey."[4]

What has become obvious to Winpisinger and others is the potential of this new source of economic power. Richard Days, who is in charge of a small $10 million UAW pension fund in New York City, sums up labor's new interest in pension fund power:

With the massive amount of pension-fund assets belonging to union members, it comes to the point now that they have to recognize us as an awakening giant, even though we're a denuded giant at this moment. Nonetheless, with control over pension funds, we could change the whole course of history.[5]

These were the same kinds of words thrown out nearly a hundred years ago by Eugene Debs, Samuel Gompers, and other early labor leaders. Back then, when they talked about an awakening economic giant, they were referring to the fusing together of the sweat and muscle of millions of working people who kept the economy going; when they talked about a new social weapon, their attention was focusing on the power of the strike; and when they talked of changing the course of history, they were talking about a movement of working people, united in their efforts to right the economic injustices perpetrated by a system based on profit first and people second. That inherent power which first launched the great labor movement organizing drives exists once again, but in a transformed state. A hundred years ago the workers' only inherent power was their own labor, which could be sold as property on the open marketplace. Their property, their backs and hands and bodies, is what made them a potential giant. Today, as a result of that labor, American workers have accumulated a "derived" property, the billions of dollars of deferred savings in their pension funds. This is what makes them, once again, a potential economic giant. A hundred years ago, the only effective weapon available to workers to bargain for their economic rights was the strike; through it they could withhold their "property," that is, their labor, from the marketplace, until their demands were met. Today, even as the strike is losing its impact, American workers have a new weapon at their disposal, their accumulated pension capital. By withholding and selectively applying their new derived property in the marketplace, they can once again have their demands met.

Unions hold other large sums of money, in addition to pension funds. For instance, the UAW has a strike fund worth about $200 million and the steelworkers' strike fund exceeds $100 million. Collectively, union assets are worth over $4 billion. This includes strike funds, death benefit funds, vacation pools, annuities, various properties and investments directly owned by the unions, and so forth. Unions also have a yearly income of $5 billion, which is used to pay for all of the programs they administer, including some insurance and health programs.[6]

Like a hundred years ago, what is needed now for labor to take advantage of the new situation before them is the kind of visionary leadership that can change the course of history. "Some labor leader is going to emerge and he'll be the Ralph Nader of pension funds—by opening people's eyes to the fact that they have ownership but no rights about that ownership. We could very well make our thrust the salvation of America. It's that simple," says one local labor official. Salvation will not come, however, without first educating the rank-and-file membership. Right now, admits Smedley of the AFL-CIO, most union members don't think at all about how their pension funds are being invested. But he contends: "If they got the idea that their pension funds were being invested in runaway shops abroad, or in non-union companies that were using low wage labor to take away their jobs, they would certainly react. They would see it clearly."[7]

The very first steps in that education process are going on right now as union leaders begin to look into the various ways that this new form of social capital could be used to further the interests of the union movement. Joseph Keenan, former international secretary of the International Brotherhood of Electrical Workers (IBEW), points out that "some pension funds are being used for foreign capital investment. Such use of these funds," argues Keenan, "will jeopardize American jobs and thus defeat the primary purpose of a pension—security in old age." [8] Other labor people are voicing the same concern about runaway shops to the Sunbelt. "My own feeling is that unions should try to have more of a voice in pension investments, especially when it comes to financing runaway shops," says Leonard Lesser, former UAW pension expert. "These pension funds can exert tremendous economic power, and I would argue that a program which discourages investments in runaway shop companies is really for the benefit of the employees too." [9]

Turning off the spigot, that is, effectively stopping the flow of pension-fund capital to companies that are pursuing either a runaway shop policy or an antiunion policy in general, is being talked about increasingly among union people. Henry Foner, president of the Joint Board of the Fur, Leather and Machine Workers, suggests that organized labor draw up an index of "recommended investments for union pension funds." Foner, like others, thinks it's ridiculous that a good portion of union pension portfolios are in nonunion companies. "Why shouldn't we invest in union companies that will mean more jobs for our people." [10] To some union people like Kevin Kistler, of the AFL-CIO organizing department, there are parallels to be drawn between the union label concept and the selective investment of pension fund capital in prounion companies. "Certainly it has always been a policy of the labor movement to follow the union label when buying and not buying products and services, and I think this is a continuation of the union label policy." [11] Robert Tilove, vice president of Martin E. Segal and Company, the biggest union pension consulting firm, argues that investing union pension funds in nonunion firms is really a moral issue.

I know there are churches which will not buy certain stocks and I can't argue with them. Now to a union member, investing heavily in a nonunion outfit that happens to be fighting an organization drive is the moral equivalent of church funds buying shares of a company in South Africa. [12]

A case in point is the du Pont company, which is nonunion and which has pursued an antiunion policy since its inception. In November 1974, *Pensions & Investments* magazine reported that du Pont had just secured $350 million in thirty-year debentures and that 75 percent of the total was purchased by pension funds. IBM is still another example. Run totally as a nonunion operation, it relies heavily on pension-fund capital in its equity and debt financing. Dow, Kodak, and many other major nonunion firms also rely heavily on pension-fund capital. In fact, according to the Union Label Department of the AFL-CIO, of the top twenty-five companies in which pension funds are invested, sixteen are classified as having predominantly nonunion shops or antiunion policies. [13]

In the fall of 1977, the late Senator Lee Metcalf of Montana, one of labor's staunchest congressional allies, delivered a speech calling on unions to demand a voice in the investment and stock-voting policies of their members' pension funds. Metcalf noted that union-bargained pension money is being used against union members when such funds are invested in runaway and nonunion companies. "Unions have been indirectly supporting unfair labor practices," he observed, "through use of financial managers closely tied to such corporations with antebellum attitudes toward workers." He concluded: "I believe that it is time for beneficiaries of all pension funds—private and public—to review arrange-

ments that have been made in their behalf regarding investment and management of those funds, and the voting of
stock in their portfolios. They should have a voice in these
matters." [14]

A month and a half later, the AFL-CIO national convention in Los Angeles adopted a resolution recognizing the
immense economic clout of union members' pension funds.
This resolution called for increased union fund investment
in mortgages and construction. It also urged "that the substantial financial power of AFL-CIO unions and negotiated
plans be entrusted to financial institutions whose investment
policies are not inimical to the welfare of working men and
women. . . ." While not a clarion call for change, this resolution does represent a significant step toward investment policies that bolster the economic security of union members.[15]
Observed veteran labor commentator Victor Riesel: "Translated, this means that labor plans to use its billion-dollar
clout as pressure on banks, insurance companies and asset
managers to refrain from investing in corporations labor is
striking or attempting to organize." [16]

Winpisinger of the Machinists is one labor leader who is
already taking the AFL-CIO resolution seriously. He believes that it's time to show nonunion companies that organized labor means business, both figuratively and literally.

"If you got a choice [of investing union pension funds] between Kodak and Xerox, for example, why take Kodak,
when there's not a union member present in the whole god-
dam place, with 18,000 people working there! We should
go with Xerox. They are just as productive an investment
and they employ union people." [17]

By selectively investing in unionized companies, say
many labor people, it will not only give those firms a financial edge over nonunion firms, but will also provide an impetus for the antilabor companies to accept unionization.
This will be especially true as the equity and debt markets
become even tighter in the years ahead. "If the employer

knows that there is money available for unionized work, it would probably make organizing for the unions much easier," says Robert Connerton, general counsel of the International Laborers Union.[18] In the meantime, argues Winpisinger, many already unionized companies are not about to complain because, aside from the financial advantage they will enjoy by being favored in union investment policies, they will enjoy another advantage as well; that is, a better competitive edge as this new union leveraging strategy succeeds in organizing more nonunion firms and bringing wages up to union scale. In addition, as more workers are organized through this financial leveraging, more union pension plans will be set up and more funds will then be available to unions for increasing their financial power over capital investments.

Just as organized labor is beginning to perceive the power of pension funds, so too are politicians in the northern industrial states. Of the $135 billion in the state and local public pension funds in the United States today, over one-half belongs to the funds of the sixteen states that make up the Graybelt region.[19] Virtually all of these funds are turned over to the banks which, in turn, shuffle much of them out of the region to investments in the Sunbelt or overseas. In a sense, the northern states are getting the capital kicked out of them from both ends: first, by the federal government, which takes their tax revenue and then parcels it out to other regions; and second, by the banks, who do the same thing with their public pension funds. It's a case of legalized looting that is fast turning this once lush capital oasis into a giant debt-ridden desert. Congressman Harrington, who was among the first to sound the alarm over the pillaging of northern state treasuries by Washington, is now beginning to turn his attention to the attack being waged from the private sector flank. "The idea of reinvesting pension funds in the region from which they come is a very attractive one," says Harrington.[20] Representative Henry Reuss of Wisconsin, chairman of the powerful House Banking Committee, agrees.

"Pension funds represent a viable means of helping to meet the fundamental needs of the Northeast and Midwest." Reuss feels that the entire issue "deserves serious consideration." [21]

That serious consideration is being given now among labor people and politicians. For the most part it is still in the talk and speculation stage, although several concrete programs are already being launched [22] (a more detailed look at these efforts is contained in Chapters 17 and 18). Sooner or later, however, the claims and counterclaims over control of this new form of social capital are going to come to a head. The outcome of such a confrontation is hard to predict. Still, the manner in which both labor and state governments have shadowboxed with this new type of power over the past thirty years provides a crude barometer of the way each is likely to behave as they begin aggressively to press their claims to control this pool of pension-fund capital.[23]

Chapter 17: Union Claims

With all of the flap over possible union control of pension-fund investments during the Taft-Hartley debates in 1947, one would expect even more intensified debate and confrontation in the ensuing decade as pension funds began to tally up into the tens of billions of dollars. For the most part, however, the concerns voiced by Taft and his fellow Republicans did not materialize in the 1950s. It was not so much the passage of the Taft-Hartley Act that was to blame. After all, it still provided for 50 percent labor representation on pension-fund boards, which was more than enough to wage an aggressive campaign for the control and use of these assets. More than anything else, it was the broader social environment of the 1950s that was instrumental in cooling off any serious labor initiative regarding pension-fund controls. Eisenhower jackets were in, radicals and commies were out. The once-firebrand CIO was being coopted to the right by its federation with the AFL; sociologists were busy studying the classless, middle-class suburban society, and in general everyone was in agreement with Daniel Bell's contention that we had, in fact, reached the "end of ideology."

This doesn't mean that there wasn't any interest at all in pension-fund investments on the part of organized labor. There was. But for the most part it was exercised in a more roundabout fashion. Joe Swire summed up the dominant feeling within the labor movement during those years. According to Swire, labor didn't want to get directly involved in the investment decisions because if something went wrong, the rank and file would undoubtedly put the blame on the union leadership. Of course, this wasn't the only reason. Says Swire:

Union trustees were scared; they didn't know anything about it [the investment business]. The union guys have a large inferiority complex. A lot of them come out of the slum. So when they meet these guys from Chase Manhattan, they're overwhelmed. It takes guts to stand up to these people, who are highly specialized and fluent in investment matters.[1]

Then too, because many union pension trustees tended to narrowly define their role as an entrepreneurial one, they failed to take into consideration the ways in which these funds could be used to advance the interests of the union movement.[2] So instead of making demands, labor leaders settled for making suggestions. Their suggestions were generally given a polite audience by the investment bankers and then quietly dumped into the nearest wastebasket. Still, their suggestions at least demonstrated an awareness on their part of the potential power that pension funds represented.

Walter Reuther of the UAW brought the question of pension-fund investments to the surface in his contract negotiations with Ford in the summer of 1958. Among other things, the company had been investing the workers' funds in the construction of luxury high-rises in Houston. Reuther argued that it would make more sense to invest the funds in middle- and low-income housing in Detroit and other cities where UAW members lived, so that their own money could be used to benefit them directly. The company disagreed and Reuther did not push his suggestion. It is important to note, however, that the UAW was not demanding direct control over investment decisions concerning the funds, but only suggesting that the financial trustees incorporate such considerations into their overall investment policies.[3]

This kind of concern, that funds should be invested in socially responsive ways whenever possible, popped up over and over again during the 1950s. In hearings held before the Senate Subcommittee on Welfare and Pensions in 1955, labor pension experts suggested that a portion of workers' pension funds be used to build such things as hospitals, health clinics, and housing. In a few instances this happened. The Ladies' Garment Workers fund put up $15 million for a housing project on Manhattan's East River and the United Mine Workers' fund lent $31 million to build medical facilities for its workers.[4]

Several union pension plans began investing portions of their funds in low- and middle-income housing in the 1950s, and one union, the International Brotherhood of Electrical Workers (IBEW), established a policy under which 50 percent of its fund assets would be put in FHA and VA insured mortgages. The IBEW fund, which is an in-house membership plan, has also established a firm policy that all of the homes it puts up money for must be built by union labor. In this way, says the union, it is not only providing a sound return on investment and investing in socially useful ways, but it is also maintaining job security for its members and trade unionists generally.[5]

There is even a union-owned insurance company, Union Labor Life, capitalized to an extent with pension-fund investments. Although it was founded in 1927, at a time when trade unionists found it difficult to get insurance because of job risks and antilabor bias, the company now has assets totaling $350 million and has a policy of only investing in prolabor companies. According to Robert Daley, of the ULLICO, one of the reasons many unions invest their funds in a union insurance company is the "idea that the money is staying within the labor movement."[6]

While most union involvement with pension funds during the 1950s centered around what labor leaders considered to be secondary or peripheral interests, broadly defined as "social investments,"[7] there were instances where funds were used directly as a leverage to foster the organizing objectives of the union. These instances, though few in number, demonstrated the real value of social capital as a weapon in labor's arsenal.

In 1954, the Teamsters were trying to organize Montgomery Ward. Its chief executive, Sewell Avery, was an out-

spoken critic of organized labor and had vowed never to
allow a union inside his operations. At the same time the
Teamsters were battling it out with Avery, another man,
Louis Wolfson, initiated a proxy challenge with Avery for
control over the company. Taking advantage of the flank
opened up between Avery and Wolfson, the Teamsters immediately bought up 12,500 shares of Montgomery Ward
stock (worth a million dollars) and let it be known, by
grapevine, that truck firms and banks with sizable Teamster
deposits held over 100,000 additional shares. Avery was suit-
ably impressed, so much so that just three weeks before his
proxy showdown with Wolfson at the annual board meeting,
he reversed his long-standing opposition to a union shop and
signed a collective bargaining agreement with the Teamsters.
Shortly thereafter, the Teamsters announced that their shares
in the company would be voted for Avery at the board meeting. Needless to say, no one was a bit surprised by the decision.[8]

The United Mine Workers, which had been the center
of attention during the Case Bill debates in 1946, also used
its pension funds as an organizing tool. In the mid-50s, the
UMW launched an ambitious campaign to force public utility companies to purchase union-mined coal. In 1955, the
UMW pension fund bought 30,000 shares of the Cleveland
Electric Company. That same year, the union lent Cyrus
Eaton, the industrialist, enough money to buy an additional
20,000 shares in the utility. Eaton was then elected to the
Board of Directors of Cleveland Electric. The union repeated the same procedure with Kansas City Power & Light
that same year, purchasing shares for itself and lending
Eaton money to buy additional shares. For the next nine
years the UMW gave a general proxy for all its shares of
both utilities to Eaton to vote. Eaton, in turn, used his proxy
influence to pressure both companies into buying only union-
mined coal. A federal judge later ruled that such activity
amounted to self-dealing and constituted a breach of trust
with the beneficiaries of the fund, mainly because one of the

trustees of the UMW fund was also president of one of the major coal companies that stood to benefit by the utilities accepting union-mined coal. The case, nonetheless, highlighted the incredible potential of pension funds as a tool to maximize union organizing objectives.[9]

The polite suggestions and the isolated skirmishes of the 1950s, though hardly impressive at the time, nonetheless set the stage for labor claims on social capital in the two following decades. By 1970, a representative of organized labor was telling a congressional committee hearing on pension investment policies that "it is our hope, in the AFL-CIO, to try to get control of a sizable amount of the pension funds." Mr. Keenan of the IBEW told the committee that pension funds should be invested in socially useful purposes, even if it meant accepting a lower rate of return.[10]

That same year a bill was introduced in Congress to free pension-fund capital for socially useful investments. Sponsored by Congressman Wright Patman of Texas, chairman of the powerful House Banking and Currency Committee, the bill reflected the growing popularity of the "double benefit" idea; the notion that pension funds should provide a benefit for the beneficiaries during their working lifetime as well as during their retirement years.[11] Patman proposed a provision to the Emergency Housing Finance Act that would have "required pension funds to invest up to 2.5 percent of their total assets in the obligations of a federally funded bank created to finance housing for low and moderate income families." While the provision was later discarded, Patman's arguments at the time show that, at least in some quarters, some thinking about possible counterclaims to social capital was taking shape. For example, Patman asked why pension funds were, by and large, being poured into equity investments of major corporations despite the fact that their rate of returns was extremely poor. The congressman made it clear that as far as he was concerned, the reason for this "less than prudent policy" had more to do with the financial community's need to exploit these funds in order to protect their own interests in the exchanges than anything else. Equally important, in what amounted to a thinly disguised warning, Patman pointed out that since pension-fund contributions were tax exempt, they should be expected to perform more of a socially useful function as an investment tool if they were to continue to enjoy such a privileged status in the eyes of the law. "I am introducing a bill," said Patman, "which establishes a formula by which private pension plans can be directed to make such investments [in moderate- and low-income housing] in return for the tax advantages they now enjoy." Mortgages insured by the FHA or VA were at the time yielding 8 percent, or nearly twice the return the funds were receiving in corporate equity investments. Because the interest was guaranteed by the federal government, Patman concluded, and rightfully so, that his bill made absolute sense as a sound business investment as well as a sound social investment.[12]

His was not the only sound bill, however, to be introduced but subsequently defeated. In 1972, Senator William Proxmire introduced a piece of legislation with similar objectives in mind. Proxmire was concerned with the increasing difficulty that state and local governments were having (especially in the Midwest and Northeast) in securing investment funds for their securities. His bill would have "allowed states and municipalities to issue taxable securities with interest rates competitive with corporate issues" by having the "federal government provide a subsidy of one-third of their interest costs." During hearings on the bill by the Senate Banking, Housing and Urban Affairs Committee, the Proxmire proposal was endorsed in principle by the National League of Cities, the National Conference of Mayors, the Municipal Finance Officers Association, and even the Securities Industries Association, but that still wasn't enough to secure its passage.[13]

Even with these defeats, it is obvious that a change in thinking had begun to take place between the late 1950s and the early 1970s over the control and use of pension funds. Organized labor and some of its friends on Capitol Hill were beginning to sit up and take notice of this new form of wealth, and more importantly, were beginning to outline some tentative claims to it. But it is not correct to assume that their new consciousness was primarily self-inspired. In fact, labor was, to some extent, reacting to other forces that were pressing it and the established political powers to assume a greater social responsibility over economic decisions. These forces, which were generated out of the turmoil of the civil-rights and antiwar movements and further refined in the environmental, consumer, and women's campaigns, created the overall environment out of which labor began to press its own claims.

Beginning in the late 1960s, church and student activists hit upon a new strategy to address the plethora of social grievances that were rocking the country. The idea was to complement their movement in the streets by opening up a second front inside the corporate boardrooms of America. It was argued that churches and universities were indirectly acting in complicity with militarist and racist policies pursued by major corporations by owning stock in those firms. Activists in both communities began to push their respective institutions to begin using their proxy power as a social weapon against corporate policies.

In 1971, the Episcopal Church introduced a proposal at the General Motors annual stockholders meeting demanding that it cease its business dealings in South Africa. While the resolution only received 1.2 percent of the shareholders' votes, the favorable attention it received in the press and among the liberal community spawned similar interest in the front offices of other major church denominations.[14]

About the same time, a consortium of churches joined together to form a clearinghouse for church investment policies. The Interfaith Center for Corporate Responsibility began introducing dozens of shareholder resolutions on behalf of these churches in annual stockholders' meetings. The issues raised have run the entire waterfront from civil rights and antiwar to environment and women's concerns.[15] For example, in 1972 the Corporate Information Center released a report listing twenty-nine major defense-contracting corporations in which churches were investing their funds. Months after the report was made public, the Church of the Brethren announced that it was divesting itself of over $2 million in defense-corporation equities and U.S. Treasury bonds; other churches followed suit.

Other shareholder resolutions have been introduced to protest strip-mining in Appalachia and the West by large coal companies, to challenge business dealings with military dictatorships like Chile's, and to support the demands of minorities and women for equal employment opportunities.

Similar efforts have been pressed on the university campuses. Dozens of university administration buildings were seized and occupied between 1968 and 1972 as student activists (and some faculty) demanded that university trustees redirect their investment policies away from defense-related corporations, or from financial investments in right-wing dictatorships.[16]

For the most part, such demands have gone unheeded or at best have only been appeased in the most token ways possible. Even in those few instances where universities and major churches have acted really aggressively in using their investment funds as a social weapon, the results have been generally disappointing, mainly because their holdings in corporate America, though hardly paltry, are still insignificant in terms of effecting a real change. Overall, the pressure tactics employed by universities and churches have been more public-relations hype than anything else. Sometimes, however, the public embarrassment engendered by such efforts has paid off. When the Corporate Information Center published a series of confidential documents revealing that forty American, European, and Canadian banks were secretly lending the white-minority South African government some

$210 million, the public clamor was enough to convince nine American banks to withdraw from the consortium.[17]

Still, the real success of church and university involvement has not been so much in what they have been able to accomplish, which has been very little, but in the ideological and strategic paths they have opened up. They have succeeded in introducing a new lexicon, which has broadened the definition of investment to include social and moral considerations in economic decision-making. By doing this they have helped to break the long-standing ideological stranglehold that the financial community had exerted over the economic language of the nation. The orthodox catechism which asserts that the only criteria for economic behavior is "what's good for General Motors" and "maximum return on investment," no longer reigns supreme.[18]

While church and university activists deserve a great deal of credit for raising this alternative investment language, others like Ralph Nader and the consumer and environmental movements deserve an equal amount of credit for popularizing it in the public's mind. Environmental and consumer suits against irresponsible corporate and banking policies and the introduction of new regulatory legislation on the state and federal level to protect the consumer and the public against unsafe products, industrial pollution, and other antisocial business practices have all served to establish the concept of social responsibility in the economic thinking of the country. Twenty years ago, the term social investment was used more as a throwaway line and conjured up the image of token do-goodism and charity. Today, it has come more and more to represent an alternative way of looking at economic decision-making and planning.

The emergence of a new ideological frame of reference for using capital is only one side of the coin. By using their investment power as a social weapon, these activist groups also pointed to the strategic possibilities of challenging capital with capital. The concept of social investment as an alternative approach to economic thinking and as a weapon to exert power, has not gone unnoticed by organized labor. That doesn't mean that labor has been an easy mark for conversion. Quite the contrary. Early on (and to a lesser extent now) many labor leaders and rank-and-file members associated social concerns over the war, defense contracting work, the environment, and consumer issues as a direct threat to jobs. Opposition to these groups and their demands was often bitter and in many quarters still is. Nonetheless, as social activists have continued to press unions to assume more of a direct social responsibility on investment policies, a noticeable change in labor's attitudes has been apparent. For example, many unions are now supporting environmentalists in protesting pollution hazards that put their own workers in daily jeopardy on the job and in the community. In August 1977, the Oil, Chemical and Atomic Workers joined with Ralph Nader's Consumer Health Research Group in petitioning the Occupational Safety and Health Administration to ban the further production and sale of the chemical DBCP because of its toxic effects on union workers who manufacture it and on consumers who use it as a pesticide in the gardens.[19]

Other unions are just beginning to speak up more forcefully in matters that affect the rights of minorities and oppressed people around the world. For example, in July of 1977, national union leaders issued a statement supporting U.S. churches' efforts to end bank loans to South Africa. Both of these examples of forged alliances would have been unthinkable just fifteen years ago.[20]

Equally important, unions are beginning to see the value of using investment power as a strategy to achieve their own organizational objectives. This is partially attributable to the example set by social action groups and partially to the frustration felt inside the labor community itself; frustration over loss of political clout, runaway shops, and sophisticated technologies which have rendered its more traditional weapons, the laws and the strike, increasingly impotent.

For all these reasons unions have taken the unprecedented step of bringing their demands directly into corporate shareholder meetings, just as the churches, universities, and public-interest groups have done in the past. Acting in their dual role as workers and owners, unions, for the first time, have been placing resolutions on corporate dockets.

In 1977, Roger D. Wenthold, president of Local 81 of the International Federation of Professional and Technical Engineers, presented a resolution before the AT&T annual board meeting calling for a representative from one of the employee organizations to be placed on the board of directors of the company. Employees of AT&T now own over 5 percent of the company's 600 million outstanding shares, which makes them one of the largest single ownership blocs.[21]

A similar proposal was presented to the Chrysler board of directors in 1977, by an employees' committee affiliated with Local 412 of the UAW. The committee represented over 100,000 shares of Chrysler stock. Because of a technicality which "allows a company to omit from its proxy, material proposals relating to an election to office," the SEC ruled that the resolution could not be presented at the annual shareholders' meeting.[22]

Taking a different tack, Mel Rubin of Local 1371 of the Retail Clerks, placed a resolution before the Bank of America board asking for disclosure of information concerning the trust department's "influence and ownership power in corporations in which it has stock." [23]

Even tiny union locals like the Oil, Chemical and Atomic Workers of Beaumont, Texas, are beginning to exercise their investment muscle in corporate matters. The president of the local, J. S. Burchfield, has put a proposal before the Union Oil Company board requesting that the firm "ship its oil only in U.S. vessels manned by unionized Americans." [24]

While most of the resolutions being put forth by unions at shareholders' meetings have tended to be more of a dessert than of a bread-and-butter kind, there are a few instances where the unions have begun to use shareholder resolutions and proxy fights as a major weapon in their organizing and bargaining efforts. One such example is the Graphic Arts Industrial Union. Faced with a series of strikes, unresolved labor disputes, and a recalcitrant employer unwilling to bargain seriously (in this case, the Western Printing Company), the union decided to embark on a new organizing front in 1977. The idea was to go directly over the management's head and to the shareholders in an effort to convince them that the labor policies pursued by company officials were costing them millions of dollars in unnecessary losses. The union drew up a series of stockholder resolutions, ran ads in the local papers in towns where the company's plants were located and sent out several mailings to thousands of stockholders. While the union resolutions failed, the impressive shareholders' response to their campaign efforts have encouraged them to use the proxy battle again in the future as a means of forcing management to come to terms with the union's bargaining demands.[25]

The upsurge of shareholder resolutions and proxy challenges by unions shows a clear intent to become involved in economic matters in an investor or ownership capacity. But up to now, these scattered skirmishes have been more like a dress rehearsal for the big battles ahead. However, in 1974, one incident did take place in the town of Charlotte, North Carolina, that effectively demonstrated the explosive potential of union control over social capital.

The United Mine Workers were on strike against a Duke Power Company plant in Harlan County, Kentucky. Duke officials in Charlotte refused to come to terms with UMW demands. The union decided to break the deadlock by the threat of mounting a massive capital boycott against the company. Fifty-nine national labor unions joined the UMW in pledging not to buy Duke Power stock with their pension funds unless the company signed the contract in dispute. The company caved in almost immediately, but not before it was forced to withdraw a proposed $5 million new stock offering from the market. That little demonstration of raw economic power sent shock waves through the financial community. Within the labor camp it signaled (for some at least) the first real wave of recognition of this new and awesome form of potential power that was within their grasp.[26]

From adversary of capital to junior partner with capital to owner and manipulator of capital—for some old-time AFL-CIO organizers who remember first-hand the bloody street battles of the 1930s, the transformation of the giant has been difficult to accept. Still, accept they must, because private- and public-sector union members now own well over $200 billion in social capital through pension funds that their own leadership fought to establish. While some labor leaders would like to ignore this new reality, it is becoming increasingly obvious that if they continue to do so, it will further jeopardize the union movement and eventually make a mockery of organized labor itself. Imagine the reaction of rank-and-file unionists when they begin to find out who their employers really work for.

Consider the following hypothetical scenario. All of America's labor leaders and millions of rank-and-file members are assembled together in one mammoth outdoor rally. One by one the leaders take to the microphones to explain to their members that American companies are closing their union shops in the North and moving their operations overseas or to nonunionized Sunbelt states. Naturally they lament the sad state of affairs that has crippled their movement, and forced their own members into unemployment lines, but they plead for forgiveness on the grounds that changing political and economic circumstances have weakened their ability to use the strikes, the courts, and the politicians to advance their demands. A lone hand pops up from somewhere deep in the crowd of blurred faces that dot the audience. A worker has a simple question to put to his leaders. "Who," he asks, "are the major owners of these giant corporations that are taking away our jobs and our livelihood?" Is there a single labor leader who would dare to come forward and explain to this worker that he and the millions of other unionists in the audience are, in fact, the partial owners of the very companies that are doing them in?

Nowhere has this contradiction become more evident than in the battle with the J. P. Stevens Company. Here is a firm whose policies epitomize many of the problems facing organized labor. First, Stevens is a runaway shop. In transferring its operations from New England to the South, it eliminated thousands of union jobs and replaced them with low-wage, nonunion labor. Second, Stevens is a company that has repeatedly manipulated and violated national labor-relations law to thwart union organizing efforts over the years. The labor movement, in an effort to force the company to come to terms, has called for a nationwide consumer boycott of all J. P. Stevens products. So far so good. But there is only one major wrinkle in all of labor's well-intentioned plans, a wrinkle that is so embarrassing that even an Art Buchwald couldn't do justice to the irony of it. This same company, this vicious symbol of antiunionism, this roadblock in the path of union efforts to organize the South, is, in fact, partially owned by none other than tens of thousands of rank-and-file union members.

"We have met the enemy and they are us." "Us" in this case is billions of dollars of *union members' pension funds* deposited in Manufacturers Hanover, Irving Trust, and New York Life Insurance Company, institutions which in turn have loaned J. P. Stevens over $147 million.[27] "Us" is also a large percentage of *union members' pension fund* assets invested in J. P. Stevens stock by banks and other institutions who now control 25 percent of all the outstanding shares of the firm.[28] Pam Waywood, a coordinator of the unions' boycott campaign, puts it bluntly: "Labor unions are paying for their opposition."[29]

Unions, then, are financing, either directly or indirectly, a good chunk of the very company they are fighting. Millions of dollars are being spent in trying to unionize a company they partially own. J. P. Stevens, in a nutshell, represents the contradiction now facing organized labor, which finds itself in the position of being both owner and adversary. Unions are sooner or later going to have to deal with this Catch-22. Take the Machinists, headed by outspoken William Winpisinger. His union has virtually all of its pension-fund assets, some $170 million, deposited with Manufacturers Hanover. Not only does this same bank have loans outstanding to Stevens totaling $29 million, but until recently two of its directors also served on the board of the Stevens Company. One, in fact, James Finley, happens to be chairman of the board of the Stevens Company. It doesn't stop there, however. Ralph Manning Brown, chairman of the board of New York Life Insurance Company, which also has billions of dollars of union members' pension-fund assets, and which has $97 million in loans outstanding to Stevens, is also on the textile company's board of directors. The list of embarrassing interlocks goes on, and in each instance, it is partially organized labor's own money that is responsible for placing these gentlemen on the Stevens board.[30] L. Philip Sipser put his finger on the problem when he remarked of the banks: "They sup at labor's table, but after eating our food and drinking our liquor, they then go ahead and help to smash us." [31] The bankers, for their part, treat the whole contradiction with an aloofness, one might almost say smugness, that would make even the robber barons of bygone days wince. Witness the following exchange with Harrison Smith, the vice president of Morgan Guaranty Trust:

Question: How did you end up voting your stock in the Stevens proxy battle? [Supporters of the boycott hand presented resolutions challenging the anti-union practices of the company in the 1977 annual shareholders meeting.]

Mr. Smith: We don't actually discuss how we voted stock in terms of the individual company. We did listen to the

management of J. P. Stevens as well as to the representatives
of the groups who offered those proposals in the proxy.
Question: Do you make known to your individual pension
funds how you vote?
Smith: No.[32]

Union members' pension funds are being invested in the
Stevens Company, and Mr. Smith, of Morgan Guaranty,
doesn't believe he has any obligation even to inform the
owners of the stock how *he* has decided to vote *their* proxies.

A vice president of Manufacturers Hanover is no less
sanguine on the matter. "I was asked whether I am going to
vote on the Stevens proposition," said the official. "You [I]
have to determine whether a yes or no vote is in the best
financial interest of the corporation." [33] Manufacturers Hanover has to decide! No wonder Mr. Winpisinger of the
Machinists, whose $170 million in pension funds are in part
being used by the bank, is more than outraged by the
thought of his own banker turning his own union's funds
against him. "It seems to me to be idiotic for our pension
fund to have something upwards of $80 million in that insti-
tution [Manufacturers Hanover] and to have $25 million of
it technically on loan to the most vicious antiunion employer
in the country, which does violence to the very guys that
created the money in the first place, our members. . . . [I'm]
ready to kick Manufacturers Hanover in the balls." [34]

The new strategy developed to isolate J. P. Stevens from
the rest of the corporate/financial community shows the
potential of the unions' economic clout. The first stage of this
campaign was to focus on the links between Manufacturers
Hanover and Stevens. With over $1 billion in union pension
assets and millions of dollars in other union moneys, Manufacturers Hanover was considered vulnerable to union pressure. Following Winpisinger's lead, hundreds of union officials wrote the bank expressing their outrage over its ties
with Stevens. In addition, thousands of letters poured in
from rank-and-file unionists, religious and women's groups

and others with savings and checking accounts at the bank. As the pressure mounted the bank finally announced that neither Finley or David Mitchell, another joint Stevens-Manufacturers Hanover director, would run for reelection to the bank's board—a sign that the message of union pension power came through loud and clear. In fact, shortly thereafter Mr. Mitchell also resigned from the Stevens board.

The contradiction facing organized labor is not going to go away with the resolution of the J. P. Stevens battle. Win or lose, Stevens is no more unique in its relationship to the unions than any one of the other major U.S. corporations. Through pension funds, unions and their members own a substantial portion of American industry. When companies engage in unfair labor practices, or ship their operations South or abroad to avoid union shops, it is not just some phantom abstraction called "the owners" who are making those decisions. The owners, in part, are unions and unionists, and when companies engage in a systematic campaign to break the trade-union movement in this country, as they are presently doing, they are able to succeed in large measure because the unions have given over their control of pension-fund capital to the private banking sector to use against them.

Union leaders are beginning to wake up to this monumental contradiction. Whether they will be able to do so fast enough to effectively claim control over the great pool of social capital that they and their own members have created is still a matter of conjecture. But one thing is no longer a matter of conjecture: if they fail to launch a serious challenge for control over capital the unions will, in the not too distant future, cease to be with us as a significant force.

Chapter 18: State and Local Government Claims

In August 1976, Governor Milton Shapp of Pennsylvania announced that he had provisionally convinced Volkswagen, the giant German auto maker, to locate its first major U.S. assembly plant in his state. This was no small feat for Pennsylvania, whose rising tax load and high union wages have been causing a major exodus of industry out of the state. How did Shapp perform this minor economic miracle? He used the state's public pension funds. Shapp convinced two large Pennsylvania pension funds to put up a $135 million loan to help the West German company set up shop in the state. Along with the pension-fund loan, the Commonwealth of Pennsylvania has agreed to put up an additional $40 million to buy up an old Chrysler plant and then lease it back to VW, and will also spend $30 million on rail and highway links to the facility. To top it all off, Shapp has agreed to waive 95 percent of local taxes that the company would normally have to pay during its first two years of operations. He has also agreed to assist in employee training.[1]

This unorthodox use of public funds did not sit well with the private financial community. *Pensions & Investments* magazine dashed off a frenzied editorial castigating the governor for using public pension funds in a less than proper manner. Quoting from *P & I*'s editorial:

We've said it before, but we'll say it again—public employee pension funds should not be looked on as a captive pool of capital which can be applied to politicians' favorite social projects.[2]

Never mind that such funds can be and are used all the time as a captive pool for the banking community's favorite projects. Much more interesting than *P & I*'s stock rebuttal, however, was the stance taken by the *Wall Street Journal*. The businessman's Bible argued that by laying such massive amounts of public funds at the feet of a private firm (and a foreign one at that) Pennsylvania was using the Commonwealth's public pension funds virtually to subsidize private investment in the state. A curious argument, considering that this has long been a part of the *modus operandi* of all local and state governments anxious to curry favor with private industry. The *Wall Street Journal* was, of course, partly right in its arguments, but for all the wrong reasons. The *Journal's* sudden revulsion to the Shapp plan was not really inspired by any sense of conviction that state governments should not help underwrite private ventures with state money. It was just the particular state money he chose to use. Pension funds, after all, are supposed to be controlled by the private sector, argues the *Journal*. That's the way it's always been, and as far as the *Journal* is concerned, that's the way it should continue to be. By exercising direct control over state pension funds in an investment decision of this size, Shapp had set a dangerous precedent, according to the *Journal*, one that other states might begin to copy. That, of course, would mean big trouble in the future for the banking and investment community, which has become used to having these public funds at its own direct disposal for its own particular uses.[3]

The long and the short of it is that Shapp pressed his state's claim to control of its employees' pension capital, and the *Journal* concluded that this was economically irresponsible. Translated, this means that only the private-sector financial fraternity is equipped to determine where investment dollars should go. If they decided to stay out of Pennsylvania and the VW deal, then it must have meant that it was not a promising investment in the first place. This bit of reasoning, of course, is of little value to Shapp and the governors of other northern states who find themselves increasingly abandoned by the private financial sector. The governor of Pennsylvania did what he thought he had to do in order to bring private industry and jobs into his beleaguered state. Shapp had to get investment capital from somewhere to keep his state economy afloat, so he chose public pension funds, probably with the rationale that they would be doing more good in the long run for both their beneficiaries and the state if they were used directly to improve the overall economic health of the region.

The Shapp initiative is both a good and bad example of what can be done when state governments press for control of social capital investments. Good, in that the state realized that its own public pension funds should be used by it directly to advance the economic interests of the state. Bad, in that by using these funds as a subsidy to attract private industry, the state continued to accept its dependency relationship with the private capital sector. Because of this dependency psychology Pennsylvania ended up receiving far less in return for what it shelled out. At least in the private sector, when banks sink hundreds of millions of capital dollars into a venture, they demand and receive a degree of control over the operations in return. At the minimum, they often get a director or two placed on the board of the company. All Pennsylvania received in return for its capital investment was a pledge by VW to pay interest on its $135 million outstanding loan and a few thousand jobs brought into the state, jobs that VW could decide to move out of the state five or ten years hence if the company receives a better deal from some other state or country.[4]

Shapp's approach of using public funds as a lure or subsidy to private industry is likely to catch on more and more, simply because state and local governments are both desperate to attract business and ideologically programmed to accept the notion that the private sector must ultimately be relied on to manage overall economic affairs. Still, some like John Harrington, special consultant to the California State Senate Committee on Investment Priorities and Objectives, are beginning to question continued governmental dependence on the private sector as the ultimate arbiter of eco-

nomic planning. "If you look at every program at the state
and federal level where public moneys have been channeled
to the private sector, you see that very little of the money
ends up getting to the people who need it, and the private
sector ends up making money on the deal." [5] Harrington (not
to be confused with the congressman from Massachusetts)
and a growing number of government consultants and officials around the country are beginning to discuss ways in
which local and state governments can take on a more direct
role in economic planning, using pension funds and other
public revenues to exercise increased ownership and control
of economic operations and activities within their regions.

The motivations here are more pragmatic than ideological. With private industry increasingly reluctant to stay in
the northern corridor, and with the financial community
equally reluctant to invest capital to keep industry in the
region, state and local governments find themselves up
against the economic wall. The sheer costs of luring industry
into staying by heaping more and more public subsidies on
them are fast reaching the point of diminishing returns. The
fact that Pennsylvania had to pay out over $135 million in
order to secure a measly 2,000 to 5,000 private-sector jobs
with VW is indicative of the tightening economic straitjacket
these northern states are now in. At some critical point, which
is fast approaching, these governments will have to come to
the realization that the amount of public funds being spent
to attract business is greater than the economic returns they
receive back in terms of private-sector involvement.

Many people in government agree with the *Wall Street
Journal* that the cities and states shouldn't be using public
pension funds for the purpose of aiding the state economy.
Rather, they contend, public pension funds should be entrusted only to the private sector to invest wherever they
think the best returns for the beneficiaries can be had. The
problem lies in the shortsighted way in which they define
"best returns." First, the private sector has, for all intents
and purposes, begun to redline the northeast/midwest cor-

ridor of the country, forcing billions of dollars of public pension funds to flow out of the region to the Sunbelt or other places. Secondly, this outflow of funds further damages local economies in the North, which, in turn, results in a further erosion of the tax base and a decline in public revenues. Less public revenues, in turn, mean further cutbacks in pension-fund contributions and in public employee jobs. So, in the end, it doesn't mean much to the individual beneficiaries to know that their money was invested in some other state to maximize its return, when they are out of a pension altogether, or, even worse, out of a job as a result.[6]

In fact, the same argument about maximizing returns applies to the problem of unfunded liabilities. There is great concern now because many public funds (like the private pension funds) are woefully unfunded, with some states and cities owing billions of dollars to their pension-plan accounts. This dangerous state of affairs is being used by the financial community to warn against the existing funds being used for any purpose other than maximum returns. Some officials of public employee unions agree. Jim Savarise, head of AFSCME's Public Policy Department, says:

If it were a choice between an investment that returns 9 percent without any social benefit and an investment at 7 percent that is also socially useful, I would be hard-pressed to recommend that we go for the 7 percent at this point. I think we would be ill-advised to make a point of questioning these funds' investment procedures.[7]

Mr. Savarise and the bankers fail to recognize that two of the main reasons the funds are in such big trouble (aside from their past neglect by the governments involved) are because their assets have been depleted by bad investment practices on the part of the banks that use them and because the funds have been taken out of the states of their beneficiaries and invested elsewhere, thus further undermining the already capital-starved local economies. As already mentioned, this outflow of capital further weakens the tax base of these states and reduces the amount of state revenues that could be used to bring the pension plans up to an adequate level of funding. The pension plans of northern states can only begin to recover their deficits if the existing funds are redirected back to investments designed to improve the North's local economies.[8]

The financial community argues that local and state governments should not become involved in economic planning and participation under any circumstances. On the other hand, what alternative is there if the private sector refuses to maintain its own involvement? Someone and some set of institutions will have to step in to fill the economic vacuum —unless the states are to be turned into nonproductive, nonfunctioning welfare wards of the federal government. The only other alternative is to reduce the standard of living, the social services, and the wages of labor to such a great extent that the local regions become competitive with North Carolina, Mississippi, or Taiwan. You can bet your bottom dollar that private industry will then come knocking at the door again. Short of that, there's little reason to expect much cooperation from the private sector.[9]

Today over 80 percent of all public pension-fund assets are invested by the financial community in corporate stocks and bonds.[10] For the most part these investments, like private pension-fund investments, are concentrated in several hundred major American corporations listed on the New York Stock Exchange. (These are some of the same multinational firms that are moving their operations out of the Graybelt region to the South and overseas.) Unlike private pension plans, state and local funds have not always been heavily invested in major industrial securities. Until the late 1950s, most government pension funds were concentrated in federal treasury notes and state and municipal bonds. While many funds did invest in high-grade corporate bonds, almost none invested in corporate equities. In fact, most government funds were restricted by law from such investments. The assumption behind these restrictions was that equity investments were too risky and that the funds were better off pursuing a more conservative approach to returns on investments. This strategy changed radically between the late 1950s and early 1960s, as the private financial community began a vigorous campaign to convince state and local governments to ease their legal restrictions to allow more public funds to flow into the equity markets.[11]

Oregon was the first state government to liberalize its investment formulas. In 1959 it raised its equity ceiling to 25 percent and hired several professional investment firms to manage its portfolio. Other state and local governments immediately followed.[12] By 1976, state and local governments had poured over 23 percent of their $117 billion in funds into corporate equities. At the same time, their holdings in corporate bonds had increased from 33 percent to over 57 percent since 1961. This has had a crippling effect on state and local bond investments, which used to be a major part of their portfolios. In 1976, public funds only invested $4.4 billion, or 4 percent, of their total assets in state and local bonds.[13]

For public funds, this change in investment policy has proven to be less than ideal. The original rationale used by the banking community to lure public funds into equity markets was that such investments would provide a better hedge against inflation. As the record now shows, not only have equity investments, on the whole, not been a hedge against inflation, but they have actually experienced lower returns over the past ten-year period than many high-grade state and municipal bonds. What's even worse is that, by directing public funds away from the municipal and state bond markets, the private sector has made it even more difficult for the already suffering northern states to find the capital needed to help rebuild their regional infrastructures and to pay for their rising costs of operations. This problem is compounded when the banks simply refuse to buy state and municipal bonds unless the governments hike up their interest rates to the point of usury. Unfortunately, the governments find that they have no recourse but to capitulate to such extortions because their own public pension funds, which could provide a cheaper alternative form of capital financing, are generally being used and controlled by the same banks making the demands. The ever higher interest rates charged by the banks force local and state governments to dig deeper into their already diminishing till of public revenues in order to pay off the loans and the high interest rates being exacted. It's a case of high-finance loansharking, where the victims, state and local governments, fall deeper into debt and become even more dependent on the very banks that are using the state's funds.[14]

Many public officials are starting to realize the insanity of having their own public pension-fund moneys used against them by the banking community. Some have begun to initiate alternative investment and capitalization strategies based on taking back and exercising more direct control over their own pension-fund capital. For example, New York City Controller Harrison Goldin believes that it's time for state and local government pension plans to begin actively exercising their stockholder voting rights in the equity holdings of their funds. As it stands now, the voting rights of almost all public-fund equity holdings are given over to the banks and other financial institutions to dispose of as they see fit. Goldin would not only like to redirect that power back to the city and state funds, but also believes that "the social impact on a community of the investment of a public employee system" should be considered along with the question of maximizing returns in deciding how and where public moneys are placed.[15]

Some city council representatives in Washington, D.C. also agree with the concept of imposing social guidelines over pension investment policies. City Council chairman Sterling Tucker believes that the lending practices of banks, for example, should be one of the social criteria for determining where to deposit public pension funds. Tucker argues that banks that pursue a policy of making loans in depressed areas of the city should be given first preference because that's where the public moneys most need to be channeled. "I would be willing to get a smaller return on an investment," says Tucker, "if it produces another kind of return for the city that we need just as much." [16]

In Hartford, Connecticut, a public-interest organization has succeeded in getting a strict disclosure ordinance passed that would require the city managers and the city treasurer to report on where all city funds (pension funds and general funds) are being invested. An earlier report by the group had shown that public pension-fund moneys were being invested in the stocks and bonds of corporations that, for the most part, didn't even have plants in the state.[17] Connecticut is also the first state to set up its own publicly owned brokerage firm. The Connecticut Nutmeg Securities firm handles a portfolio of over $650 million in stocks, mortgages, and other securities and even has a seat on the Philadelphia-Baltimore-Washington stock exchange. According to state treasurer Henry Parker, the state-owned brokerage house saves Connecticut a great deal of money by bypassing the middleman functions of the private-sector investment firms. It is estimated that the publicly owned investment firm saves the state over 25 percent in transaction charges and brokerage fees that it would normally have to pay if it were using a private investment company.[18]

One state that has been particularly hard hit by the shift of jobs and capital to the Sunbelt and overseas is Massachusetts. The state's Social and Economic Opportunity Council (an independent state agency) did a study of how the state's two biggest pension funds were being invested by the First National Bank of Boston and found that a good deal of the money was being invested out of state. In fact, First National has announced that they are considering investing up to one-third of their deposits overseas in the next several years because that's where they believe the best returns will be had. The council has issued a report to the state government recommending that the Commonwealth's general funds be invested in accordance with four criteria: first, that in-state investment should be given priority; second, that unemployment and income levels should be considered in determining where to invest funds within the state; third, that low-cost housing should be a priority for funding; and fourth, that loans to cooperatively owned or community-controlled labor-intensive business should be given top consideration in investment decisions.[19]

In devising various alternative ways in which public pension-fund investment can aid the local economies of a region, the states are also looking to how they can more immediately benefit the beneficiaries as well. Some states, like Hawaii, are beginning to broaden the concept of "returns on investment" to include the two-benefit notion discussed earlier (namely, the idea that a pension fund should aid the recipient during both his work life and his retirement years). Hawaii's public pension system already invests in home mortgages at bargain rates and with liberal down payments for its own members.[20] It is also interesting to note that Hawaii has become the first state to use its pension funds to acquire a portion of direct control over a private company in which it has heavily invested. The state fund owns 16 percent of the stock of the Hawaiian Independent Refinery, and as a result successfully placed a representative of the state fund on the company's board of directors.[21]

Placing public representatives on private company boards is seen by the financial community as a major architectural blueprint for public ownership and control over industry. Their perception is right. In fact, all of these intermediary constructions—establishing social criteria for pension investments, setting up state-owned and operated brokerage houses, directing public funds into priority economic areas like low-income housing and community-controlled business and coops—mark the first tentative building blocks toward publically designed economic structures where financial planning and capital allocation are taken over by local and state governing bodies.

Although intellectuals on both the left and right are likely to exchange many thousand printed words arguing about the implications and nuances of this transformation of economic power, the dynamic that is beginning to unfold is not very difficult to anticipate or explain. Simply put, those private interests that now control public economic planning and allocation decisions have decided to withdraw productive commerce and industry, over a phased period of time, from the midwest and northeast sections of the continental United States. This leaves the states and localities without a significant capitalist base and without a productive economy. Whether it leaves them without capital as well depends on whether they press their claims for control over their own pension fund assets. A growing number of political officials are beginning to argue that if the capitalist sector continues to move out of the region and if it proves impossible to buy them back with sufficiently substantial public subsidies, then at least they should not be allowed to take the state's own capital funds (pension-fund assets) with them. That money, they contend, should remain with the states and be used to rebuild regional economies. The only real alternative to either capitalism or local public ownership and control over the economy, as they see it, is becoming a ward of the federal government.

Unfortunately, a great number of state government officials still continue to pin their hopes for economic survival on convincing the private sector to remain in the region, through the bestowal of more and more public gifts. Yet even this strategy has begun to reach a point of no return as public treasuries have run out of gifts to give. This is exactly what happened in New York City in 1975, when the country learned that it was facing imminent bankruptcy. For several years, financially troubled New York was floating bigger and bigger bond issues to pay for its increasing debts and its skyrocketing costs of operations. Part of the reason for both the debt and the high costs was that industry and middle-class taxpayers were pulling out of the city and banks were taking billions of dollars of public pension funds and investing them outside the locality (and the state), where they could get a so-called better return. Naturally, this further depressed the economic base of the city, diminishing the revenues, increasing the taxes, and forcing the municipality into greater debt financing to maintain its operations.[22]

As the city's financial position worsened, it found the banks increasingly unwilling to buy its bonds. This forced the city into agreeing to pay ever higher interest rates, again in the hope that they could somehow keep the private sector involved. The banks continued to bleed the city by exacting these higher interest rates until they figured that they had all but busted the city itself. Then the banks quickly unloaded over $2 billion in city bonds on unsuspecting small investors over an eight-month period, and at the end of this maneuver announced that they would no longer buy bonds issued by the City of New York at any price because of its disastrous financial plight; a plight they helped, in part, to create by their policies.[23]

The city was at the end of the line in 1975. The capitalist banking sector had squeezed it for every last ounce it could extract and then had pulled out. The only option left for the city was either to file bankruptcy and become a ward of the state and federal governments or find an alternative means of financing its bonds. The only large capital pool that the city had any claims over was the municipal pension funds, amounting to some $11 billion. Through some rather complicated manipulations, including the enactment of special legislation by the state and a special exemption granted by the federal government, New York was able to secure commitments for the investment of $3.1 billion of public employees' retirement funds in the city's bonds, allowing it, at least for the moment, to forestall collapse.[24]

The public employees, needless to say, were not thrilled at having to bail the city out, but were as entrapped by the situation as the rest of the government. They realized that at that point there was little choice. Without the pension-fund loan, the city would not have enough operating funds to pay the thousands of New York employees their future paychecks.[25]

The New York City bail-out is a good example of what can happen when local and state governments wait until it is almost too late to assume control over their own social capital. The city had allowed the banking community to use the city's public pension funds for its own ends for years. The city had also continued to allow itself to be extorted by these same banks as they raised their interest demands and lowered the financial lid on the local region. The city did all this because the elected officials were wedded to the ortho-dox notion that their survival depended on currying the favor of the private banking sector. Even when it finally be-came obvious that it was this same private banking sector that was putting its financial knife to the city's throat, the only response was continued capitulation, more groveling, and greater victimization. Only when the banks pulled out altogether did the city finally take action on its own, and then only because it was now truly alone and abandoned.[26]

Had New York taken the initiative years earlier and be-gun to reclaim control over its own social capital pool, using these moneys to rebuild the economy and the infrastructure of the city, it might never have reached the point of insol-vency. Like other city and state governments, it saw what was happening but refused to react. The flight of jobs and capital out of the city did not occur overnight. It took place over two decades, plenty of time to begin preparing an alter-native approach to economic planning and capital allocation, using public pension funds as a tool. It failed to prepare, and as a result the city itself failed in the end. This is a lesson for other governments in the northern tier who are facing the same long-range prospects as the City of New York. They can continue to allow themselves to be blackmailed economi-cally by the private financial community, even letting it continue to use their own pension-fund moneys as its chief economic weapon. Or states and cities can begin pressing their claims now for control over this social capital pool as well as for increased control over economic planning and participation as the private sector phases out its business dealings in their local regions.

If municipal and state governments do begin to push for a greater role in economic planning and capital allocation, they will need the support of working people in their regions. With organized labor directly representing the interest of 32 percent of the work force in the Graybelt sector, it is the single most important potential ally in any plans to restructure these regional economies.[27] Labor's problems are virtually the same as the problems facing the states. The solution to both their problems lies along the same path. Their mutual survival depends now on their forging an economic alliance. With each working together as coequal partners, they can begin to lay the groundwork for worker and community control over capital, economic planning, and production.

Chapter 19: The Legal Question

Many labor leaders and local public officials say they would be willing to move much more aggressively to claim control over their own pension-fund capital if they thought they could do it legally. Well, for the most part, they can.

First of all, public pension funds are presently only accountable to local and state statutes. There has been some noise in Washington over the possibility of bringing them under federal supervision, but it is questionable whether or not such action would violate the constitutional rights of the states. In a landmark decision handed down by the Supreme Court in 1976 in the *League of Cities vs. Usery*, the justices ruled that "the federal government cannot tell the states what to do in employment matters such as minimum wage and overtime pay." [1] Many observers believe this ruling effectively prohibits Washington from regulation of state and local public pension funds as well. Still, some members of Congress believe there might be other ways to bring the federal government in. For example, Congress might be able to legislate a change in the IRS laws governing public pension funds. They could conceivably "eliminate the tax deferral on a participant's accrued benefits" unless the plans met certain standards. Congress might even try to pass a law declaring that the beneficiary's interest in his pension fund is the same as a property right and therefore subject to federal standards under the Fourteenth Amendment to the Constitution. This course of action is considered highly unlikely by Capitol Hill insiders. So, as it stands now, state and local governments have virtually complete discretion as to how their public pension funds are used. [2] The real confusion about legal restrictions arises over private funds which are regulated by the federal Employee Retirement Income Security Act of 1974. Labor leaders who are seriously discussing the idea of mounting a major offensive to claim control over pension-fund capital are unsure of what things they can legally do and what things are prohibited under ERISA.[3]

Much of the caution exhibited thus far, admit some labor spokespeople, is because of the advice being given to the unions by investment counselors. Lawrence Smedley, of the AFL-CIO Social Security Department, is quick to point out that such advice is almost always given with a corporate perspective in mind. "These counselors are in all likelihood corporate rather than union people and have their heart somewhere else than with the union member." [4] As a result, says Smedley, they almost always tell the union that it can't do anything with its own funds. Many union leaders have been willing to accept such pronouncements in the past because they didn't want to accept the fiduciary obligations that go with taking over management of their own funds. Under ERISA, unions can rid themselves of any fiduciary responsibility over what happens to their own funds if they turn them over to an asset manager and give him exclusive control. This legalism has given banks (and insurance companies) a virtual *carte blanche* over control of these assets.[5] Nevertheless, an objective reading of the law suggests that unions can do just about everything they would like to do with these funds, if they choose to. The fact that they haven't thus far has been more a result of timid leadership and lack of imagination than of legal prohibitions. Russ Allen, for a long time the AFL-CIO's chief expert in the field, is unequivocal on this score.

Union pension trustees are being told that they can't even keep their investments out of antiunion companies, to say nothing of promoting unions. I say they can. And even if their lawyers aren't telling them that, they should be doing it. These conservatives have got everybody so scared about fiduciary responsibility that they're not opening their mouths. I think they could be directing these funds into areas that would help the unions, and away from areas that are antiunion.[6]

Under the provisions of ERISA, trustees of private pension funds are charged with the responsibility of maximizing the returns of the funds in accordance with the prudent man rule. As long as the principles of maximum return and prudent investment are faithfully followed, there is nothing to preclude the trustees from exercising other considerations in their investment strategies. For example, if both IBM stock and Xerox offered the same current rate of return in the market, there would be no reason why trustees of a fund couldn't decide to invest in Xerox rather than IBM, on the grounds that its management had a prounion policy. Even Ian Lanoff, the administrator of the Pension and Welfare Benefits Program of the U.S. Department of Labor, has argued that "as long as all things are equal" with respect to rate of return, there is no reason why unions couldn't direct investments in ways that would help workers.[7]

The irony is that by the very investment standards commercial banks currently apply there would be virtually no conflict in any of the potential investments union funds might want to make, at least in the stock market. Consider the fact that banks invest almost all of their pension-fund assets in the equities and bonds of the Fortune 500 companies, and their investments are considered prudent by both the asset managers and the government lawyers. While there are many reasons to question whether such investments are indeed always prudent, the fact remains that the banking establishment and the government consider them to be. Since virtually all of the companies that labor might want to influence in its investment policies are also listed in the Fortune 500, they would be applying their funds to the very same field of businesses as the banks do now—although more selectively—taking into consideration which firms are unionized, which are pursuing runaway shop policies, and other matters of importance to them. How then could it possibly be argued that union investments in this or that Fortune 500 company are less prudent than the same investments by a commercial bank? Obviously, it couldn't be. About the only thing that could be argued is that unions might try to use their ownership position to influence company policy. But such reasoning assumes that labor should somehow be penalized for exercising the same ownership rights as every other stockholder or investor. It is an established feature of American business that stockholders have every right to buy, sell, or vote their stock in ways that accomplish their own ends. Certainly banks and insurance companies do this every day. The investment community might argue that a union decision to buy, sell, or vote stock, because it would be in part motivated by the desire to advance the interests of union organizing, is not being made on the grounds of strict investment merit, or for the exclusive benefit of the participant. This, however, is merely an opinion—some might say a prejudiced opinion. Unions could just as easily argue that any investment strategy that helped to broaden union membership or insure the preservation of a strong labor movement is of great economic benefit to workers, the economy, and the companies themselves, and could cite judicial precedent, federal laws, leading authorities, past presidents of the United States, and any number of other sources to more than back up their claim.[8]

The point is that the financial community can't have it both ways. If they want to continue to buy, sell, or vote stock to advance their own interests, they can't preclude labor from doing the same, especially when its investments are securing no less a return than theirs. The same argument extends to the question of electing company boards of directors. Banks believe they have an obligation to protect large investments they have in firms by placing some of their representatives on the boards to look after their interests. Why shouldn't union funds or public funds with similar large investment holdings be allowed to do the same thing?[9]

What about investments outside the stock market? As far

as home mortgages go, with an 8 percent guaranteed return, there isn't a lawyer in the country who could possibly argue against such investments on the grounds of returns or prudence. Compared to almost all major corporate equities and many corporate bonds, they're simply a better deal.[10]

The one area where union investments might be challenged on the basis of return and prudence is municipal and state bonds. Averaging 4 to 6 percent, and because there is no tax advantage in a pension fund investing in them, they are no better a risk than many corporate equities and a worse investment than some. Does this mean that private pension funds should continue virtually to ignore the municipal and state bond market, cutting off cities and states from the largest single source of investment capital that exists in the country? If ERISA argues that an increase in such investments is a strict violation of the principle of maximum return and prudence, then the cities and states might as well fold up their operations, declare bankruptcy, and become wards of the federal government, because they will have no other choice. Simply speaking, someone has to provide the investment funds for these economically troubled governments— if not the private-capital market, then the federal government. Since the burden of countless future bankruptcies of local and state governments is not a very prudent proposition for the federal government to want to entertain, it makes sense for ERISA to relax its standards of prudence and maximum return in this area now, while there is still hope of fending off economic collapse. Or better yet, the federal government should help subsidize and guarantee the interest rates on municipal and state bonds so that private pension funds can continue to infuse needed capital into these local and state governments. A 1976 report in *Pension World* magazine has suggested just that. It proposes that ERISA allow private funds to invest up to 15 percent of their assets in municipal issues, with the federal government granting a federal income tax credit of 3 percent of the amount invested. Such a plan, according to the report, could free an additional $30 billion of available pension money for investment in the bonds of America's cities, right at the very time when they are in such desperate need of funds to maintain and rebuild their local infrastructures and economies.[11]

As it stands now, organized labor and the northern industrial states have the legal power to begin exercising direct control over pension-fund capital. It is possible that the battle for control over social capital might lead to the question of nationalization of these funds. "It is not inconceivable to me," says Michael Clowes, editor of *Pensions & Investments* magazine, "that one day the assets of this nation's private and public employee pension system would be nationalized." [12] Most observers believe that day is a long way off or will never come at all. Still, there is already some talk about absorbing pension funds into the social security system.[13] With the costs of maintaining private and public pension funds becoming increasingly high, many are beginning to question whether the business community and local governments will be able to maintain their plans. Similarly, the nation's social security system is in deep financial trouble. The increasing number of Americans reaching retirement age and the pressing need to continue upgrading benefits to adjust for inflation is putting a serious squeeze on the solvency of the fund. The present administration has already secured an increase in the contribution requirements of private employers and wage-earners in an attempt to meet the crisis. The business community is angry over this since contributions to social security will probably have to be paid by the companies out of their corporate earnings. Even with the increase, there is a recognition by all concerned that some type of basic overhaul in both social security and pensions is going to have to take place sometime in the next decade. The big question is whether it is economically possible to continue paying for both pensions and social security at the same time.[14]

Still, the debate over nationalization of pension funds is not likely to be precipitated by the concern over retirement benefits, although it is likely to be used as a convenient cloak. The plight of senior citizens is more apt to be the excuse for the debate, with the question of control over social capital being the underlying catalyst. As labor and northern state governments begin successfully to press their claims for control of pension capital, the American business community might see the wisdom in advocating the nationalization of these funds. While at first glance it seems strange that the nation's private sector would entertain such a position, a closer look at the dynamic suggests the value in their adopting such a strategic course.[15]

The Congress is increasingly controlled by the Sunbelt states who represent the interests of the private business sector. As a consequence, any plan to nationalize pension funds is likely to work to the advantage of the business community. First, even if these funds are nationalized, they would have to continue to be used as a capital investment fund simply because if they were withdrawn altogether from the marketplace, the economy would not have sufficient investment money left to survive. No one with any economic sense is even suggesting that pension funds be absorbed into a nonusable fund, like social security funds are now. The question then becomes, who would control the capital investment policies of these nationalized funds and for what ends? With the federal government virtually under the control of the Sunbelt states after 1982, and with the Sunbelt states virtually under the control of the private business community, it is not difficult to imagine who would control a nationalized pool of capital. In fact, even though many business leaders are now rattling their sabers against nationalization, they have much to gain if it comes to pass. The private sector would not only be able to direct this enormous pool of capital in ways that benefit the interests of America's major banks and corporations, but it would have the entire federal government as a guarantee. For the private sector, this form of state capitalism would be the answer to their prayers.[16]

This is why some labor people like Reese Hammond, of the Operating Engineers, worry about the prospects of nationalization.

The government will move in and they're going to serve the interests of the business community, who will be saying: "Hey, these son of a bitches [unions] are getting too big for their britches. Let's get pension funds into the public domain. Let's change social security. Because we know that big business will *always* be controlling the government. And if we can get the government to control these pension funds, we won't have to worry about some smart-ass union guy coming along and hurting us." [17]

Other labor leaders, like William Winpisinger of the Machinists, are more equivocal on the question of which side would benefit from nationalization.

As poor as our influence with the government is, it's probably higher than our influence with the capitalists. So I think I'd opt for the government doing it [taking over pension funds] because it does create some leverages that can be used. [18]

Even Winpisinger, however, is tentative on the question and realizes that the labor movement would have to be very careful to make sure "the government didn't stick it into our shorts like they so easily can do." [19]

Still, Winpisinger and other leading liberals and socialists are likely to opt for nationalization of social capital if and when it gets down to the wire. Many of them will argue that nationalization would at least be a first step toward federal planning of the economy. For many economic reformers, federal planning is the takeoff point toward an inevitable journey to socialism. Their faith in that inevitability is based on some long-held assumptions concerning their own influence in federal government. For liberals and socialists alike, Washington has been the arena to push for social and economic reforms since the early days of the New Deal. For close to four decades liberals, poor people, trade unionists, and northern city dwellers have successfully coalesced as the dominant force in the national political life of the nation. Their alliance has been responsible not only for the major social reforms of the period but also for whatever curbs have been placed on the rapacious policies of big business. But all of that is now becoming past history. The old liberal left coalition is no longer the dominant voice in Washington. The New Dealers no longer control the legislative machinery of government. Their power to affect the life of the nation through the federal government has been greatly reduced and will be reduced even further after the 1982 reapportionment. In spite of that they talk of effecting a transformation of control over the economy, and the more left-leaning among them even talk about the prospect of legislating in a socialist society through the Congress of the United States. Such talk is mere illusion on their part. Imagine the question of nationalization of pension funds coming up for consideration in the Congress of the United States a few years from now. By what stretch of the imagination do some liberals and socialists believe that they would prevail in any knock-down drag-out legislative fight concerning who should sit on the boards that plan how these funds should be invested? Are Sunbelt politicians likely to vote for a board that takes control out of the clutches of the American business community and puts it into the hands of left-leaning liberals or socialists? [20]

Liberals are right in assuming that nationalization of pension funds would mean a concrete step toward state planning. The question is who would be doing the planning. A careful reading of the shifts in power that are taking place in Washington suggests that those who would do the planning would be planning for state capitalism, not state socialism. However, nothing is written in stone. A major and prolonged depression that is equally traumatic in its effects on all regions of the country could so alienate the entire body politic that a truly *national* movement for socialist alternatives would emerge and be triumphant. Short of that, the reality is that those parts of America that are already being abandoned by the private capitalist sector—the unions and the North—are ready to pursue a new and independent economic course, one based on the principles of worker/community control. If they begin to use their own pension-fund capital to establish alternative economic mechanisms and the beginnings of an alternative economic system for their region, it can serve as a model of economic democracy for the rest of the country, when their own situation becomes sufficiently grave to turn their attention to new possibilities.

Pension Capital and an Alternative Economy

Chapter 20: Laying the Base

A base is already being laid for an alternative economic system within the United States. Cities and states throughout the northern tier are becoming increasingly involved in economic functions that have traditionally been the exclusive preserve of the private sector. The pattern of involvement has run the gamut from greater regulation of private industry to direct public ownership of economic enterprises.

For the most part, the economic initiatives undertaken by local and state governments have lacked any coherent long-range design. Instead they have a patchwork approach intended both to penalize and reward the private sector and at the same time to fill the gaps where the business community has opted out. Still, seen in total, the array of legislative initiatives being proposed and implemented adds up to an impressive potential blueprint for an alternative economic system. Whether the result is just that or will merely provide a convenient safety value for the private capital sector depends on two related factors: first, the degree to which organized labor and public officials begin to perceive the urgency of developing a close economic relationship with each other; secondly, the extent to which new leadership in both these camps is able to develop a clear and unified political perspective regarding long-range economic alternatives to private-sector capitalization. Without these two factors, it is doubtful whether either bloc can reverse its present downward spiral regardless of what claims each makes on the control and use of pension-fund capital. However, with a strong alliance and a shared philosophical commitment, each bloc can provide the other with something they desperately need to create an independent economic

base. Organized labor has the potential to marshall the votes
needed to elect politicians to public office who are committed to passing alternative economic legislation. Elected
officials, in turn, can continue to create the legal mechanisms
necessary to transform local economies from private to public control. Together, organized labor and the northern
states have sufficient claims over a large enough pool of pension capital to make such an economic transition possible.
While skeptics are likely to question the probability of this
kind of alliance, the reality is that with the private sector
severing its relationship with both these blocs, they have virtually nowhere else to turn but to each other. Certainly the
federal government, which increasingly reflects the interests
of the Sunbelt states and the private sector, cannot be expected to champion the interests of organized labor and the
North. At best, it can be relied on to do little more than
cushion their decline.

Some public officials on the state level have already come
to understand, at least in part, the need to exercise greater
control over the economies of their region. As a result, there
has been a flood of legislative proposals, and in many instances legislative enactments extending public participation into the economic realm.[1] As a starting point, many
local and state governments are increasing their regulatory
powers over the private sector. A few years ago, public authorities were primarily concerned with regulating such
business abuses as consumer frauds, industrial pollution, and
unsafe work environments. Today, many public authorities
have begun to broaden their regulatory powers to include
checks and restrictions on private capital planning and allocation decisions.[2]

In Ohio, legislation has been proposed that would penalize large corporations who flee the state. The bill before
the Ohio legislature would require runaway shops to pay
severance benefits both to the employees and the affected
communities. The payments to the community would be
used as matching funds to secure federal job-creating aid

and redevelopment projects as well as being used for emergency tax relief.[3] A similar bill proposed in the Michigan legislature would, in addition, require the corporation to allow its employees first option to purchase the facilities. The bill also provides for the state to financially assist employees in making such a purchase.[4]

Industry is not the only target of these new regulatory restrictions. Many cities and some states have begun to enact strict regulatory legislation against the redlining practices of commercial lending institutions. Typical of this kind of legislation is the new city ordinance in Cleveland which would penalize local banks who pursue a redlining policy by withdrawing public funds deposited in those institutions. With $300 million in public funds deposited in just five major commercial banks, the city of Cleveland is in a strong position to make its voice heard.[5] In Colorado, the state treasurer took a somewhat different tack by agreeing to accept lower interest rates on state funds deposited in commercial banks on the condition that they be used to assist minorities, small businesses, women, and rural residents.[6]

While regulatory restrictions over the uses of private capital can have some marginal effect, the only way really to influence capital planning and allocation decisions is for public authorities to begin exercising a measure of direct control. Some state governments have begun to use public funds as a capital investment tool. States like Pennsylvania have set up industrial development funds or credit corporations. For the most part, these institutions have served as a lure to entice private companies to locate plants in so-called high-risk communities. In return for bringing business operations into highly depressed areas, the companies are amply rewarded with low-interest loans from the state funds. For example, Pennsylvania's Industrial Development Authority provides loans at only 4 percent interest and will finance between 30 and 50 percent of the entire package for any given company who qualifies. As Peter Bearse, former director of the New Jersey Council of Economic Advisors, points out, these development programs are "biased towards the established industries and larger firms." Pennsylvania has used this form of public subsidy to lend more than $325 million to private businesses in the state.[7]

Massachusetts, on the other hand, has set up a development fund of a very different kind. Capitalized at $30 million, the Massachusetts Community Development Finance Corporation is designed specifically to avoid the kind of public subsidies to large private businesses that are found in other state financing programs. The CDFC makes loans and direct grants only to nonprofit community development corporations, mostly in impoverished areas of the state. These grass-roots organizations, in turn, invest the funds in economically useful projects that will be of benefit to the community at large. To qualify for financial assistance, the local CDCs must be governed by a board representing a cross-section of the community's interests to insure a real measure of democratic participation and community control over the disposition of capital funds.[8]

Similar types of community development corporations now exist in over thirty states. A study done a few years ago showed that about two-thirds of these CDCs have proven successful. Still, their outreach is greatly limited by the amount of capital available. Commercial banks have generally refused to make loans to these projects, preferring instead to keep their investments in traditional private-sector businesses. It is not difficult to understand why CDCs are being shortchanged by the financial fraternity. Ideologically, they are anathema to many of the principles held dear by the banking establishment. Being nonprofit and community controlled, they represent an alternative form of economic planning, one controlled directly by the public. Interestingly enough, they have been formed to fill the vacuum left when the private capital sector abandons particular neighborhoods or communities. In this sense, their existence and success provide a model for an alternatively structured and democratically run economic system for the entire northeast region. The commercial lending institutions are not anxious for such models to gain a popular audience because, more than anything else, they demonstrate both the feasibility and desirability of alternative approaches to private capitalist planning.[9]

Up to now, CDCs have had to rely on token funding assistance from the federal government and the states and to some extent private philanthropists. However, even the small amounts of funds made available have proved helpful on one level. They have provided the necessary research and development that can now be applied to larger, more comprehensive alternatives in the future. State and local involvement with CDCs has also set a precedent for greater public participation in capital planning and allocation decisions. In fact, as far as precedents are concerned, even those states which have opted for financial development agencies to subsidize large private industries have at least established the notion of direct government involvement in capital markets. Whether the precedents and the mechanisms already established can be redirected in a substantial way to replacing, rather than subsidizing, private-sector hegemony over capital planning depends on the disposition of the general public and the determination of elected officials and organized labor.[10]

The first major test of that determination is likely to come over the battle to establish state-owned and operated public banks. Proposals for state-owned banks have been introduced in Massachusetts, New Jersey, New York, the District of Columbia, and several other states. The furor aroused over the proposed establishment of a state bank for New York is indicative of the passions that such proposals are likely to arouse throughout the northern states. The state of New York has over $6 billion in public funds deposited in a handful of New York commercial banks. Almost 50 percent of those funds are invested out of state, much of them in the Sunbelt or overseas. State officials, angry over the refusal of New York commercial banks to infuse desperately needed capital back into the state's depressed economy, introduced a bill into the state legislature in 1975 which would establish a public bank whose purpose would be to use state funds for investment in New York. The fear that the state might transfer $6 billion in public moneys out of commercial lending institutions into a state-owned bank has created near-pandemonium within the private financial sector. That fear was compounded when the proposed bill passed the state assembly in 1975. Only a last-ditch lobbying effort of unprecedented proportions by the commercial banks prevented the bill's passage in the state senate.[11] But since the private banking community continues to direct billions of dollars of public moneys out of the state, many observers believe it is only a matter of time before New York succeeds in enacting legislation to establish a state public bank. With $6 billion to start with, a New York state bank would automatically become one of the largest banks in the United States.[12] Commercial banks realize the implications, and the precedent it would set for other northern states. Controlling billions of dollars of public revenues would pose a potentially serious challenge to the private capitalist system. According to Kenneth Buhrmaster, president of the New York State Bankers Association,

this so-called bank [state bank] would constitute unfair and destructive competition for most commercial banks in New York State. . . . No longer would commercial banks . . . be able to use *public funds* to help finance businesses. . . . It would undermine the private financial system so vital to a dynamic, growth economy.[13]

Of course as far as the New York state legislators are concerned, Mr. Buhrmaster's claims that the commercial banks are necessary to promote "a dynamic, growth economy" mean very little if that dynamic, growth economy happens to be in Tampa or Hong Kong.

New York state officials argue that with control over public funds, a state bank can invest in municipal and state bonds without having to demand the usurious interest rates extracted by commercial banks. In addition, by investing directly in business enterprises in the state, a public bank would not only be improving the regional economy, but would also be improving the overall revenue-producing picture for the state as a whole.[14]

One of the dangers, however, is that state banks like that proposed for New York could end up taking over only those business enterprises that have been abandoned by the private sector because of their inherent unprofitability. The dangers of what some critics refer to as "lemon socialism" are very real. If state banks begin to serve merely as subsidizers of ailing industries, they will be unable to turn the corner and rebuild their sagging economies. In the end, they will have indirectly aided the private financial sector by having freed them to invest funds only in the most lucrative business ventures. To prevent this from happening will require a combination of public vigilance over state bank investment policies and shrewd and innovative approaches to economic planning and capital allocation by those in charge.[15]

Naturally, the commercial bankers argue that state-run banks would be incapable of exercising the kind of seasoned judgment necessary to survive and prosper. Their argument seems to rest on the two-fold assumption that the states do not have the necessary talent to manage their own banks and that it would be impossible to insulate these institutions from purely political motivations. On the first count, it should be obvious that for the right price states could purchase the best professional banking talent available. With billions of dollars of assets, they could certainly out-compete the private sector for salaries and wages. For the right price, Harvard and Wharton business graduates would flock to their doors, especially if they could make a good salary and at the same time believe that they were working for the public good and not just for the profit of a small business elite. As to the question of political interference in bank policies, it is certainly a double-edged sword. On the one hand, political interference is not all bad. The public, through its elected representatives, should have the final say on how public pension funds are being used. Of course, politically motivated self-dealing is another matter. While there is no way to guarantee against such abuses—they exist to some extent at every level of private and public life—there are still ways to protect state banks from such excesses.[16] In fact, the only existing state bank in the country, North Dakota's, is a model of sound financial management, divorced from political self-dealing. At the same time it has pursued a socially conscious investment policy designed to aid both the state economy and the residents. For example, it gives priority to loans for small farmers, people needing housing loans, and students seeking to finance their higher education. These are the kind of priorities that are important to people and important to the state, but not necessarily important to commercial banks, whose interests are generally focused on the business community.[17]

With the establishment of public banks, the northern states would become increasingly involved in the economic enterprises they invest in. Like private banks, they could be expected to place public representatives on the boards of directors of private firms they hold equity in. On occasion they could buy out existing companies altogether or set up entirely new enterprises which would, in effect, be constituted as public enterprises.

While the concept of local and state governments taking an active role in semipublic or public enterprises is likely to conjure up images of bureaucratic mismanagement such as occurs in the postal service, the fact is that they have been successfully managing their own enterprises for a long time and with few complaints from the public, or at least no more complaints than the private sector usually gets. Many cities and states own and manage their own public utilities, almost all of which have proven to be more cost effective than their private-sector counterparts. They also own and operate bridges, airports, garbage companies, parking garages, mass-transit systems, water works, industrial parks, sports stadiums, convention halls, and scores of other revenue-producing public enterprises. While some of these enterprises are highly profitable, others by their very nature have required public subsidies to maintain their ongoing operations. Still, for the most part, these public enterprises have operated effectively and efficiently as long as the overall private economy in which they functioned was healthy as well. Where public management of public enterprises has deteriorated, it is usually because the private economic base of the area has begun to deteriorate first, drying up needed revenues and causing a general breakdown in the public infrastructure of the region.[18]

State banks could extend the involvement of the public sector beyond these traditional public enterprises into areas that have always been the exclusive domain of the private sector. In some states this has already happened, and if the performance record of some of these novel public enterprises is any measuring stick, the private sector is in for some stiff competition.

Take, for example, the Wisconsin State Life Insurance Fund. Founded as a self-supporting state-owned business in 1911, this insurance company provides Wisconsin residents with the least expensive life-insurance costs in the United States. While an ordinary ten-year private insurance policy might cost somewhere around $3.50 per $1,000 of coverage, a comparable Wisconsin Fund policy costs only 15¢ per $1,000. This incredible difference is partially a result of the fact that the Wisconsin Fund has such a small overhead compared to private insurance companies. Because it has no advertising costs and no sales commissions to pay out, its administrative expenses are virtually zero compared to industry giants like Prudential. Unfortunately, because of a strong lobby by the private insurance industry over the years, the fund has been unable to expand its mandate to cover larger premiums and to diversify into other insurance areas. As a result of that and its legal restrictions on advertising and solicitation, it has remained small. Nonetheless, its viability and sound business practices over a fifty-year span are a good example of the possibilities that exist for state governments entering the insurance field. In fact, since most states are already heavily involved in regulating such items as auto insurance, there is good reason for them to set up natural monopolies in these areas. A state auto insurance firm would not only mean a reduction in premiums, but would also provide a large pool of ready capital that could be reinvested in other state revenue-producing public enterprises.[19] The Canadian provinces of Saskatchewan and British Columbia already have mandatory public auto insurance operations and their rates are significantly lower than commercial rates.[20]

One of the most unique public enterprises to date is the Connecticut Product Development Corporation. Created in 1972 as an autonomous agency within the State Department of Commerce, the CPDC is authorized to extend interest-free loans of up to $200,000 to small and medium-sized Connecticut businesses to be used for the research and development of new products. If the products are successful, the CPDC and the state receive a royalty on all future sales. This makes Connecticut the first state in the country officially to launch its own public-venture capital operation. For the state the advantages of the CPDC are two-fold. Aside from the direct revenues it can expect from royalties on successful new products, the CPDC's investment policy will mean new jobs for Connecticut residents as well—when, and if, the new products really take off.[21]

States are also entering the retail markets directly with competing public enterprises. New Hampshire's state-run liquor stores produce millions of dollars of revenue for the public kitty (and cheap prices for the consumer); New York State runs highly profitable public ski resorts; and the state of Pennsylvania sponsors "farmers' markets," bringing produce directly to the consumer at a much-reduced price by bypassing the enormous middleman costs.[22]

Public enterprises can serve several functions. They can

provide a needed good or service that the private sector either can't or won't provide or provides inadequately. State-run businesses are also a source of employment for the residents of the state and a source of revenue for the public treasury. In addition, public enterprises allow the state to become directly involved in economic planning and capital-allocation decisions.

Aside from setting up public enterprises, state banks could also help finance the conversion of existing private companies to worker ownership and control. In communities throughout the northern industrial corridor giant multinational firms are closing up their local plants. While some of these operations deserve to be closed down because of their inherent unprofitability, others are still potentially sound business operations. In the past, when plants closed, there were loud complaints from those directly affected, but little else. Today, communities, workers, unions, and public officials are increasingly unwilling to accept shutdowns as the inevitable, though unfortunate, by-product of industrial progress and economic expansion. Haltingly, and with little previous experience as a guide, these threatened communities are beginning actively to seek out alternative forms of ownership and production that will maintain their economic lifeblood and offer hope of stability and security in the years to come.

A striking example of this trend was the response of the residents of the Mahoning Valley in Ohio to the Lykes Corporation's announcement that it was closing its Youngstown Sheet and Tube facilities, thus throwing over 5,000 people out of work. Even before the initial shock wore off, angry steelworkers could be seen on national television demanding that the Lykes Corporation give them a chance to take over the plant themselves. Soon, some local union leaders were echoing this demand by asking the Western Reserve Economic Development Agency to look into the feasibility of such an effort.[23] At the same time, over 200 local clergy and lay people in the Youngstown Religious Coalition signed a statement deploring the company's decision. They endorsed, and financed, two preliminary feasibility studies on community and/or worker ownership of the plant. Equally as important, these church people developed an explicitly religious response to the crisis confronting their community— and many others:

We believe that the performance of the Lykes Corporation, in this instance, fails to meet ... fundamental moral criteria. ... We believe that industrial investment decisions ought to take into account the needs and desires of employees and the community at large. In its refusal to invest in new equipment or necessary maintenance, the Lykes Corporation failed to do this. Human beings and community life are higher values than corporate profits.... Our traditional teaching points out that economic decisions ought not to be left to the judgment of a few persons with economic power, but should be shared with the larger community which is affected by the decisions.... We have begun a process of seriously exploring the possibility of community and/or worker ownership of the Sheet and Tube plant or other positive alternative use of the facilities to employ the workers.... The idea of worker and community ownership is not foreign to our religious and national traditions. It ought to be explored as a creative response to abandonment of the mill by outside interests.[24]

There have been many instances like Youngstown's over the past several years, where communities and employees, faced with plant shutdowns, have wanted to buy up these operations and manage them as worker- or community-run companies. Unfortunately, without an alternative financing mechanism, this was mostly impossible.[25] State banks or other appropriate financial development agencies could provide part or all of the necessary capital for worker- and community-owned enterprises like the one proposed for Youngstown. In fact, there are already examples of local communities and workers joining together to buy out plants and businesses from large conglomerates that were abandoning them.

A good case in point is the Vermont Asbestos Group. In January 1974, the GAF Corporation, one of Fortune's 500 leading industrials, announced a decision to shut down its asbestos plant in Lowell, Vermont, rather than meet federal antipollution requirements which the company said would be too costly. Closing the plant would have resulted in the loss of 178 jobs at the mine and an equal number in the nearby town, as virtually the entire area depended on the asbestos operation for economic survival. Unwilling to sit passively by as the New York–based conglomerate signed a death warrant for their company, workers banded together to buy the plant and became the sole owners. Employees raised an initial fund of $78,000 by purchasing a minimum of one fifty-dollar share each in the joint business venture. Additional shares were purchased by friends, relatives, local retailers, and the high-school student council. Still, all of their efforts fell short of providing the financing they needed to buy up the plant, and the commercial banks were unwilling to extend any financial assistance. This is where the state's development agency stepped in. Only when the state agency agreed to guarantee all commercial loans for the buy-out venture did the commercial banks go along with requests by the workers and the community for a $2 million loan. Had the state had its own public bank, it could have made the loans directly without having to rely on the private financial community.

Still, the Vermont Asbestos story demonstrates the great potential in worker and community buy-outs of private business operations. On March 12, 1975, the employees became the official owners of the asbestos plant. One year later the worker-owned and -operated plant had repaid its original loans, turned a handsome profit, provided a dramatic pay boost to its working members, and installed $250,000 worth of environmental-protection equipment. The Vermont Asbestos Group, as it is now called, is managed by an elected board of directors which includes seven union members, seven management representatives, and one community member.[26] Today, the Vermont Asbestos Group is a thriving business. Critics nevertheless point out that its success is

more a result of external economic conditions than of increased efficiency and productivity resulting from worker
ownership. Within a year or so of the worker/community
buy-out, world asbestos shortages forced prices to skyrocket.
Thus, the Vermont Asbestos Group found itself on top of a
gold mine, and the profits have been rolling in ever since.
Not all worker buy-outs are as blessed by such fortuitous
market reversals. Nonetheless, there are many examples in
recent years of marginally profitable or even losing concerns
whose balance sheets have been dramatically improved after
worker and community takeovers.

The Library Bureau furniture plant in Herkimer, New
York, is a good example of what can be accomplished with
worker/community buy-outs, even when market conditions
are only marginal. In the spring of 1976, Sperry Rand announced that it was going to shut down its library furniture
plant in Herkimer, even though it had been considered a marginally profitable operation. For this tiny upstate community,
already facing 13 percent unemployment, the shutdown of
one of its largest plants (employing over 250 workers) would
have plunged the entire area into near-depression conditions.
Consequently, the community decided to buy the plant from
Sperry Rand. Local business and civic leaders needed to
raise $6 million in initial capital in order to take over the
plant from the conglomerate. After employees gave the go-
ahead, public subscriptions were sold. First, the workers
themselves invested an average of $1,000 each. Then, the
general public was asked to buy shares in the new company.
An aggressive public stock offering campaign in the Mohawk
Valley was waged and proved successful. In all, the workers
at the Library Bureau plant and local residents of the Herkimer area purchased some $1.5 million in common stock.
This was augmented by a $2 million loan from the U.S.
Government Economic Development Administration and another $2 million in loans from local banks. The plant never
missed a single day of operations and after the first year
under worker/community ownership, production was boom-

ing, with $11.8 million in revenues. Looking back at what the town was able to accomplish, former mayor Henry Enea said: "By saving this one, I think we've shown people that other plants can be saved too." [27]

The Vermont Asbestos and Herkimer Library Bureau plants represent small worker/community buy-outs. There are, however, a number of examples of large worker buy-outs that demonstrate the feasibility of such an approach on a grand scale. In 1972, for example, a broad cross-section of the 13,000 employees of the Chicago and Northwestern Railroad bought out their own company. After five years of worker ownership, the large rail line has passed the other major midwestern railroads to become the strongest financially in the region.[28]

While there are dozens of examples of successful worker and community buy-outs, they are overshadowed by the countless shutdowns of other plants and businesses that could have been saved if they had only had an available pool of capital to finance takeover bids. Private and public pension assets could provide the necessary funds, and state banks could provide the mechanism to negotiate such takeovers in the future.

Of course, these Band-Aid, stopgap, or ambulance-chasing strategies have very definite limits. The more important and difficult task will be to prevent future shutdowns from happening at all. This means that workers and communities must become directly involved in a process of long-range democratic economic planning and capital allocation. They will need to explore new, appropriate, job-creating industries. Again, the redirection of pension assets would obviously greatly facilitate this process.

Whether states buy into existing private firms or help finance a transition to worker-owned and -operated companies, or set up their own enterprises to compete with the private sector, or in some instances (like utilities and insurance) replace the private sector altogether with state-run monopolies, two major and related problems must be addressed. First, the problem of how to assure real worker and public participation in these enterprises. Secondly, how to prevent these alternatively run operations from being taken over and exploited by the private sector. One major danger facing successful worker/community buy-outs is that controlling interest in the companies can be bought up by outsiders, if ownership is *stock* ownership—stock that can be bought and sold outside the workplace and community. This is precisely the situation at both Vermont Asbestos and the Herkimer Library Bureau. A much better method is to establish a perpetual trust, where ownership is held in common and control of the firm remains firmly in the hands of the workers and the community, being based only on *membership*, either in the company or the community.

One of the major criticisms to date of employee and publicly owned enterprises in this country is the lack of worker participation in the economic policy decisions and day-to-day operations. Few of these kinds of enterprises have developed the structural mechanisms through which employees could have a direct voice and role. Even when such enterprises are operating efficiently and cheaply, the failure to include workers in the policy formulations of these businesses prohibits the development of any kind of meaningful democratic economic alternative to the present private capital system. Without direct worker and citizen involvement, alternative enterprises are likely to develop many of the same characteristics of privately managed businesses. As the history of other economic systems has demonstrated, bureaucratic self-dealing and self-aggrandizement can be just as dangerous to the interests and well-being of the general public as the exploitation for profit experienced under a private capital system.[30]

Some worker-owned companies are already worker-controlled as well, and they provide some useful models for broad implementation of direct employee democracy at the workplace. Take, for example, the International Group Plan insurance company in Washington, D.C., a company selling group insurance plans to organizations ranging from the American Association of University Women to the National Rifle Association. The firm was started with three employees and a $3,000 investment twelve years ago. It now employs 350 workers and has a yearly volume of $60 million.

IGP is a worker-owned, self-managed company. All employees, from file clerks and secretaries to the president and other officers, have an equal vote in making company policies. The employees work in committees and are responsible for appointing management, setting working hours, fixing salaries and incomes, and determining long-range financial policies. Employees are free to join many committees and to attend and take part in meetings of committees they have not joined. According to IGP president Jim Gibbons, the guiding philosophy of the community is that the company exists to serve the working members. At IGP, "providing an opportunity for self-fulfillment is the real goal, much more than just having discontented workers making piles of money."

IGP workers have voted themselves a thirty-five-hour work week (with some working a four-day week), unrestricted sick leave, and unspecified days off with team agreement. The in-house guidebook suggests that employees should take no less than two weeks' vacation annually to protect their physical and mental health. IGP has a Human Resources Committee that "plans ways to maximize humanness and to safeguard participatory democracy in the firm." During a recent business slump, the employees at IGP were faced with the choice of laying off a number of low-seniority workers or taking an across-the-board pay reduction. In a vote, IGP employees overwhelmingly favored the pay reduction (which lasted for several months before full wages were reinstated).

New employees at IGP need have no special educational background. They are just ordinary people. Half are black and a majority are women. The only requirement at IGP is that people take responsibility for themselves and their community. The company is a functioning classroom where employees train themselves in the exercise of democracy. Part of the training includes instruction and community education about the broad business objectives of the firm, the market, and the industry. Community members learn about themselves as they work. New talents are discovered and nurtured. Personal relationships are encouraged. IGP is working on a strategy to replace hierarchical management with operating teams, development of a food co-op, and building exercise and shower facilities in the office to allow for daily physical development.

Strange as it may seem, IGP does not sell insurance just because it's profitable. Its members feel they are responsible for selling customers only services that satisfy a real need. IGP people feel so strongly about providing real insurance service to their fellow citizens that they are currently devising a plan to turn over 50 percent of the stock to the clients. One IGP employee summarizes the feeling of this unique community in these words:

I know I am not sacrificing my personhood here. At IGP we're not all little ants doing our jobs. The company really does exist for the good of the people—both clients and employees.

In just a few short years, this unique community of people has made IGP one of the largest supplemental group insurance companies in its field.[31]

Three thousand miles way in the Pacific Northwest, sixteen worker-owned plywood factories have been operating under the principle of self-management for several decades. The firms, which vary from 80 to 450 workers, gross from between $3 million to $20 million annually. Worker-owned and -controlled plywood factories presently account for 12 percent of the nation's plywood output. More interesting, however, is the fact that their average production is 30 percent greater than standard industry productivity levels. Much of their success is directly attributable to their organizational structure.

In most of the worker-owned plywood firms, employee shareholders meet annually to elect their own board of directors. The boards are generally made up of the workers themselves. While the boards of directors are responsible for setting overall company policy, the employees usually reserve the right to approve any major expenditure or policy change. Flexible work hours and job rotation are an integral part of the work environment in these democratically owned and operated enterprises. Most of the plants also operate under the principle of equal pay. That is, no salary distinctions exist between older and younger workers, or between higher-skilled and lower-skilled jobs. Yet take-home pay in worker-owned and -operated plywood factories is almost always higher than that in the traditional plywood firms, and, of course, year-end division of the surplus among the worker owners boosts income even more.[32]

Community and employee ownership and democracy at the workplace is a concept that is increasingly being discussed. According to a 1975 national survey conducted by the Peter D. Hart polling firm, two out of three Americans would actually prefer working for companies owned and controlled by the employees themselves. In fact, the same survey showed that a majority of Americans believe that if "the people who worked in the companies selected the management, set policies, and shared in the profits," such an arrangement would improve the economic condition of the country.[33]

The success of existing worker-owned and -controlled businesses and the enthusiastic support of the general public suggest both the feasibility and desirability of incorporating the principle of workplace democracy into alternatively financed union and public enterprises. It is important to note, as Erwin Knoll, editor of the *Progressive*, succinctly put it, that "worker control means more than the election of workers to a board of directors, though this can certainly be a start. It means a process under which workers have the opportunity to redesign their jobs and the essentials of their work life, creating processes in which they have an opportunity to do the day-to-day planning as well as the execution of tasks." [34]

Related to the problem of securing democratic participation at the workplace is the equally important task of preventing private capital interests from co-opting and taking over public enterprises for their own commercial ends. The solution to both sets of problems rests in the type of commitment made by the general public, organized labor, and public officials. Again, it gets back to the willingness of the parties involved to work together in a unified campaign to replace what's left of the private-capital sector with a truly alternative worker- and community-based economic system. Most importantly, it depends on how adept organized labor and public officials are at mapping out and executing a jointly sponsored step-by-step approach to democratic economic alternatives.

Certainly there are already sufficient alternative mechanisms in place and enough precedents already firmly established to begin a serious campaign for public control over economic planning in the northern states. With claims of over $200 billion and more in pension-fund capital between them, both labor and the northern states are in a good position to turn these various mechanisms and precedents into the beginnings of a viable alternative system. To succeed will not only require a close working partnership between the unions and the individual states and cities, but also a working alliance between all the states and cities of the region and between all the unions as well.

Chapter 21: Pensions, Politics and Power: A Strategy for the 1980s

Modest proposals are for gentle times. These are not gentle times for organized labor or for the old industrialized states of the North. Each faces their own dance of death as the private sector begins to sever the all-important economic lifeline on which they have both depended for their survival. That lifeline is capital. Without its constant infusion there are no jobs, no incomes, no revenue, no public services.

Organized labor and the Graybelt states share the same plight as colonies the world over. Namely, it is their own native resources that have been used to create that capital and that lifeline in the first place. Now their colonial masters —the private business community—are moving on to exploit new colonies, using the wealth they extracted from each as the major weapon in their drive for new conquests. When labor leaders and public officials begin to assert their claims over pension-fund capital, they are affirming their right to expropriate that wealth which is theirs in the first place.

Justice notwithstanding, humanity's historical ledger is littered with many such rightful claims, some of which were never forcefully pressed, others of which were brutally put down. The difference between claims affirmed and claims realized is the difference between the first thoughts of rebellion and the successful act of revolution itself. Rebellious thoughts are, after all, momentary, unfocused, and undisciplined. Successful revolutionary actions, on the other hand, are the result of methodical calculation and an unwavering commitment to a well thought out objective.

Organized labor and the old industrial corridor will not be saved by rebellious thoughts alone. It is not enough for union leaders and public officials to lament the fact that their own pension capital is being used against them by the private sector. Nor is it enough to speculate about the ways such capital could be used if only they had control over it. The distance between speculation and materialization is a light year. When that speculation is transformed into positive action the distance to be traveled is reduced to a long march.

For labor and the North, positive action means laying the groundwork for both the takeover of pension capital and the implementation of an alternative economic base, one independent of the private-capital sector. To be successful, this kind of positive action needs a revolutionary commitment commensurate with its revolutionary objective. That commitment, in turn, means careful planning. While there are many ways to wage a war for control over capital and the economy, there are several important battles that labor and the northern states will have to win along the way.

First, both unions and state governments must be able to convince their own constituents of the desirability of using pension funds to advance their interests. For the unions this will require a broad educational effort among rank-and-file members, informing them of how their pension assets are often being used by the financial community to undermine union jobs. Many labor leaders believe that once their members realize that their own funds are financing runaway shops and antiunion employers, they will be angry enough to demand that their unions take a more active role in determining how their moneys are being invested. Still, there is apt to be some concern over the possible mismanagement of funds by union leaders, especially in light of the past abuses of the teamsters' and mineworkers' pension funds.[1] Assurances by union leaders are not likely to be enough to calm such fears. The only effective antidote is to bring the rank-and-file in on the investment process itself. If they have access to investment information and a real voice in establishing overall policy on how the funds are to be used, there is a greater chance of building the necessary bonds of trust between the leadership and the membership.[2] To avoid any semblance of corruption or self-dealing, unions would be well advised to pursue alternative pension investment strategies completely in the open. By publicizing the funds' activities in advance, unions could not only alleviate fears about misuse of pension assets, but they could also generate broad public support for these efforts. Then too, letting union members know how poorly the commercial bankers have managed their funds will go a long way to dispelling the mystique of objectivity and expertise that surrounds these so-called professional asset managers. In the final analysis, the ability to win over the rank-and-file will depend not only on how well the leadership remains open and accountable to the members, but also on whether or not it is able to point to real concrete victories in its use of pension funds. If, for example, the unions are successful in saving or creating union jobs through selective use of their capital investments, the rank-and-file is likely to be sufficiently impressed.[3]

Since only one in four workers belong to unions, it will also be necessary to educate and win over the general public. While this will be difficult to do in the Sunbelt and other regions where unions have enjoyed little support in the past, it should be somewhat less difficult in the troubled Northeast and Midwest, especially if unions make it very clear that they plan to pursue an investment policy designed to keep capital and jobs in those regions. There are other ways as well in which labor can convince the public at large that an alternative investment strategy in labor's hands makes sense. For example, housing is a major concern of most Americans. At present, however, banks invest less than 2 percent of pension-fund moneys in VA and FHA mortgages. Imagine the effect if on the next Labor Day holiday, America's major unions bought television and radio time to announce to the public that they were shifting 5 percent of their pension investments into mortgages so that millions of Americans could afford their own homes. This represents a commitment of at least $2 billion in the housing market by organized labor. Since VA and FHA mortgages are both insured and bring over 8 percent interest, labor could also rightfully claim that such an investment is more prudent than most investments in corporate equities. This gesture alone would help reestablish labor's claim to leadership as a progressive voice of all working Americans. It would certainly go a long way toward convincing the public that labor's interest is their interest.[4]

Public officials will also have to convince the voters of the importance of using public pension funds as a capital tool to rebuild the regional economies. Informing the public of the fact that billions of dollars in public funds are being invested in jobs and production out of state and out of the region by the commercial banks should have a powerful impact on public opinion. The more difficult job will be to convince the general public and the beneficiaries of the public employee pension funds that these pension moneys should be invested within the local community or region, even if the returns proved to be slightly less than what they might get on investments out of the region or out of the country. The public and the beneficiaries of these funds will have to realize that if they don't make a financial commitment to rejuvenate their own economies, no one else will do it for them, least of all the private business sector or a Sunbelt-dominated Congress. As for using public pension funds to rebuild local economies, it will be necessary to redefine the concept of prudent investment to include long-range considerations, including the impact of "recycling" scarce capital within the region. For the general public and the beneficiaries of public pension funds, a marginal increase in return on investments in the short run will, in fact, be imprudent if it is made at the expense of the long-run economic stability of their own city or state. Public officials, then, are going to have to convince the citizenry and public employees that limited sacrifices in the short run are preferable to harsher sacrifices in the long run. There is simply no other way out if these regional economies are to be saved from further collapse.

In the final analysis, both rank-and-file unionists and the general public must decide whether it makes more sense to continue to allow the banks and insurance companies to invest their pension funds, or to give their unions and local and state governments that power. If the financial community continues to invest these funds, the first and only priority will be the dollar return on investment, and even then, their own financial self-interest will come before the interest of the beneficiaries. On the other hand, if unions and local governments begin taking responsibility for these investments, their priority will not only be maximizing returns but also insuring jobs and production. Unlike the banks, unions and local governments will have to give as much thought to employment and local economic development in investing their funds because their primary loyalty is to the economic security of their constituents. It is true that in a declining economy, unions and state governments are not likely to do any better at maximizing returns on investment than the private financial institutions, if returns are measured solely in terms of short-run profit. For the millions of workers trapped in the northern industrial corridor, however, the issue boils down to choosing one of two options. Beneficiaries can continue to allow banks to set the priorities for pension capital —investing their pension money in other regions or other countries and guaranteeing the long-run loss of their jobs and their pensions altogether. Or the pension beneficiaries can choose to have their funds invested—with investment priorities that serve *their true interests*—by unions and state and local governments, in ways guaranteeing continued employment and production for the local economy.

Winning over their constituents and the general public is only the opening battle. Individual unions must also be willing to join forces in a united investment front if they are to have much impact with their respective funds, and the state governments of the Midwest and Northeast must be willing to forge a regional investment alliance as well.

There is a wide range of potential strategies for alternative pension investments. Banks, insurance companies and corporations themselves have developed a staggering array of financial tools for their own use. There is no reason why many of these mechanisms cannot be adopted for use by unions and state and local governments for their own ends. All it takes is some imagination.

In most cases, unions still lack the financial skills that will be necessary for successful investment strategies. This fact has led to a whole industry of financial advisory firms for unions. Although some of these "experts" do understand and sympathize with the goals of the labor movement, most are simply traditional Wall Street financial advisers who have found working for unions to be most profitable. However, their advice tends to be quite conservative. The fault for this situation does not lie solely with these advisers. Most union pension trustees have obviously not pressed for creative and progressive investment advice in the past. But this is changing. The AFL-CIO resolution on investment of union pension assets has already spurred a series of meetings and a conference on how to change direction in investment policies. According to labor columnist Victor Riesel, "labor has moved from the picket line to the boycott into the gut of the nation's financial world." [5]

Whatever specific strategies are developed for alternative pension investments, they must strengthen the economic security of the funds' true owners and they must be implemented with other, more traditional union tools such as organizing drives, strikes, lobbying, electoral campaigns, and other activities.

Some union leaders are talking about setting up a "union label" investment list which would be used to pursue investment policies on the basis of agreed-upon priorities. Says one:

We need a list of recommended investments for union pension funds. It should say: these are the companies that are not running away from union labor, these companies are represented by unions, these companies are not polluting our neighborhoods, and so forth. It would be a Consumer's Union sort of thing for union pension funds. Union trustees need this desperately. Right now, all they have are advisers who purport to tell them how to get the best return, no matter where it's invested. But these people won't tell them how to invest the money not just for returns to the fund, but for the full benefit of union members. Our slogan should be: "The best return for our members." [6]

Following this strategy, labor could begin to classify the union policies of all companies listed on the stock and bond exchanges. It could agree to use its pension assets in any of the following ways: only investing in unionized companies; withdrawing investments from companies pursuing a runaway shop policy; buying or selling shares in companies they are attempting to organize in order to influence management to accept unionization. It could even be possible for unions to use shares to elect union representatives to the boards of directors of companies and banks in order to influence or control their investment policies, or they could even buy out companies and convert them into union-owned, worker-run firms.

Unions could also set up their own pooled investment trusts or labor banks to allow them still greater flexibility and control over investment policies. Pooled union investment trusts already exist for the purchase of mortgages of union-built structures. This same principle could well be applied to the purchase of corporate stocks and bonds. Similarly, there is no reason why unions couldn't set up labor banks geared to recycling union members' funds within the unionized sector of the economy. The Amalgamated Clothing and Textile Workers already own a bank which could—without tremendous difficulty—be used for just this purpose. Pooled investment trusts or labor banks would give union funds a more direct role in economic decision-making. By establishing viable alternatives for depositing pension assets, unions would greatly increase their leverage with existing banks. By having available to them alternative financing mechanisms, unions would be in a good position to influence commercial banks and other financial institutions to stop lending money to flagrantly antiunion companies. Needless to say, labor banks could also enter into joint projects with progressively-led state and local governments—just as banks do now with traditionally-led governments.[7]

There are many other possibilities for increasing the impact of union pension fund investments. Again, none of these can be pursued in a vacuum. They must be coordinated with over-all union efforts and goals.

Unions already have potential claims to $50 billion of jointly administered Taft-Hartley funds which, by themselves, represent a formidable economic lever if used in a concerted fashion. Still, there exists an additional $75 billion in union members' pension funds that are presently controlled by corporate plans. A few labor leaders are suggesting that such plans be converted to jointly administered funds and have expressed a willingness to make such demands a part of the collective bargaining process. If converted, giant pension funds like those of the GM union workers would greatly increase labor's potential financial power.[8]

Obviously there are many reasons why unions would want to cooperate with each other in making joint investment decisions with their funds. But the real question is why the management trustees, who comprise 50 percent of the control of most Taft-Hartley funds, would decide to go along with union plans to use the assets as a capital weapon and organizing tool. As mentioned earlier (in Chapter 16), management trustees often find that their interests coincide with labor's. For example, it would not take much convincing for management trustees to see the advantage of voting along with the union in its attempt to pressure a nonunion company into accepting a union shop. While the trustees might not have any great fondness for the union, they would be anxious to have their competitors pay union wages, in order to improve their competitive cost position. ERISA's command that trustees invest pension assets in the "exclusive interest of the participants" could logically be interpreted to mean that nonunion, runaway shop investments are not at all in the overall financial interest of union members, and that their interests are much better served with "union label" investment policies. There might even be occasions when the trustees decide to go along with labor in return for a future favor by the union. For example, the company management may face a takeover bid by an outside interest and need the union to buy shares or vote its existing shares of company stock in their favor in order to repulse the takeover bid.[9]

Unlike the unions, the states are more likely to attempt to develop unilateral pension-fund strategies, first, because their past track record of mutual cooperation is poor compared to the unions, and secondly, because the larger states like New York and Illinois have greater funds at their disposal to affect economic planning and capital-allocation decisions. Still, the value of a unified regional approach to pooling resources or at least prioritizing investment decisions would be enormous. Together, the sixteen states of the Midwest and Northeast have claims to over $75 billion in pension-fund capital. The potential power of using such a capital pool in consort would be far greater than if each state decided to go it alone. The fact that these states have already recognized the need to forge a political coalition to implement regional solutions to their shared economic problems is a sign that joint cooperation with capital investments is now within the realm of possibility. It might take considerable diplomacy and even charismatic leadership to put such an economic alliance together, but certainly the intrastate rivalries are far less severe than those among the European nations, who were still able to overcome their historical enmities and forge a European Common Market.

Organized labor and the northern state governments are each in a position to assume an ownership role in the American economy. With control over pension-fund capital, each can elect their own representatives to the boards of private firms. They can take over companies or even create wholly new economic enterprises. They can begin to take part in broad economic planning decisions. They can begin to exercise influence over what is produced, how things are produced, and where production is to be located. They can do all of this, to a limited extent, without joining together. What they can't do alone, however, is institutionalize their ownership claims in the form of an alternative economic model. Without that institutionalization, their individual forays into the economy are likely to have little lasting value. They might be able to apply pressure in one instance or plug a vacuum in another, but in total their investment policies will represent little more than an eclectic reaction to a system still controlled in private hands.

If American unions and the northern industrial states are to free themselves once and for all from their dependence on the private capital sector, then they must begin to depend on their own set of alternative mechanisms. To institutionalize their own claims over the economy will require the coming together of a unique labor/state alliance. This alliance is essential for both sectors. State and local governments will require support from labor for innovative investment programs. Unions in the private sector will need state-sponsored investment mechanisms and guarantees in order to meet ERISA's prudence standards. Many of these efforts can be modeled after the whole range of government subsidies to private industry that presently exist (industrial development bonds, loan guarantees, and other programs). Under such an alliance public planning commissions would need to be created. Public banks would need to be legislated. Public enterprises would need to be established. Community development corporations would need to be organized. Worker-run companies would need to be set up. Union and state pension funds would need to work closely together (or be pooled) in mapping out broad economic investment and capital allocation decisions. Unions and the public would need to be represented fully on the boards of these alternative institutions.

Legislating a comprehensive economic alternative will require the support of the voting public. Since organized labor already represents nearly one-third of the workers in most of these states, it is the logical vehicle to mobilize voter support behind public officials who are committed to an alternative program. With the active support of the public, organized labor and the northern state governments can begin to forge a new economic experiment: a worker- and community-controlled system that can begin to rebuild from the shattered ruins left behind by the exiting private capital sector.

The notion of an economic system where the people's interests are looked out for by the people themselves and where cooperation is the guiding principle has always seemed beyond the reach of a society that has traditionally prided itself on being more pragmatic than idealistic. Now that very strain of pragmatism that runs deep in the American character is what is calling forth a new economic order. The people of America's northern tier no longer have any choice but to look out for their own economic interests because the private sector, which has long played the role of a paternalistic (and exploitive) benefactor, has begun to leave both the people and the region behind. Similarly, cooperation, which has always played a tangential role in American economic life, has now become a practical necessity for those who have been abandoned by private capital. In the past, "cooperation" between government and industry has been almost a private affair between top corporate executives and insulated public officials. A push for alternative pension investments will require true cooperation among vastly larger and much more representative segments of society. The simple reality is that no single interest or bloc alone is now strong enough to recast the economic fortunes of the region. Organized labor, state governments, and the public will have to join together and cooperate if they are to insure their survival.

Chapter 22: The Upcoming Battle

"Inevitable!" This was the word Noel Arnold Levin chose to use in assessing the likelihood of organized labor using pension funds as a capital tool to assert its ownership rights in the American economy. Mr. Levin is the distinguished past president of the International Foundation on Employee Benefits.[1] His view on the matter is shared by an increasing number of people within the American labor movement. Union leaders are talking less about *if* and more about *when* they will begin to take control over tens of billions of dollars of union pension funds. The simple fact of the matter is that it is going to happen soon because the funds are available, unions have a legitimate claim to them, and, most importantly, they desperately need to use these moneys if they are to survive as a significant power bloc.

In states throughout the Northeast and Midwest, public officials are also talking along similar lines and for the same reason. Survival! For years the unions and the northern industrial states have been desperately chasing after capital. Now they are talking openly about grabbing hold of that capital instead, especially that part of it over which they have obvious claims—pension funds. What other choice is really open to them? The private sector is abandoning its long-standing "partnership" with organized labor and the industrialized North. The mass exodus of capital from the region means increasing loss of jobs for the majority of union members who are concentrated there and continued destabilization for the economies of the old industrial corridor.

The unions and the local governments of the northern tier need desperately to break out of the economic vacuum the private sector has placed them in. Lacking the necessary political clout in Washington to reverse their misfortunes and unable to provide the private sector with sufficient lures to attract it back to the region and the union shop, both blocs find themselves cast adrift, with their available reserves fast running out. Their future looks bleak, their options limited. If they continue on their present dead-end course, labor will lose more and more of its membership to unemployment lines and population migration, and the governments of the region will become increasingly entangled in a web of economic deterioration and financial indebtedness. The other option is to turn their economic abandonment into economic independence by asserting their ownership rights over the means of production. With billions of dollars of pension funds at their disposal, they have the essential capital they need to make this kind of fundamental transition. Common sense and self-preservation make such an option virtually inevitable. Literally starved for capital and with an abundant supply there for the taking, they simply cannot pass up the opportunity, regardless of whatever past conditioning has predisposed them against taking hold of it.

The private sector, on the other hand, is not going to roll over and play dead as unions and states attempt to seize control over these tens of billions of dollars. As in New York State, where the banks mounted an unprecedented lobbying effort to defeat a public-bank proposal, similar pitched battles can be expected wherever unions and local governments attempt to institutionalize their claims over parts of the social capital pool. The private sector needs pension-fund capital just as desperately as the unions and northern states. It is the only guaranteed pool of savings that is large enough to meet their increasing need for investment and debt capital. Without its constant infusion into the equities and bonds of America's corporate giants, the financial community and the Fortune 500 would face serious problems.

The battle over control of pension capital, and with it the control over parts of the American economy, will be one of the central economic battles of the next decade. The private sector will continue its attempt at institutionalizing control over this new form of wealth in their hands. The unions and the northern states will begin a countercampaign to socialize pension-fund capital under some rudimentary form of worker/community control. In the early stages, they are likely to use these funds in a partial attempt to lure back the private sector. However, the diminishing returns of such efforts are likely to become increasingly apparent, disposing both blocs to take on a more direct ownership role over economic planning, capital allocation, and production.

If the thought of forging a new economic system in the northern industrial corridor seems difficult to envision, it is not because the situation doesn't warrant it. On the contrary, all of the evidence suggests the wisdom of pursuing just such a course. Still, the thought of building an alternative economy within a particular region of the country while the rest remains firmly ensconced within a capitalist ethic is certainly an unorthodox notion. On the other hand, there is nothing sacrosanct about geographic, political, or even economic boundaries. In fact, contemporary European history is replete with examples of Socialist or Communist enclaves developing within the bowels of capitalist countries. In France and Italy, left opposition forces have, for years, pursued a strategy of bringing key cities and provinces under Socialist or Communist administrations. They have then used these economic spheres both as springboards for their national organizing efforts and as working models of what effective alternative economic systems could look like. Interestingly enough, most of these cities and provinces turned Socialist or Communist because their residents were no longer willing to tolerate the abuse, exploitation, and callous disregard they were suffering under capitalist control of their economies. Most of the success that the Communists and Socialists have had in transforming these regions is attributable to the support the political parties enjoy within the trade-union movements. Heavy union concentration in these cities and provinces has been the decisive factor in marshaling public support behind fundamental economic change.[2]

While there are many similarities between the conditions that have spawned alternative economic enclaves within European nations and the plight facing unionists and northern states here, there are also some notable differences. Unions do not represent as large a percentage of the working population in the northern industrial corridor as they do in most European urban centers. Then too, organized labor in this country has always had an ideological inclination different from that of its European counterparts. Equally as important, there are, as yet, no major political leaders or parties in the northern states advocating fundamental economic change.[3]

The American experience is obviously not the same as Europe's. Thus, while proposals for economic restructuring are likely to borrow some of the best features of European Socialist programs, they are just as likely to draw on well-established American institutions, such as cooperatives, community development corporations, public utilities, and others. The movement for basic economic change in this country will develop its own unique alternatives, loosely defined as "economic democracy." In other words, this movement will apply traditional American principles of political rights, duties and participation within the economic setting, both at the workplace and within the larger community and society.

If the economic decline of the northern corridor continues at its current pace, labor leaders and state officials are more likely to use their claims over pension capital selectively, investing in existing companies, buying out concerns that are being abandoned and even setting up their own public banks and enterprises—always with the intent of plugging only the most glaring holes in their regional economies. It will be a patchwork approach to public planning, narrowly designed to fill in whatever vacuums are left by the private sector, without any pretense of building a coherent strategy for a worker- and community-controlled economic order to take its place.[4]

A crucial variable in this entire equation will be the degree to which grass roots pressure is successfully mobilized around demands for sweeping economic change. With increased rank-and-file involvement in union decision-making, greater community and issue group activism, plus the development of broad coalitions around specific issues, labor, political and community leaders could be moved to take much more radical stands than they are now doing.

Of course, if a monumental economic emergency were to engulf the region without warning, it is possible that an entirely new economic and political psychology could develop overnight: one that could propel labor leaders and public officials into pursuing a course similar to that taken by the Left in European cities and provinces. For example, a new economic downturn of serious proportions nationally could, conceivably, wreak havoc on city governments throughout the North. Scores of major northern municipalities could default on their obligations, forcing a situation comparable to the one that befell New York City in 1975. A federal government controlled by the Sunbelt states might not be willing to shell out tens of billions of dollars to keep these local governments afloat. The cities would then be forced to slash public services, close down schools, fire departments, hospitals, and police stations. Panic could spread into the streets and touch off open rebellion.[5]

An emergency energy crisis could have the same effect. For example, the Arabs could impose another oil embargo on the United States, just before a long, cold winter. Without sufficient oil reserves, the nation would have to rely on its immediate supplies of natural gas. However, a Sunbelt-dominated Congress might be unwilling to supply the northern cities with adequate supplies of natural gas, forcing them to survive the winter without enough energy to operate their homes, plants, offices, and schools. Public frustration and anger could easily ignite into militant political action.[6]

Emergencies of this sort are certainly possible. They could easily come at any time. If they do, the chances are that more radical leadership will emerge within the union community and within local and state governments. With that leadership is likely to come a much more ideologically defined economic and political perspective, one predicated on using pension capital as an instrument to begin building an alternative economy for the region. Behind that leadership will be millions of people whose sense of frustration and despair has been replaced with a revolutionary vision and faith, the kind that alters the course of history.

While it is impossible to predict all of the twists and turns that are likely to influence the battle for control over social capital, this much, however, is assured. With the emergence of pension-fund capital, millions of American workers now have the power, through their unions and state and local governments, to claim control over their own economic destiny.

The claims and counterclaims of the unions, the northern industrial states, and the private business sector will soon move pension funds onto the center stage of American political and economic debate.

Footnotes

Chapter 1: The Crisis and the Opportunity

1. See *Washington Post* series on Eurocommunism, September 19–22, 1977; "Western Europe's New Left Socialism" by Bogdan Denitch and "Eurocommunism's Coalition Politics" by George Ross in *Working Papers*, Winter 1977.
2. William F. Martin and George Cabot Lodge, "Our Society in 1985—Business May Not Like It," *Harvard Business Review*, November–December 1975, pp. 143–52.
3. *Business Week*, Special Report: "The Slow Investment Economy," October 17, 1977, p. 60 ff; Tad Szulc, "Trade War: The First Skirmishes?" *Forbes*, October 15, 1977, p. 29; *Business Week*, October 24, 1977, p. 48; see also, Michael Harrington, *The Twilight of Capitalism* (New York: Touchstone, 1976).
4. "American Public Opinion and Economic Democracy," Peter D. Hart Research Associates survey done for the Peoples Bicentennial Commission, July 1975. See Jeremy Rifkin, *Own Your Own Job* (New York: Bantam Books, 1977).
5. Jeff Faux and Robert Lightfoot, *Capital and Community*, Exploratory Project for Economic Alternatives (Washington, D.C.: 1976), pp. 35–36, 72–76, 95–97; also Denitch, *op. cit.*, and Ross, *op. cit.*
6. Report of the First National City Bank Task Force of the Center for the Study of Responsive Law, cited by Paul O'Dwyer during hearings of the New York State Assembly Bank Committee on a proposed New York state bank, April 24, 1975, p. 4 of prepared statement; and *American Banker*, February 28, 1977, p. 69.
7. Ferdinand Lundberg, *The Rich and the Super-Rich* (Bantam, 1968), p. 928.
8. Harrington, *op. cit. Business Week*, October 17, 1977, p. 60.
9. In general, the "Midwest/Northeast" or "Graybelt" includes the sixteen states represented in the Congressional Northeast/Midwest Economic Advancement Coalition: Maine, Massachusetts, Vermont, New Hampshire, Rhode Island, Connecticut, New York, New Jersey, Pennsylvania, Ohio, Michigan, Indiana, Illinois, Wisconsin, Iowa, and Minnesota. There are obviously internal differences in this region and in other states (such as Maryland, Delaware, the District of Columbia, and West Virginia) as well as in large urban areas throughout the country which share many of the same problems.
10. See *Industry Week*, September 26, 1977, and October 10, 1977, and *Business Week*, October 10, 1977, for reportage on fears raised by the recent steel industry closings.
11. *New York Times*, January 23, 1976, p. 1; February 10, 1976, p. 22.

234   THE NORTH WILL RISE AGAIN

12. *Directory of National Unions and Employee Associations, 1975,*
    Bureau of Labor Statistics (1974 figures).
13. Estimate for spring 1978 based on Securities and Exchange Com-
    mission and Federal Reserve Flow of Funds Accounts year-end
    1976 figures. Unless otherwise noted, figures are book value. At
    year-end 1976, market value was about 8 percent higher than book
    value. Figures assume a growth rate of 10 percent per year, which
    was the rate for 1975–76. Industry sources, such as *Pensions &
    Investments* magazine, expect this rate to hold for the forseeable
    future.

    There are four basic categories of pension funds: private non-
    insured, private insured, state and local government, and federal.
    Federal retirement funds are exclusively invested in government
    and agency notes. For that reason, we will normally refer only to
    nonfederal funds, which total over $400 billion. With the addi-
    tion of federal pension funds, total pension assets are now over
    $500 billion. The following table lists all four types of funds at
    book and market values for year-end 1976, and estimates for
    spring 1978, assuming a 10 percent annual rate of growth:

	Book		Market	
	(Billions)			
	Year-end 1976	Spring 1978	Year-end 1976	Spring 1978
Private noninsured	160.4	182	175.5	200
Private insured	80.1	91	88.4	100
State and local	117.2	133	121.5	138
Subtotal	357.7	406	385.4	438
Federal	87.8	97	87.8	97
Total	445.5	504	473.2	535

14. The May 10, 1976, issue of *Pensions & Investments* reported that
    private noninsured pension funds held 15.3 percent of all New
    York Stock Exchange securities. State and local government funds
    held another 4.2 percent. Insurance companies held 6.2 percent,
    of which at least half (over 3 percent) were accounted for by in-
    sured pension funds. Thus, at year-end 1975, private and public
    pension funds owned approximately 22.5 percent of all NYSE
    stock. Pension funds are invested in the smaller stock markets at
    about the same level. *Pensions & Investment* (April 11, 1977)

estimates that this total is now over 25 percent, at least for the major U.S. corporations.

At year-end 1975, corporate bonds were worth $317 billion. Private noninsured pension funds held $38 billion, state and local governments held $61 billion, insurance company (pension) separate accounts held about $3 billion, and general insured funds, at least $23 billion: a total of $125 billion, or 39 percent of all corporate bonds. At year-end 1976, the figures were: all corporate bonds were worth $354.2 billion, and pension bond holdings were worth at least $140 billion, or 39.8 percent. (Federal Reserve Flow of Funds Accounts, September 1977)

15. Michael Clowes, speech to Association of Private Pension and Welfare Plans, Washington, D.C., April 21, 1977.

16. In the preparation of this book, we found that some of the data we needed on pension funds does not exist. Thus, for example, we were forced to piece together disparate bits of information in order to estimate the value of the pension assets of unionists and public employees in the Graybelt. The $200 billion figure was derived as follows:

Graybelt public employees: The Bureau of the Census (Finances of Employee-Retirement Systems of State and Local Governments in 1975–1976, May 1977) lists the assets of all nonfederal public pension funds. The funds of the sixteen northeast and midwest states account for roughly 55 percent of the total, or about $75 billion by spring 1978.

Unionists: This is a much more difficult figure to compute; there are several ways to approach an estimate. Virtually all union members are covered by some sort of pension. Ian Lanoff, administrator of pension law enforcement for the Department of Labor, estimated in an interview that roughly two-thirds of *all* workers in the private sector covered by a pension plan are in collectively bargained plans. The Bureau of Labor Statistics, in a survey of all pension plans with over 100 participants (which cover 86 percent of all participants), found that 69 percent were in collectively bargained plans ("Study of Retirement Plans as of September 1, 1974"—in progress). The most conservative estimate is that "about half" are in collectively bargained plans (Alfred M. Skolnik, "Private Pension Plans, 1950–74," Social Security Bulletin, June 1974, p. 3). Other studies show that the union membership is the most certain route to coverage by a pension plan in the private sector. But no one has attempted to determine the value of unionists' pension assets. Wayne Jett, a prominent West Coast union pension attorney, estimates that unionists' pensions are now worth $200 billion.

More conservatively, we estimate that *private sector* union members' pension funds are worth at least $125 billion (book value, spring 1978). Even adjusting for the fact that management and highly paid technical employees receive much higher pensions, the funds of the roughly 60 percent of private-sector participants who are unionists are certainly worth at least 45 percent of all private pension asset. Of this $125 billion or more, we estimate that between $45 and $60 billion are in jointly managed funds and $65 to $80 billion are in corporate-managed funds. (See Section II for an explanation of the difference between the two). Noel Arnold Levin, former president of the International Foundation on Employee Benefits, the major association for "union" pension officials, confirms this estimate.

17. *Congressional Record,* October 26, 1977, p. E 6579.
18. James Henry, "How Pension Fund Socialism Didn't Come to America," *Working Papers,* Winter 1977, p. 84.

Chapter 2: Unions in Turmoil

1. *U.S. News & World Report,* February 21, 1972, p. 28.
2. At year-end 1976, unions represented 24.5 percent of all nonfarm employees and 20.1 percent of the entire labor force. Unions and associations (primarily teachers and other public-sector groups) represented 28.3 percent of the nonfarm work force and 23.2 percent of all workers. Unions represented 19,432,000 workers. Unions and associations represented 22,463,000 workers. "Labor Union and Employee Association Membership—1976" (Press Release, USDL: 77–771), Bureau of Labor Statistics, Labor Day weekend, 1977.
3. *Nation's Business,* July 1977.
4. BLS, *op cit.* Association membership increased by about 400,000. Thus, there was a net loss of 200,000 union and association members. Labor officials blame the recent recession for a large part of this loss, from which the unionized labor force has not at all recovered.
5. Personal interview with Joe Swire, June 30, 1977.
6. "Unions Finding Organizing Efforts Are Meeting Increasing Resistance," *New York Times,* July 19, 1977, p. 1.
7. Quoted in Haynes Johnson and Nick Kotz, series on unions, *Washington Post,* April 9, 1972.
8. Jerry Wurf, president of the American Federation of State, County

and Municipal Employees, writing in the *Washington Post,* October 14, 1973.

9. Johnson and Kotz, *Washington Post,* April 11, 1972. The Organizing Department of the AFL-CIO has established a special group to coordinate bargaining efforts among unions in an attempt to head off jurisdictional disputes. While labor unions become more conscious of the need to stop raiding each others' membership, it remains to be seen whether or not unions will be significantly more cooperative in the future.

10. Johnson and Kotz, April 11, 1972.

11. *Ibid.*

12. Gil Green, *What's Happening to Labor* (New York: International Publishers, 1976), p. 19, citing *Statistical Abstract of the United States, 1972,* p. 230.

13. Phillip Ray, "Profile of a Changing Workforce," *The American Federationist,* September 1974.

14. *Ibid.*

15. Quoted in "Is the Labor Movement Losing Ground?" *U.S. News & World Report,* February 21, 1972.

16. Johnson and Kotz, *Washington Post,* April 10, 1972.

17. Phillip Ray, *op. cit.*

18. Figure supplied to authors by *Industry Week.* See Arthur Kornhauser, *Mental Health and the Industrial Worker* (New York: Wiley, 1965); Special Taskforce of the Secretary of Health, Education and Welfare, *Work in America* (Cambridge, Mass: MIT Press, 1973); and Harry Braverman, *Labor and Monopoly Capitalism* (New York: Modern Reader, 1975).

19. Quoted by Jeremy Brecher in *Strike!* (San Francisco: Straight Arrow Books, 1972), p. 265.

20. Quoted in Johnson and Kotz, *Washington Post,* April 10, 1972.

21. *Ibid.*

22. Johnson and Kotz, April 11, 1972, quoting Victor Gotbaum reading 1970 Meany Labor Day speech.

23. Brecher, *op. cit.,* quoting Monsignor Charles Owen Rice. Also see Stanley Aronowitz, *False Promises: The Shaping of American Working Class Consciousness* (New York: McGraw-Hill, 1973).

24. Quoted in *John Herling's Labor Letter,* March 30, 1974.

25. See Claudia Dreifus, "Trade Union Women's Conference," *The Nation,* March 30, 1974; Patricia Cayo Sexton, "Workers (Female) Arise!", *Dissent,* Summer 1974; "Women Unionists Meet," *Interface,* Summer 1974.

26. BLS, *op. cit.;* see also Edna E. Raphael, "Working Women and

their Membership in Labor Unions," *Monthly Labor Review*, May 1974; and "Blue Collar Women, Unions and Political Power Today," *Industrial and Labor Relations*, November 1974.

27. "Women's Participation in Labor Organizations," *Monthly Labor Review*, October 1974.

28. Quoted in *John Herling's Labor Letter*, April 2, 1977.

29. *Monthly Labor Review* (October 1974), *op. cit.*

30. The National Organization of Women (NOW) has established a Labor Taskforce, and many younger feminists are aware of the need to reach out to working-class women. But the women's movement remains overwhelmingly middle class or professional, and NOW's Labor Taskforce has been struggling just to raise a minimal amount of money to continue its operations.

31. *Industrial and Labor Relations, op. cit.*, citing 1964 Rutgers University study.

32. A May 20, 1977, *Washington Post* article quotes a letter sent by Robert A. Georgine, president of the AFL-CIO Building and Construction Trades Department, to 383 local and 33 state construction trades councils calling on them to recruit "qualified female applicants. . . ." The letter said, "Discrimination because of sex cannot be tolerated in the trade union movement any more than racial discrimination can be permitted." Since fewer than 1 percent of all construction workers are women, the building trades obviously have a long way to go.

33. William Lucy, "The Black Partners," *The Nation*, September 7, 1974.

34. *Ibid.*

35. Herbert Hill, former NAACP labor secretary, writing in *Skeptic*, May–June 1976, p. 61. The antiunion National Right to Work Committee has taken full advantage of racism in unions for well over a decade. For example, Reed Larson, president of the NRTWC, in an address to the California Negro Leadership Conference in 1967, stated: "It is in the interest of your people and all minorities to disperse, not enhance, a power structure through which the prejudice of fallible human beings can be brought to bear against the employment opportunities of your people. Compulsory unionism does exactly that! . . . What appears to be the next civil rights target is unionism itself" (see "A Major Obstacle to Full Employment Opportunity" and other NRTWC materials). Larson takes special pleasure in quoting the NAACP's Hill. Employers, especially in the South, have effectively used this approach, in efforts to convince black workers to vote against unionization.

36. "There is no union *movement*," says one veteran labor organizer with whom we spoke. "There are a lot of individual unions just like there are a lot of individual companies, and they're all protecting their own turf." Ironically, although George Meany and the top leadership at the AFL-CIO are often depicted as the dictators of labor, the opposite is more often the case. The principle of union autonomy has effectively turned the AFL-CIO into a loose coalition of independent organizations. Of course, labor's central body still has a range of powers it can exercise, but it is clear that unions do not act like they are part of a crusade whose goal is "to create an economy that will guarantee full employment, higher living standards and full security for all members of our society" (Emil Mazey, secretary-treasurer of the United Auto Workers, writing in *The Nation,* September 7 ,1974).

37. See Edgar James, "Sadlowski and the Steelworkers: Notes for the Next Time," *Working Papers,* Spring 1977.

38. *U.S. News & World Report,* May 11, 1977.

39. In an interview for this book, Winpisinger offered some of his views on the state of the labor movement:

   "I'm seriously asking out loud whether we might not have exhausted the usefulness of our out-and-out pragmatism. I'm wondering whether it might be time to stop bragging so loudly about being totally pragmatic, and adopt a few principles. Part of this business of not wanting to appear to have lost is what gets us tagged as Big and Powerful when we're really piss-weak. And we stink!

   "I think we've got to have some articles of faith pretty firmly established one of these days soon. Even if it means accomplishing a little less momentarily as we establish a firm base. I'm sick and tired of going to the polls every couple of years and trying to decide between a Republican ten degrees to the right and a Democrat ten degrees to the left. Especially when the only difference is that there are a few less working under a Republican than when you've got a Democrat.

   "The whole political game has become who can first successfully preempt the center. Well, screw that. The labor movement is the only institution in this country that has the ability to create and dramatize a choice. The labor movement belongs on the left, and we should be out there. We should be peddling our wares with an articulate voice. But that requires some principles" (personal interview, July 18, 1977).

Chapter 3: Uprooting Union Jobs

1. *Prospectus,* Northeast/Midwest Research Institute (Washington, D.C., August 1977).
2. Rep. Michael Harrington, "The Case for Regionalism," unpublished speech, 1976. See Harrington's "Organizing for Change: The Region Fights Back," *Opportunities,* August 1977, Number 18 (Durham, New Hampshire).
3. Michael J. McManus, ". . . In the Face of Dire Economic Necessity," *Empire State Report,* October–November 1976, p. 343.
4. *Viewpoint,* Industrial Union Department (AFL-CIO) quarterly, 5 (1975); *Business Week,* July 6, 1968, and July 11, 1970; *Fortune,* November 1971.
5. Richard J. Barnet and Ronald E. Müller, *Global Reach* (New York: Simon and Schuster, 1974), p. 17.
6. Harry Weiss, "The Multinational Corporation and Its Impact on Collective Bargaining," *Collective Bargaining Today,* Bureau of National Affairs (Washington, D.C., 1970), p. 299.
7. Testimony of Andrew J. Biemiller, director, Department of Legislation, AFL-CIO, before Subcommittee on Multinational Corporations of the Senate Committee on Foreign Relations, December 10, 1975.
8. Barnet and Müller, *op. cit.,* p. 303; *Viewpoint, op. cit.,* p. 11.
9. *Oriental Economist,* July 1971, p. 32; "Movin' On Up" (Cincinnati, Ohio, July 1971).
10. Gil Green, *What's Happening to Labor?* (New York: International Publishers, 1976), pp. 83–84.
11. *National Journal,* June 26, 1976, pp. 885–86.
12. Northeast/Midwest Research Institute, *op. cit.*
13. *Statistical Abstract of the United States 1977,* Table 596, p. 367.
14. Helen Dewar, "Organizing the South," *Washington Post,* June 7, 1977.
15. *Directory of National Unions and Employee Associations 1975,* Bureau of Labor Statistics, Bulletin 1937, 1975 figures.
16. "Unions in the Sunbelt," *Business Week,* May 17, 1976.
17. "Campaign to Unionize the South," *New York Times,* March 17, 1977.
18. "Conflict in Clinton," *Wall Street Journal,* June 7, 1976.
19. *New York Times,* July 3, 1973; *U.S. News & World Report,* January 10, 1977, p. 74.

There are really two Souths. In the larger urban areas, *whites* are as well off as northern workers. But it's a different story in rural areas. This is especially true for blacks. An article in the *New York Times* (February 6, 1977, p. 22) reports that "virtually all of the benefits of the new South have accrued to whites, and especially urban whites. . . . The impoverished, racially divided rural South is an easy target for nonunion employers."

20. Daniel H. Pollit, "Union Security in America," *The American Federationist* (AFL-CIO, reprint).

21. Wilfred Sheed, *Atlantic,* July 1973, p. 49. The Taft-Hartley bill was the culmination of no less than 230 attempts to repeal the Wagner Act.

22. Rep. Ed Markey (D.-Mass.) indicated in an interview that he feels it is essential for his heavily unionized—and declining—Northshore district to have Section 14(b) repealed: "My feeling is that since 1947—and the move by the National Association of Manufacturers to put 14(b) on the books—there has been a systematic reduction of union shops in the southern states. This has given them a competitive advantage over industrialized states such as Massachusetts, because of their ability to use Taft-Hartley to whip and beat the highest possible profits out of the least-unionized and lowest-paid workers in the country."

23. "Right to Work," pamphlet distributed by AFL-CIO. The NRTWC has strong right-wing connections and, not surprisingly, a federal judge has ruled that it has acted as an employer front for the purpose of harrassing unions.

24. Emil Malizia, "Earnings Gap in North Carolina," University of North Carolina at Chapel Hill, June 1975 (reprinted by the North Carolina AFL-CIO). For a comprehensive view of workers and unions in the South, see *Southern Exposure,* Spring–Summer 1976. This issue has a number of excellent articles and a state-by-state profile of the southern work force.

Chapter 4: Labor's Chief Weapons

1. Quoted in AFL-CIO Labor Law Reform Taskforce, "Speaker's Handbook," p. 31 (draft).

2. *U.S. News & World Report,* February 21, 1972, p. 28; Haynes Johnson and Nick Kotz, *Washington Post,* April 18, 1972; *The Nation,* September 7, 1974, p. 171.

3. Personal interview with Kevin Kistler, July 14, 1977.

4. Personal interview with Henry Dillon, July 7, 1977. A classic example of the decreasing effectiveness of strikes is the extended dispute between ABC and its technicians. The average television viewer was probably completely unaware that a strike was going on at all; during the summer of 1977, there was no noticeable disruption in the network's programming. The striking technicians' cause wasn't helped any by the fact that several other unions were

still on the job and refused to honor picket lines. Pickets in front
of ABC's Washington, D.C., headquarters acknowledged the utter
ineffectiveness of their strike, with one major exception: according
to them, in San Francisco, not only did the other ABC unions refuse to scab, but the sanitation workers even refused to pick up
ABC's garbage.

5. Bureau of Labor Statistics, press release, August 26, 1977.

6. Attributed to Jack London.

7. As a weapon in labor's arsenal, the strike is obviously rusty. But
it can still be labor's ace in the hole, according to Oil, Chemical
and Atomic Workers organizer George Roach. In many industries
it is still the most *direct* way to apply pressure. But in order to
be effective, the strike must be very well organized and the workers'
grievances must be made clear to the general public. Roach believes that the combination of a militantly aggressive strike with
sympathetic community support is unbeatable. The reason that
unions usually fail to gain that support is that they have forgotten
that "the community" and the union should be one and the same.
Many other labor organizers are learning, and relearning, this lesson. Unions and community organizations have often clashed in
the past, and often they ended up competing for the loyalty of the
same people. This situation seems to be easing, and recently,
the National Association of Neighborhoods and the Industrial
Union Department of the AFL-CIO announced that they were
developing strategies for joint community/union action.

8. John J. Fialka, interview with Charles Hughes, in "Discouraging
the Formation of Unions Is Big Business," *Washington Star*, June
8, 1977.

9. Cited in "Speaker's Handbook," AFL-CIO Labor Law Reform
Taskforce.

10. Kevin Kistler, *op. cit.*

11. Fialka, *op. cit.*

12. Frederick J. Naffziger, "When Management Faces a Union Orga-
nizing Campaign," *Management Review*, August 1974, p. 25. See
also "What Management Can Do During a Union Organizing
Campaign," by Steven J. Cabot and Douglas G. Linn II, *The
Practical Lawyer*, March 1, 1976; James L. Dougherty, "How to
Keep Your Company Union Free," *Conservative Digest*, May 1977,
and *Union Free Management*, also by Dougherty (The Darnell
Corporation, 1968).

13. Fialka, *op. cit.*

14. Labor Law Reform Task Force, *op. cit.*; Alan Kistler and Charles

McDonald, "The Continuing Challenge of Organizing," *The American Federationist,* November 1976.
15. *Ibid.* (Kistler and McDonald).
16. Personal interview with Al Bilik, August 5, 1977

Chapter 5: Organized Labor's Strategy
1. See "They Said It Couldn't Be Done: A History of the Textile Workers Union, AFL-CIO," Textile Workers Union pamphlet. They have now merged with the Amalgamated Clothing Workers of America into the Amalgamated Clothing and Textile Workers Union of America (ACTWU).
2. Helen Dewar, "Organizing the South," *Washington Post,* June 7, 1977; and "Civil Rights Fervor," *Time,* March 14, 1977. See also hearings and reports of Subcommittee on Labor-Management Relations, House Committee on Education and Labor, December 1976, "Staff Report on the National Labor Relations Act and Its Administration by the National Labor Relations Board"; and hearings, August 1977, in Roanoke Rapids, N.C.
3. Timothy McNulty, "Small Town Now a Battleground for the Textile Union," *Chicago Tribune,* March 14, 1977.
4. *Wall Street Journal,* November 4, 1975.
5. Ed McConville, "The Southern Textile War," *The Nation,* October 2, 1976.
6. "Campaign to Unionize the South," *New York Times,* March 17, 1977.
7. Amalgamated Clothing and Textile Workers Union of America, *J. P. Stevens Factsheet,* #2 and #8; and William Clairborne, "Textile Boycott Envisions Unionizing All the South," *Washington Post,* December 5, 1976.
8. McConville, *op. cit.;* "Fortune 500," *Fortune,* May 1977.
9. ACTWU, *J. P. Stevens Factsheet,* #4; and "It's Profits First," ACTWU pamphlet.
10. A. H. Raskin, *New York Times,* August 15, 1976, sec. 3, p. 11. "The J. P. Stevens fight . . . becomes more important in the context of an industry that has an increasing number of black workers within an overall declining workforce that still constitutes the largest group of industrial workers in the region. . . ." *Southern Exposure,* Vol. IV, No. 1–2, Spring–Summer 1976.
11. "Stevens Digs Its Heels in Deeper," *Business Week,* March 14, 1977, p. 29.
12. *Ibid.;* "Still the Union Makes Them Strong," Ed McConville, *The Progressive,* August 1975; Robert M. Bleiberg, "Cloak of Sanctity:

The Boycott of J. P. Stevens Is a Grab for Power," *Barron's,*
March 7, 1977; Mike Lavell, *Chicago Tribune,* April 5, 1977; *National Journal,* March 12, 1977, p. 378.

13. *Industry Week,* June 28, 1976, p. 31. This view is echoed by most sources inside and outside the labor movement.
14. *Ibid.*
15. Gary Dinnuno, "J. P. Stevens: Anatomy of an Outlaw," *Federationist,* 1976, p. 1.
16. Raskin, *op. cit.*
17. ACTWU, *J. P. Stevens Factsheet,* #2; Clairborne, *op. cit.*
18. Clairborne, *op. cit.; National Journal, op. cit.; Time, op. cit.*
19. "The Struggle for Economic Justice at J. P. Stevens," ACTWU pamphlet.
20. See *Pensions and Investment,* "Textile Union Mulling Use of Capital Boycott," March 14, 1977; Jeremy Rifkin and Ted Howard, "Taking Care of Business: Labor's New Weapon," *New Times,* March 4, 1977; "Textile Union Scores Bank for Its Ties to J. P. Stevens & Co.," *Wall Street Journal,* April 25, 1977; "J. P. Stevens' Woes Affect Sperry Rand Directorate," *Wall Street Journal,* July 26, 1977, p. 29.
21. "Unions in the Sunbelt," *Business Week,* May 17, 1976.
22. James W. Singer, "A Picketing Post Mortem," *National Journal,* April 2, 1977, p. 378; "Labor's New Southern Strategy," *Business Week,* February 7, 1977.
23. *Ibid., Business Week; U.S. News & World Report,* March 7, 1977; Statements on Labor Legislation, adopted by the AFL-CIO Executive Council, Bar Harbor, Florida, February 22, 1977 (AFL-CIO Press Office).
24. *National Journal, op. cit.;* "What Situs Taught the Unions," *Business Week,* April 11, 1977, p. 100. The common situs bill was controversial inside the labor movement. It was viewed as something of a parochial issue by many. Unions in the construction trades wanted it very badly, but many in the industrial and service unions felt that it was a big mistake to push situs first.
25. Walter S. Mossberg, "Carter Push for Revision of Labor Laws to Strengthen Union Organizing Efforts," *Wall Street Journal,* July 1977, p. 2; Philip Shabecoff, "Carter Sends Congress Proposals for Helping Unions in Bargaining," *New York Times,* July 19, 1977, p. 1; Helen Dewar, "House Votes to Increase Wage Floor," *Washington Post,* September 16, 1977.
26. Personal interview with William Winpisinger, July 18, 1977.
27. Philip Shabecoff, "Labor Turning from Lobbying to New Political

Tactics in Growing Struggle for Influence on Legislation," *New York Times*, June 23, 1977, p. 31.

28. Personal interview with Doris Hardesty, July 29, 1977.
29. "Labor and Grass Roots Lobbying: A Manual for Congressional District Coordinators" (DRAFT), AFL-CIO Labor Law Reform Task Force, 1977.
30. Harris poll release, "Mixed Views About Unions," January 6, 1977. The AFL-CIO commissioned its own poll and found, essentially, the same thing (Public Interest Opinion Research, June 16, 1977). Says Jim Rosapepe of PIOR, "The public has generally positive attitudes toward the role of labor protecting workers and working for social legislation. People do understand—and support—the role of unions. The contradiction is that they have quite negative perception of union leadership."
31. John Fischer, "Letter to a New Leftist from a Tired Liberal," *Harper's*, March 1966, p. 16.
32. James C. Hyatt, "Business Pushes 'Employee Bill of Rights' to Blunt Labor's Drive for Law Change," *Wall Street Journal*, June 24, 1977; *New York Times*, June 24, 1977, p. A9; AFL-CIO Special Report; "Labor Law Reform, the Right Wing"; and "Union Haters Raising Slush Fund," AFL-CIO Labor Law Reform Task Force.

The business coalition drafted its own legislative proposal, the "Employee Bill of Rights Act," which it hopes will serve to defuse major parts of the labor reform bill. Among other things, the business bill would impose even more constraints on union organizing than presently exist. For example, it contains a provision requiring a secret-ballot election before an employer has to bargain with a union. As it stands now, if the employer voluntarily recognizes the union, an election isn't required. Another provision would prevent unions from expelling members who cross picket lines or try to decertify a union as a bargaining agent. Under the proposed act, an employer could also demand a vote of employees to determine whether to call, maintain, or resume a strike. The proposal even has a provision which would permit an employee who objects to unions on religious grounds to pay the equivalent of his dues to a nonreligious charitable fund.

Chapter 6: The Decline of the Graybelt

1. Michael J. McManus, "The Need for a Northeast Coalition" (unpublished paper presented to Coalition of Northeast Governors), June 16, 1976, citing *National Journal*, June 26, 1976.

2. Quoted in "Behind the Decline in Mid-West Manufacturing," *Business Week*, May 17, 1976.
3. "Why Migrants Become a Flood Tide," *Business Week*, May 17, 1976, p. 96.
4. Rep. Michael J. Harrington's calculations cited in McManus, *op. cit.*
5. Rep. Michael Harrington, "The Northeast-Midwest Economic Advancement Coalition: An Effort to Reverse the Tide" (draft article obtained from NMEAC), April 20, 1977.
6. *Ibid.*
7. Michael J. McManus, ". . . In the Face of Dire Economic Necessity," *Empire State Report*, October–November 1976, p. 345.
8. Quoted in Neal R. Pierce, "The Northeast Battle Plan," *Empire State Report*, December 1976, p. 409.
9. Jack Newfield and Paul DuBrul, *The Abuse of Power* (New York: Viking Press, 1977), p. 55, citing David Muchnick, *Dissent*, Winter 1976.
10. *Ibid.*, pp. 50–60.
11. Tom Cochran and Randy Evans, "A Mix of Employment Programs for the Urban Industrial States," *Empire State Report*, October–November 1976, p. 394.
12. Newsletter of Rep. Michael Harrington, September 22, 1974, p. 4.
13. Richard M. Rosenbaum, "Perspectives on the Northeast Region," March 25, 1976. Mimeograph obtained from NMEAC.
14. Richard Morris, mimeograph obtained from NMEAC office.
15. Personal interview with John Moriarty, July 7, 1977.
16. Susan Sanders, "Dallas Dawns as a Sunbelt Leader," *Dallas*, December 1976, p. 28.
17. *Ibid.*, pp. 28, 29.
18. Dr. James M. Howell, "A Four-Point Program for the Northeast," presented before the Boston Citizen Seminar: The Northeast Means Business, March 2, 1977 (p. 2 of prepared remarks).
19. Edson D. deCastro, "The Massachusetts Economy," presented before the Boston Rotary Club, February 2, 1977.
20. Michael J. McManus, "How the Northeast Finances Southern Prosperity," *Empire State Report*, October–November 1976, p. 351.
21. *Ibid.*
22. *National Journal*, June 26, 1976, p. 886.
23. McManus, "In the Face of Dire Economic Necessity," p. 344.
24. "Energy Shortage Is Said to Pose Lasting Threat to North," *New York Times*, February 1, 1977.
25. Richard Morris, *op. cit.*

26. McManus, "The Need for a Northeast Coalition"; Neal Pierce, "Northeast Battle Plan," p. 409.
27. Pierce, *op. cit.*
28. See David T. Stanley, *Cities in Trouble* (Cleveland: National Urban Policy Roundtable, Academy for Contemporary Problems, 1976), discussion paper #7.

Chapter 7: The Graybelt Strategy

1. Personal interview with John Moriarty, July 28, 1977.
2. "The Shift to the Sunbelt: What It Means for Cities," The National Urban Coalition, *Network*, Summer 1976, p. 1.
3. "The Second War Between the States," *Business Week*, May 17, 1976, p. 92.
4. Rep. Michael Harrington, "The Northeast-Midwest Economic Advancement Coalition: An Effort to Reverse the Tide," draft article from NMEAC.
5. *National Journal*, June 26, 1976, p. 889.
6. *New York Times*, March 21, 1977, p. 43; Neal R. Pierce, "Northeast Battle Plan," *Empire State Report*, December 1976; Timothy B. Clark, "Politics: A New Northeast Togetherness," *Empire State Report*, October–November 1976, p. 336.
7. Neal R. Picrce, *op. cit.*
8. Paul A. Landon, "Regional Parity: Time for a Northeast TVA," *Empire State Report*, October–November 1976, p. 386.
9. Frank Comes, "Regional Development Bank: Credit Where Credit Is Due," *Empire State Report*, October–November 1976, pp. 381–90.
10. Rep. Michael S. Harrington, Newsletter, September 22, 1976, p. 6.
11. Comes, *op. cit.*
12. *Ibid.*
13. Personal interview with John Moriarty, July 28, 1977. Moriarty doesn't see a significant role for public ownership of industry. "I don't see this country socializing industry. . . . We do it backhandedly. Look at railroads, for example."
14. "U.S. Planning Bank for Cities' Borrowing," *Washington Star*, May 8, 1977.
15. *National Journal*, June 26, 1976, p. 889.
16. "A Counter-attack in the War Between the States," *Business Week*, June 21, 1976, p. 71.
17. Sandra Kanter and Bennett Harrison, "The Great State Robbery," *Working Papers*, Spring 1976.

18. *New York Times,* December 29, 1977, p. 16; *Washington Post,* January 30, 1977, p. 23.
19. Rep. Harrington indicated, in an interview for this book, that he was concerned with the slow pace of his coalition's efforts. "I don't see a willingness to really go far beyond very predictable kinds of initiatives. I think we'll have trouble selling the whole development bank concept to some of our own constituency," says Harrington. What will it take, then, to convince his colleagues and constituency to go beyond very limited kinds of programs? "More trauma," he says.

Chapter 8: A Catch-22

1. Quoted in Haynes Johnson and Nick Kotz, *Washington Post,* April 11, 1972.
2. Many unionists reacted with embarrassment to the part of George Meany's 1977 Labor Day speech where he castigated multinational corporations for abandoning "free enterprise" doctrines.
3. Gil Green, *What's Happening to Labor?* (New York: International Publishers, 1976), p. 27.
4. *Ibid.,* p. 163.
5. Personal interview with John Moriarty, July 18, 1977.
6. Personal interview with Rep. Michael Harrington, July 28, 1977.
7. For example, economic geographers have found that between 1947 and 1972, six major, highly unionized, northern metropolitan areas (New York City, Chicago, Detroit, Philadelphia, Boston, and Pittsburgh) suffered a 30 percent decline in their share of national new-capital expenditures (going from a combined share of 25 percent to one of 17.5 percent). Peter B. Corbin and Murray Sabrin, *Inflation and the Spatial Structure of Production* (forthcoming), using the data from the *Census of Manufacturers* and *The Annual Survey of Manufacturers.*
8. While data is not yet available, it is almost certain that most of the 600,000 members unions lost from 1974 to 1976 were from Graybelt areas. Many observers feel that these jobs are lost forever, even with a full economic recovery—an unlikely event in itself.
9. See footnote 14, Chapter 1.
10. See footnote 13, Chapter 1.
11. To this may be added hundreds of billions of dollars of individual savings and insurance accounts also controlled by banks and insurance companies.
12. From dozens of interviews, it became clear that most labor leaders have begun to think about the impact of their members' pension-

fund investments. As we shall demonstrate, while there are many reasons for labor's relative lack of involvement in pension-investment policies, it seems clear that, one way or another, this issue will become a very important one to them in the years to come. Similarly, we found strong interest, and some action, on the part of state and local officials and their advisers in such states as Massachusetts, Connecticut, Pennsylvania, Ohio, Michigan, Wisconsin, and California.

Chapter 9: A New Form of Wealth

1. The term "social" capital or "social property" was first applied to pension funds in an incisive book by Paul P. Harbrecht, S.J., *Pension Funds and Economic Power* (New York: The Twentieth Century Fund, 1959). "[Pension funds] are owned by no one in any meaningful sense of the term. Such a phenomenon in a capitalist society, which has traditionally considered the distinction between public and private ownership to be adequate and complete, challenges us to find a rational framework to accommodate it. The old conceptual framework has no room for the pension trusts. The old bottles are now bursting with new wine" (p. 2).
2. *Congressional Record,* September 29, 1976, S.17084, 94th Congress, 2nd Session.
3. See footnote 13, Chapter 1.
4. Speech by Michael Clowes, executive editor, *Pensions & Investment,* before the Association of Private Pension and Welfare Plans Convention, Washington, D.C., April 21, 1977 (tape of speech).
5. Federal Reserve, Flow of Funds Accounts, September 1977.
6. *Washington Post,* July 17, 1977, p. E1; and *Business Week,* July 18, 1977, pp. 86–88.
7. *Institutional Investor,* April 1974.
8. *Dun's,* June 1974.
9. William C. Greenough and Francis P. King, *Pension Funds and Public Policy* (New York: Columbia University Press, 1976), p. 28 ff.
10. *Ibid.,* p. 69 ff; Personal interview with Murray W. Lattimer, July 14, 1977; *American Labor,* May 1971; Bert Seidman, "Social Security—40 Years Later," *American Federationist,* July 1976.
11. *Business Conditions,* Federal Reserve Board of Chicago, September 1950; American Labor, *op. cit.;* Welfare and Pension Plans Investigation, Senate Subcommittee on Welfare and Pension Funds, 84th Congress, 1st Session, Interim Report, 1955, pp. 6–8.
12. Harbrecht, *op. cit.,* pp. 91–96.

13. "500," *Fortune,* May 1976; and "1977 Pensions Directory," *Institutional Investor,* January 1977, listing of top 350 corporate pension funds. Based on a comparison of these figures (the closest sets of data available). The April 1974 *Institutional Investor* lists the following companies with pension funds worth approximately the same, or more, in market value as all the company's stock: Allis-Chalmers, American Standard, Colt, General Dynamics, Grumman, Jones & Laughlin, LTV, Lockheed, Northrop, Pan Am, Rockwell, TWA, United Aircraft, U.S. Steel, Wheeling, Pittsburgh.

14. At year-end 1976, federal retirement funds were worth $87.8 billion, and state and local government funds were worth $117.2 billion (book value). By spring 1978, they will be worth some $97 billion and $133 billion respectively.

15. *The Statistical Abstract of the United States* (1976), Table No. 596 (source: U.S. Bureau of Labor Statistics).

16. Walter W. Kolodrubetz and Donald M. Landay, "Coverage and Vesting of Full-time Employees under Private Retirement Plans," *Social Security Bulletin,* November 1973, pp. 20–21. "Thus for a large proportion of the population—especially among women, blacks, the low-paid and workers in small firms—the major, if not the sole source of retirement income is Social Security, or for some supplemented by Supplemental Security Income. While in time, some people in these categories will begin to be covered by private pension plans, Social Security and SSI will continue to be their dominant sources of income for many years to come." Seidman, *op. cit.,* p. 18.

17. Personal interview with Robert Tilove, June 16, 1977. This is supported by the findings of Kolodrubetz and Landay.

18. "Study of Private Pension Plans as of 1974" (in progress), Bureau of Labor Statistics.

19. "1977 Pension Directory," *Institutional Investor,* January 1977, pp. 49–76.

20. Greenough and King, *op. cit.,* p. 109, citing Harry E. Davis and Arnold Strassen, "Private Pension Plans, 1960–1969—An Overview," *Monthly Labor Review,* July 1970, p. 46.

21. *Institutional Investor, op. cit.*

22. Jack Barbash, "The Structure and Evolution of Union Interests in Pensions," in Joint Economic Committee, Subcommittee on Fiscal Policy, *Old Age Income Assurance Part IV,* December 1967, p. 67 ff.

23. "Study of Retirement Plans as of 1974," *op. cit.*

24. Strassen and Davis, *op. cit.,* p. 47.

25. Michael Clowes, personal interview, April 21, 1977.
26. See footnote 16, Chapter 1.

Chapter 10: Propping up the American Economy
1. *Pensions & Investments,* April 25, 1977 survey of 449 "tax-exempt" money managers.
2. *Pensions & Investments,* May 9, 1977, p. 3, year-end 1975 figures. *P&I* noted that this figure was an increase of 29.5 percent for the $112 billion at year-end 1974.
3. *Pensions & Investments,* April 25, 1977, p. 1. From the survey of 449 tax-exempt money managers (pensions represent about 75 percent of tax-exempt assets). The article also notes that the twenty-five largest manage 54 percent of all tax-exempt assets; the average individual portfolio manager handles some $230 million in total investment assets (including non–tax-exempt) and that tax-exempt assets account for about half of all assets managed by banks, insurance companies and independent money managers ($345 billion of total $709 billion in assets managed by the 449 major investment firms).
4. To a degree, recognition of this phenomenon has been hindered by the attention focused on "institutions," the "two-tier" market, etc. What is usually not pointed out, though, is the fact that pension funds account for well over half of institutional holdings in equities.
5. American Bankers' Association brochure, reprinted in: William Alexander (vice-president, ABA), "Crisis in Capital Formation," *Pension World,* February 1976, p. 10.
6. *Ibid.,* p. 11.
7. Cited in Michael Clowes, *Pensions & Investments,* October 13, 1975, p. 27. The NYSE estimates that of the $3 trillion needed for new capital expenditures from 1975–1985, $800 billion will have to be raised externally.
8. Cited in *Pensions & Investments,* February 28, 1977, editorial; see also Jason Epstein, "Capitalism and Socialism: Declining Returns," *New York Review of Books,* February 17, 1977, pp. 35–39.
9. "Rollercoaster to Nowhere," *Time,* August 19, 1973, pp. 44–49; see also Warren Buffet, "How Inflation Swindles the Equity Investor," *Fortune,* May 1977, pp. 230–67; "A Ticking Time Bomb," *Newsweek,* August 29, 1977, pp. 57–58; Leonard Silk, "Lagging Capital Spending and Investment Incentives," *New York Times,*

October 17, 1977; and "The Issue of Profitability and Capital Spending Lag," *New York Times,* December 15, 1977.

10. James Roscow, "How We've Been Turning Off Investors," *Pension World,* February 1976. According to Roscow, if you count the peak, early 1972, when individual shareholders numbered 32.5 million, the decline actually amounted to 7.3 million, or 22.4 percent in a little over three years. See also "The Wall Street Dropouts," by James W. Davant, *New York Times,* November 30, 1977, and "Behold the Stock Market," *Wall Street Journal,* October 20, 1977, editorial.

11. Roscow, *op. cit.,* p. 16.

12. Michael Clowes, "Funds Role Is Vital in Corporate Drive for New Capital," *Pensions & Investments,* October 13, 1975, pp. 27, 30.

13. *The World Almanac and Book of Facts 1977* (New York: Newspaper Enterprise Associates, 1976), p. 113.

14. Equity holdings for private noninsured pension funds went from $21 billion in 1964 to $79 billion in 1974 (book). State and local government holdings went from under $2.6 billion in 1964 to $17 billion in 1974. And, although no precise figures are available, insured pension-fund equity holdings increased by at least $8 billion. *Flow of Funds Accounts, 1964–1974,* Federal Reserve, 1976; *Pension Facts 1976,* American Council of Life Insurance, New York. Internal documents supplied to authors by the Securities Exchange Commission.

15. Jason Epstein, *op. cit.*

16. Clowes, *op. cit.; Pensions & Investments,* October 15, 1975, p. 30.

17. Editorial, *Pensions & Investments,* June 7, 1976, p. 12. *Pensions & Investments* also had this to say: "The private pension system is, in fact, the most efficient accumulator and distributor of investment capital the U.S. economy has. Anything that weakens it must weaken the nation's economic system" (*P & I,* editorial, March 28, 1977, p. 2).

"Pension funds are a form of saving that provides a significant part of the capital required for the future growth of the American economy" (*P & I,* editorial, November 10, 1975).

This was a dominant theme of the Joint Economic Committee's hearings on "The Impact of Pension Investments," Hearings, Subcommittee on Fiscal Policy, Joint Economic Committee, April 27, 1970. See pp. 1, 10, 11, especially. See also Norman D. Ture and Barbara A. Fields, "The Future of Private Pension Plans" (American Enterprise Institute, Washington, D.C., 1977).

18. Says Harrison Smith, executive vice-president, Morgan Guarantee Trust: "We don't really know, but we think that probably the

pension funds that we administer have three million beneficiaries" (personal interview, June 16, 1977).

19. Anonymous personal interview at the convention of the Association of Private Pension and Welfare Plans, Washington, D.C., April 1977. This individual, who is quite well known within the pension "industry," believes that pension assets have become much too important to the economy to be left in the hands of corporations, banks, and insurance companies: "The immense size and the projected growth of pension funds has put a tremendous amount of power in their hands—especially when you talk about the control of corporations and voting of stock."

Chapter 11: Setting the Precedent

1. See *American Labor*, May 1971; *Welfare and Pension Plans Investigation*, Senate Subcommittee on Welfare & Pension Funds, 84th Congress, 2nd Session, #1734 4/16/56, pp. 167–70.
2. *Congressional Record*, May 13, 1946, pp. 4891–911.
3. *Ibid.*, pp. 4892–93; see Jack Barbash, in *Old Age Income Assurance Part IV*, Joint Economic Committee, December, 1967; Richard Blodget, *Conflict of Interest: Union Pension Fund Asset Management* (New York: Twentieth Century Fund, 1977), p. 4.
4. *Ibid.*, p. 4892.
5. *Ibid.*
6. *Congressional Almanac*, 1946, pp. 293–98.
7. *Congressional Record*, May 8, 1947, p. 4747.
8. *Ibid.*, p. 4749 ff; *Congressional Record*, May 13, 1946, pp. 4892, 4903. Kentucky's Alben Barkley, who became Truman's vice-president, said that what the sponsors of the amendment were really saying was that union members who elect their representatives "must be protected against themselves"—although, noted Barkley, the good senators had much more confidence in the wisdom of the democratic process when it came to electing them to office. Barkley put the Senate on notice that the essence of the Taft amendment was that the employees had no right to control these funds and "therefore the employer ought to take it over" (1947, p. 4753).
9. Paul P. Harbrecht, *Pension Funds and Economic Power* (New York: Twentieth Century Fund, 1959), pp. 134–39.
10. *Ibid.;* James Henry, "How Pension Fund Socialism Didn't Come to America," *Working Papers*, Winter 1977.
11. Most progressive criticism of the 1958 and 1974 reform legislation has focused on its shortcomings in terms of protecting the rights of individual beneficiaries to their pension (see *Pensions & Invest-*

ments, Sept. 9, 1974, p. 20). There is no question that this is true. But the mandate that social capital be invested only in absolutely traditional ways has had an effect on *all* workers, not just retirees. Without this "legislated capitalism," it is likely that workers would not only own a quarter of American industry, but they would control it as well.

12. The term "prudent man" was written into the law when ERISA was passed, but had been used since trusts were formed. Essentially, the prudence clause is a mandate to all pension trustees to mimic the behavior of their peers. A trustee can show that he has not been imprudent in investing the funds if he can show that he is simply doing what everyone else is.

13. Personal interview with William Winpisinger, July 18, 1977.

14. Personal interview with Joe Swire, June 30, 1977.

Chapter 12: A Corporate "Asset"

1. See A. H. Raskin, "Can Anybody Clean up the Teamsters?" *New York Times Magazine,* November 7, 1976; Richard Blodgett, *Conflicts of Interest: Union Pension Fund Asset Management* (New York: Twentieth Century Fund, 1977); *Wall Street Journal,* July 22, 1975; *Oakland Tribune,* reprinted in *Congressional Record,* November 20, 1969. Many local union trustees have come to regard pension funds as their own personal domain. They also become more concerned with the business aspects of the pension fund than with the economic impact these funds' investments have on their membership. This is one aspect of what rank-and-file activists have called "business unionism."

   It seems clear that a rejuvenated democratic labor movement would be much less prone to these kinds of abuses. Certainly, an active and involved rank-and-file would not stand for them.

2. John Brooks, *Conflicts of Interest: Corporate Pension Fund Asset Management* (New York: Twentieth Century Fund, 1975), p. 6.

3. *Ibid.,* p. 57.

4. *Ibid.,* p. 13.

5. *Ibid.,* pp. 1, 15–16.

6. *Ibid.,* p. 16.

7. *Ibid.,* pp. 27–34, 47–53; Edmund Faltermayer, "A Steeper Climb up the Pension Mountain," *Fortune,* January 1975.

8. Brooks, *op. cit.,* pp. 32–33.

9. *Ibid.,* p. 31.

10. *Ibid.,* p. 30.

11. A. F. Ehrbar, "Those Pension Plans Are Even Weaker Than You Think," *Fortune,* November 1977, p. 105.

12. Brooks, *op. cit.*, pp. 47–53; *Mercer Bulletin*, July 1975.
13. *Business Week*, July 18, 1977, pp. 86–88; *Pension & Investments*, July 18, 1977, "Many Large Pension Plans Are Plagued by Acute Unfunded Vested Liabilities," Michael Clowes; Ehrbar, *op. cit.*
14. *Ibid.*
15. "The Big Pension Fund Drain," *Dun's*, July 1975; *Washington Post*, July 17, 1977, p. E1; see also Merton C. Bernstein, *The Future of Private Pensions* (London: The Free Press of Glencoe, 1964), p. 41 ff.
16. *Business Week, op. cit.* When Bethlehem Steel closed its facilities in Johnstown, Pa., and Lackawanna, N.Y., it took a one-time writeoff of $483 million to pay the accumulated unfunded liabilities it owed the 12,000 workers it was laying off (*New York Times*, November 8, 1977, p. 45).
17. There is some dispute about what, exactly, is a defined benefit plan and what is a defined contribution plan. The prevailing view appears to be that only traditional profit-sharing plans and "money-purchase" plans (where an annuity is purchased from an insurer) are defined contribution plans, while both single-employer and multiemployer plans are defined benefit plans. The confusion arises because multiemployer plans usually contain, in the contract language, both specified levels of contributions *and* benefits. While some local multiemployer plans and participating employers maintain that they are not defined benefit plans, ERISA clearly states that pension benefits, once vested, are not forfeitable. Thus, the participant is guaranteed a specific level of *benefits* regardless of contract language to the contrary.
18. Ehrbar, *op. cit.*; see also *Pensions & Investments*, "PBGC May Be Hit with Big Liability," October 10, 1977.
19. George Getschow, "UMW Health and Pension Funds' Plight Could Have Impact beyond Coal Industry," *Wall Street Journal*, December 1, 1977; John J. Fialka, "How an Obscure U.S. Agency Almost Became Coal Power," *Washington Star*, December 21, 1977; Paul R. Merrion, "Mandatory Coverage Bill in Peril," *Pensions & Investments*, November 21, 1977.
20. Ehrbar, *op. cit.*
21. See "Economist Warns of Dying System," *Pensions & Investments*, November 21, 1977, and "Social Security Revisions Must Consider Importance of Private Pension System," editorial in same issue.

Chapter 13: A Boon for the Banks

1. According to Michael Clowes (in a speech before the Association

of Private Pension and Welfare Plans Conference, Washington,
D.C., April 21, 1977) private noninsured pension funds were invested 58 percent in equity and 26 percent in corporate bonds.

2. The book value of insurance reserves, at year-end 1976, was $80.1
billion; $15.4 billion of this was in "separate" accounts—which are
mechanisms to allow insurance companies to invest more heavily
in stock than they normally can. The remaining insured pension
assets are in general insurance accounts, and are heavily invested
in corporate bonds (*Pensions & Investments*, May 23, 1977).

3. "Commercial Banks and Their Trust Activities," House Banking
and Currency Committee, Vol. 1, p. 2, July 8, 1968, 90th Congress, Second Session. Also known as the "Patman Report." See
also *Voting Rights in Major Corporations*, The Senate Subcommittee on Reports, Accounting and Management (The Metcalf Committee) January 1978.

4. *Ibid.*, p. 25.

5. *Ibid.*, p. 23.

6. *Ibid.*, pp. 1–3.

7. *Conflicts of Interest: Commercial Bank Trust Departments*, Edward
S. Herman (New York: Twentieth Century Fund, 1975), p. 35,
citing Patman Report data (Vol. 1, Chapter 3, pp. 484–85).

8. Adolph Berle, *Power Without Property* (New York: Harcourt,
Brace and World, 1959), pp. 52–55, cited in Patman Report (see
pp. 17–18). See also Berle's article "Economic Power in a Free
Society," in Andrew Hacker's *The Corporation Takeover* (New
York: Harper & Row, 1964).

9. "Chase's Rocky Road," *Latin American and Empire Report*, April
1976, p. 20. North American Congress on Latin America (NACLA).

10. Herman, *op. cit.*, notes: "From its inception corporate trust business was regarded by bankers not only as a direct source of profits
but also as a source of other loan and deposit business. Bank pre-
eminence in the corporate trust field has been maintained up to
the present day by a combination of experience, legal requirements that banks act as trustee, and the power of the banks' relationships with the corporate community" (p. 16). "As recently as
1962, a bankers' association survey reported that 'in determining
what objectives of the trust department were most important to
their bank the heaviest votes were for . . . (bank trust departments
serving) as a device to hold and increase commercial bank business'" (p. 28).

11. *Ibid.*, p. 52. Herman used data from the Patman Report made
available to him by the staff of the House Banking and Currency
Committee.

12. *Ibid.*, pp. 28–29.
13. *Ibid.*, p. 54; also p. 29.
14. *Ibid.*, pp. 62–63.
15. *Ibid.*
16. "Citibank Suit Not Filed Lightly: Steel Fund Manager," *Pensions & Investments,* June 3, 1974, p. 3.
17. Herman, *op. cit.*, pp. 54–55; *Wall Street Journal,* March 29, 1973, p. 20.
18. Herman, *op. cit.*, p. 55; " 'Chinese Wall' Suit Remains Undecided," *Fensions & Investments,* May 23, 1977, p. 7.
19. A case in point was the proposed "Ag Land Trust." Continental Illinois Bank of Chicago wanted to invest $50 million in prime Midwest farmland. According to the *Washington Post*: "Small farmers fear this would be a first step in a massive corporate land purchase that would push up the price of land to a level they couldn't afford and would either push them off the farm or back to the status of tenant sharecropper of Depression days" (Feb. 17, 1977, p. 2).

    Although the ensuing furor caused Continental to cancel this proposed investment the bank made it clear that farmland is the next logical place for billions of dollars in pension funds to go. If this happens, the social fabric of the entire Midwest could be drastically transformed. See George McGovern, *Congressional Record,* Feb. 2, 1977, p. S-2105.
20. "S & P Out Performs Most Banks in Hansen Study," *Pensions & Investments,* March 28, 1977, p. 11.
21. A. F. Ehrbar, *Fortune,* June 1976, p. 148. "*Fortune* estimates that pension funds, profit sharing plans, and employee thrift plans are worth *$13 billion* [emphasis in text] less today than they would be if their stock portfolios had done as well as the S&P during the last ten years" (p. 146).
22. *Pensions & Investments,* January 5, 1976; Edward Malca, in *Pension Funds and Other Institutional Investors* (Lexington, Mass.: Lexington Books, 1975, p. 21), estimates that for 1973, pension portfolios lost an additional $30 billion. *Pensions & Investments* estimates the 1973 loss at $22 billion.
23. Speech by Michael Clowes before the Private Pension and Welfare Plan Conference, Washington, D.C., April 21, 1977.
24. *Pensions & Investments,* May 23, 1977, p. 15. *Pensions & Investments* regularly publishes its own in-house performance measures plus those of a number of other analysts—almost without exception, these findings show bank and insurance equity funds significantly underperforming the market.

25. See *Time*, August 29, 1977, p. 44 ff; and *Newsweek*, August 29, 1977, pp. 57–58.
26. See Frank L. Voorheis, "How Well Do Banks Manage Pooled Pension Portfolios?" *Financial Analysts Journal*, September–October 1976, p. 35. Voorheis concludes that big banks, with huge research budgets, did worse than smaller institutions with less sophisticated, less expensive, and fewer managers.
27. Ehrbar, *op. cit.*, pp. 145–54; Malca, *op. cit.*, pp. 107–109. Ironically, the random walk theory works precisely because the market is dominated by institutions. Since they all have huge research budgets, there is little information about the market that is not known by all institutions within a very short time.
28. Ehrbar, *op. cit.*, p. 152.
29. Speech by Michael Clowes, *op. cit.*; the August 15, 1977, *Pensions & Investments* was almost entirely devoted to indexing.
30. Ehrbar, *op. cit.*, p. 146.
31. The trend toward computerization of all financial transactions is growing rapidly. In all likelihood, there will be one large, computerized national exchange in the next few years (see "Turmoil on Wall Street," *Time*, August 29, 1977, p. 46).

    Pensions & Investments carried a rather whimsical short story on 1985 computerized investing by a leading indexing proponent ("A Look at Your Job in Eight Years with G. Rodney Scattergold IV," by Dean Le Baron, president, Batterymarch Financial Management Corp., Boston, May 9, 1977, p. 25). See also the *P&I* April 12, 1976, issue on the future of investing, in which Steve Yahn speculates that by 1985, there will be major international index funds. And *P&I*, September 9, 1974, "O. Neil and His Computers Challenge Wall Street," p. 3; *P&I*, January 17, 1977, "Firm Designs Computerized Stock Program."
32. Cited in *Voices of the American Revolution*, Peoples Bicentennial Commission (New York: Bantam Books, 1974).

Chapter 14: Who Are the Real Owners?

1. Figure excludes federal plans. There are about 38 million private-sector active and retired pension participants and about 11 million active and retired state and local government participants. With private, state, and local pension assets worth more than $400 billion, the average employee's pension is worth $8,000. Source: Social Security Administration, *Pension Facts 1976;* American Council on Life Insurance (New York, 1976).

2. Ralph Nader and Kate Blackwell, *You and Your Pension* (New York: Grossman, 1973), p. 5.

3. Although it is claimed that the 1974 pension reform act (ERISA) eliminated most pension abuses and "horror stories," this is not at all the case, according to the Pension Rights Center (Room 1019, 1346 Connecticut Ave., NW, Washington, D.C. 20036). This group continues to be deluged with complaints from individuals who had thought they had earned the right to a pension, but were sadly mistaken.

4. Merton C. Bernstein, *The Future of Private Pensions* (London: The Free Press of Glencoe, 1964).

5. According to Karen Ferguson of the Pension Rights Center, between one-third and one-half of all covered pension participants will never collect a dime. Preliminary figures from the Bureau of Labor Statistics indicate that fewer than 45 percent of all covered participants will collect a pension, even under ERISA.

6. Nader and Blackwell, *op. cit.,* p. 23.

7. Very few companies vest their employees voluntarily before ten years. According to Michael Clowes, editor of *Pensions & Investments,* most companies are choosing the longest possible period for vesting their employees (personal interview, April 21, 1977).

8. Merton C. Bernstein, letter to the *New York Times,* April 2, 1974.

9. *Coverage and Vesting of Full Time Employees under Private Retirement Plans, From the April 1972 Survey,* Bureau of Labor Statistics, September 1973. This survey shows that the median length of employment for covered pension participants was 8.6 years in 1972. There are strong indications that this figure is significantly lower today.

10. Although ERISA requires full vesting of earned pension benefits after a maximum of ten years, few participants collect the maximum pension. First, since, in most instances, pension credits are not transferable—or portable—from one employer to another (except in multi-employer plans, and only then within the same union), a worker must start over again at each new job. Thus, it is quite conceivable that a worker could become vested in two or even three different pension plans. But the total of those separate benefits will almost never equal what it would if those pension credits had been applied to only one plan.

11. Anonymous interview, June 1977. This banker continues: "The beneficiary of a pension is the true owner of that property, but he can't act as an owner—so he has a lot of people acting on his behalf."

12. Former Chase Manhattan vice-president Esmond Gardner says, "I don't quite agree that it's their [the workers'] money. Because it's contingent, deferred. It's the fund's money, a separate entity" (personal interview, June 15, 1977).

John English, who oversees AT&T's $17 billion pension system, makes this comment: "The difference between the fact that a worker does not have any control over his investments and the fact that an individual investor does have that control would be that the worker did not write out a check to a broker to buy the shares. I know that's a fine line. But, there's a difference in my mind between making an active decision on your own—like taking some of your paycheck to buy a security—as opposed to having an impersonal investor do it for you" (personal interview, June 17, 1977).

13. Cited in William C. Greenough and Francis P. King, *Pension Funds and Public Policy* (New York: Columbia University Press, 1976), p. 64.

14. Cited in Merton C. Bernstein, *The Future of Private Pensions* (London: The Free Press of Glencoe, 1964), p. 120.

15. Paul P. Harbrecht, *Pension Funds and Economic Power* (New York: Twentieth Century Fund, 1959), pp. 269–70 ff.

16. See footnote 16, Chapter 1.

17. *Pensions & Investments* (1976 figure) May 23, 1977, p. 12.

18. See Harbrecht, *op. cit.*, pp. 107 ff, 119 ff, 211 ff, and 267 ff. Observes Harbrecht: ". . . another type of owner has emerged in the evolutionary process of property organization. This is the financial institution. Through the acquisition of stock in corporations for income purposes the financial organizations have begun to gather to themselves the atomized rights of control that have always been attached to shares of stock. . . . In the financial institution the concept of ownership has reached a dead end and no longer has any functional meaning, whereas the control over property which resides in the managers of these institutions is a dynamic and powerful force" (p. 4).

19. Anonymous interview, June 1977.

Chapter 15: No Investment without Representation

1. "Denial of a Teamster Pension Stirs Furor in Varied Groups, Poses Changes on Retirement," *New York Times,* January 20, 1977, p. 53.

2. *Ibid.;* "Court Rules Pension Funds Are Subject to Securities Laws," *Pensions & Investments,* March 15, 1976; "Appeals Court Upholds

Daniel; Pension Ruled to Be a Security," *P&I*, September 12, 1977, p. 1.

3. Decision of the 7th Circuit Court of Appeals, reprinted in *Benefits and Pension Reporter*, Bureau of National Affairs (Washington, D.C.), August 29, 1977, p. 10 of reprint.

4. From text of Judge Kirkland's decision, reprinted in *Pensions & Investments*, March 15, 1976, pp. 24–33.

5. "Labor and SEC May Square Off in John Daniel's Class Action Suit," Paul R. Merrion, *Pensions & Investments*, November 8, 1976, pp. 1, 35.

6. "SEC Brief Comes on Strong for Daniel," Paul R. Merrion, *Pensions & Investments*, February 14, 1977, pp. 1, 41.

7. Seventeen years earlier, Paul P. Harbrecht had this to say: "... great social advantages may be derived from treating pension funds as the property of the pensioners. A property interest in the pension fund would return to the worker some of the economic independence which the pension system has taken from him. As acknowledged owners, employees would be given some share in the direction and control of the pension funds. This would mean that they should have some voice in the investment of these assets. ... A voice in investment policy would allow the employees to help direct fund investment into channels beneficial to them, such as housing and savings and loan activities." (*Pension Funds and Economic Power*, Paul P. Harbrecht (New York: Twentieth Century Fund, 1959).

8. Already, several members of Congress are talking about voiding the *Daniel* decision through legislation. Senators Javits, Williams, and Long, and Rep. Ehrlenborn have decried it. However, it remains to be seen whether millions of individual pensioners will remain silent while these lawmakers legislate away their rights to their deferred wages.

9. Personal interview with Karen Ferguson, August 24, 1977.

10. See *America's Birthday* (New York: Simon and Schuster, 1974); *Common Sense II* (New York: Bantam Books, 1975) and *Voices of the American Revolution* (New York: Bantam, 1975) all by the Peoples Bicentennial Commission, for an expanded argument along these lines.

11. A 1975 Institute of Life Insurance survey reported that over 90 percent of the public felt that they had a *right* to an adequate pension upon retirement. This sentiment notwithstanding, at most one in four American workers will ever get a pension to supplement a meager Social Security check. Even for this fortunate mi-

nority, these pensions are hardly likely to provide an adequate retirement income (*Mercer Bulletin*, November 1976).

12. Teamsters for a Democratic Union literature (TDU, Box 99133, Cleveland, OH 44199).

13. Most labor pension officials we interviewed were critical of unions such as the UAW and Steelworkers for not pushing for greater control over their members' funds.

14. Telephone interview with Jean Lindberg, June 14, 1977.

Chapter 16: Vying for Economic Power

1. Telephone interview with Ray Rogers, June 3, 1977.
2. Personal interview with Lawrence Smedley, July 5, 1977.
3. Personal interview with I. Philip Sisper, June 20, 1977.
4. Personal interview with William Winpisinger, July 18, 1977.
5. Personal interview with Richard Days, June 17, 1977.
6. "Money Is Muscle With '78 Labor," Victor Riesel, *Birmingham (Ala.) News,* January 3, 1978; also see the four articles in "Symposium—Union Financial Data," *Industrial Relations,* Vol. 14, No. 2, May 1975, pp. 131–157.
7. Personal interview with Lawrence Smedley, July 5, 1977.
8. Statement before Joint Economic Subcommittee on Fiscal Policy, "Investment Policies of Pension Funds," April 27–30, 1970, p. 214.
9. Personal interview with Leonard Lesser, July 1, 1977.
10. Personal interview with Henry Foner, June 20, 1977.
11. Personal interview with Kevin Kistler, July 14, 1977.
12. Personal interview with Robert Tilove, June 16, 1977.
13. The Union Label Department classified a list from *Pensions & Investments,* December 6, 1976, p. 3, of the top twenty-five stocks held by bank trust department pension accounts. Included in the sixteen predominantly nonunion or antiunion companies were IBM (1), Exxon (2), Kodak (4), Sohio (6), GE (7), Dow (10), Procter and Gamble (11), Sears (12), Kresge (14), American Home (15), Standard of California (17), J. C. Penney (18), Texaco (20), Mobil (22), Schlumberger (24), and Citicorp (25). Seven of the top twenty-five companies were rated as being relatively well unionized and having adequate labor relations: GM (3), AT&T (5), Ford (9), Merck (17), Caterpillar (16), Xerox (19), and Arco (21). Only two were rated as having "reasonably good" or "good" labor policies: 3M (8) and Kellogg (23). All of the industrial companies were considered to be runaway corporations, to one degree or another.

14. *Congressional Record,* October 26, 1977, p. E 6579.
15. Text obtained from AFL-CIO Union Label Department. It is interesting to note that the original resolution, as proposed by Earl D. McDavid, president of the Union Label Department, differed significantly from the final form. Two significant changes were made: first, reference to "third parties" who invest union members' pension moneys was watered down (evidently because some delegates felt uncomfortable attacking their advisers and bankers); secondly, the resolution was changed to read that pension moneys should be entrusted to financial institutions whose policies are "not inimical" to the welfare of working men and women. The original resolution asked that these institutions investment policies be "compatible" with their welfare. Clearly, this whole subject is still a very touchy one with some union officials.
16. "Money Is Muscle With '78 Labor," Victor Riesel, *Birmingham (Ala.) News,* January 3, 1978.
17. Personal interview with William Winpisinger, July 18, 1977.
18. Personal interview with Robert S. Connerton, July 8, 1977.
19. See footnote 15, Chapter 1.
20. Personal interview with Rep. Michael Harrington, August 2, 1977.
21. Rep. Henry Reuss, written reply to submitted questions, August 1, 1977.
22. A brief telephone survey produced information on proposals by public officials for alternative uses of pension funds in Massachusetts, Connecticut, New York, Pennsylvania, Ohio, Michigan, Illinois, Wisconsin, Minnesota, California, and Oregon.
23. In Europe, pension funds are already being used to help workers directly. For example, in France, pension funds are used to build workers' housing. In Scandinavia, they build hotels both to provide low-cost accommodations for workers and to attract tourists. In Great Britain, pension funds have become the focal point of labor's drive for more accountability of capital. Labor is demanding 50 percent control over the investment of all $40 billion of British pension funds.

Chapter 17: Union Claims

1. Personal interview with Joe Swire, June 30, 1977. Swire emphasizes that unions, up to this point, have been too involved in securing benefits to do anything about how their members' pension funds are invested.
2. Personal interview with Richard Days, June 17, 1977.
3. Paul P. Harbrecht, S.J., *Pension Funds and Economic Power* (New

York: Twentieth Century Fund, 1959), pp. 97–99; personal interviews with Woodrow Ginsberg and Leonard Lesser, former union
pension experts, July 1, 1977.

4. See *Welfare and Pension Plans Investigation*, Senate Subcommittee on Welfare and Pension Funds, 84th Congress, Second Session, #1734, pp. 42, 302 ff; *Pension Funds and Economic Free-
dom*, Robert Tilove (New York: Fund for the Republic, 1959);
Business Week, Special Section on Pension Funds, January 31,
1959, p. 14 ff; and "It's Bound to Happen . . . ," Wayne Phillips,
Pensions, Fall 1972, p. 33 ff.

5. *Pensions & Investments*, November 10, 1975; and testimony of
Joseph Keenan before the Joint Economic Committee, Subcommittee on Fiscal Policy, April 27–30, 1970, pp. 215–18.

6. Personal interview with Robert Daley, July 19, 1977.

7. The term "social investments" or "socially responsible investments"
is something of a misnomer, especially when it concerns the funds
of union members and "Graybelt" public employees. "Economic
accountability" would appear to be a more descriptive term.

8. Robert Tilove, *op. cit.*, p. 70; *Pension and Welfare Plan Investigation*, *op. cit.*, p. 43; Noel Arnold Levin, *Labor Management Benefit Funds* (New York: Practicing Law Institute, 1971), #4 in
corporate practice series, p. 212.

9. *Blankenship v. Boyle*, 329 F. Supp. 1089 (1971); Richard Blodgett, *Conflicts of Interest: Union Pension Fund Asset Management*
(New York: Twentieth Century Fund, 1977), pp. 21–22; see
"Public Employee Pensions in Times of Fiscal Distress," *Harvard
Law Review*, March 1977, vol. 90:992, p. 1008 ff, for a well-rea-
soned argument that the *Blankenship* decision itself does not at all
preclude the use of funds in similar ways, providing that trustees
responsibly, methodically, and openly chart their course of action.

10. Keenan, "Investment Policy of Pension Funds."

11. Phillips, *op. cit.*, p. 33 ff.

12. *Congressional Record*, December 22, 1969, p. 40933.

13. Phillips, *op. cit.*, pp. 33–35.

14. John G. Simon *et al.*, *The Ethical Investor: Universities and Corporate Responsibility* (Yale University Press, 1972), p. 55 ff. The
Eastman Kodak company was probably the first to be pressured
in a stockholder meeting in this way. The issue was Kodak's hiring
and other employment practices.

15. *The Corporate Examiner*, Interfaith Center for Corporate Responsibility, September, 1976 (475 Riverside Drive, N.Y., N.Y. 10027).

16. See *College Press Service* (Denver), April 22, 1977; *Corporate*

Examiner, July–August 1977; "Regents Should Use Proxies for Social Clout," Bruce McWilliams, *Los Angeles Times,* May 20, 1976.

17. *Corporate Examiner,* September 1976, July 1976, *op. cit.*
18. *Wall Street Journal,* March 23, 1977; *Wall Street Journal,* May 23, 1977; and *Washington Post,* Marjorie Hyer, February 10, 1977; and articles in the following issues of *Pensions & Investments:* April 8, 1974; July 1, 1974; July 15, 1974; October 21, 1974; November 18, 1974; March 1, 1976; June 7, 1976.
19. Letter from Oil, Chemical and Atomic Workers to the Occupational Safety and Health Administration.
20. Press release, National Council of Churches, July 6, 1977.
21. *Washington Star,* March 15, 1977, p. 1.
22. *Ibid.;* Richard Days, administrator of a United Auto Workers' local fund in New York City, has expressed his strong support for the auto workers' using funds to push for a form of codetermination.
23. *Ibid.* Rubin, from Bakersfield, California, is actively working to convince West Coast unions to use their pension investments strategically.
24. *Ibid.*
25. Personal interview with Henry Dillon, July 7, 1977.
26. *Pensions & Investments,* March 14, 1977, p. 31; *P&I,* April 22, 1974. The UMW took out full-page ads in *P&I, Wall Street Journal,* and other papers, warning stockholders not to invest in Duke Power.
27. Company "8K" Reports to the SEC.
28. *Pensions & Investments,* March 14, 1977, "Textile Union Mulling Capital Boycott."
29. *Ibid.;* telephone interview with Pam Woywood, June 29, 1977.
30. Company "8K" reports to the SEC.
31. Personal interview with I. Philip Sipser, June 20, 1977.
32. Personal interview with Harrison Smith, June 16, 1977.
33. Anonymous personal interview.
34. Personal interview with William Winpisinger, July 18, 1977.

Chapter 18: State and Local Government Claims
1. "Pennsylvania Pension Funds Offer VW $135 Million Loan to Help Set Up Plant," *Wall Street Journal,* September 9, 1976, p. 1; "VW Negotiations with Pennsylvania Funds Chugging Along," *Pensions & Investments,* July 19, 1976; telephone interview with Richard Witmer, secretary, Pennsylvania State Public Employees Retirement Fund, August 18, 1977, and September 5, 1977.

2. "Don't Look to Funds to Support Social Projects," *Pensions & Investments,* June 21, 1976, p. 6.
3. "Rabbits in the Cabbage Patch," *Wall Street Journal,* August 13, 1976.
   As a result of the outcry by the *Journal* and others, Shapp was eventually forced to cut the proposed $135 million to a token $6 million.
4. See Ron Chernow, "The Rabbit that Ate Pennsylvania," *Mother Jones,* January 1978.
5. Telephone interview with John Harrington, August 18, 1977.
6. This is a "redlining" issue writ large. The issue of redlining in mortgage lending has become a major one because people have seen their money shipped out of their communities and states in the name of higher returns. For a graphic description of bank redlining practices, see Jack Newfield and Paul DuBrul, *The Abuse of Power* (New York: Viking Press, 1977), pp. 98–106.
7. Telephone interview with Jim Savarise, July 7, 1977.
8. One of the major reasons that this has not been done before is that the administrators of public funds are uniformly conservative, "hard-headed investment managers" who operate just like any other investment managers. According to Richard Witmer, secretary of the Pennsylvania fund, public-fund administrators are coming under increased pressure to help rejuvenate local economies. In fact, according to Witmer, it was one of the main topics of conversation at the annual convention of the National Association of State Retirement Administrators, August 1977.
9. A constant theme among all of the investment managers we interviewed—bankers, corporate administrators, public fund managers—was that until taxes and spending were cut back, investment would not return to the region.
10. *Flow of Funds Accounts,* Federal Reserve, September 1977, Sector Statements of Fiscal Assets and Liabilities.
11. Louis M. Kohlmeier, *Conflicts of Interest: State and Local Pension Fund Asset Management* (New York: Twentieth Century Fund, 1976), p. 7 ff.
12. *Ibid.* See also Barbara A. Patocka, "The Herculean Task Is Under Way," *Pensions,* May/June, 1973, p. 34 ff.
13. *SEC Statistical Bulletin,* April 1977, p. 42. About half of this total is New York City public employee fund holdings of NYC paper.
14. See ·Newfield and DuBrul, *op. cit.;* and *The Bank and the Municipal Crisis: Public Responsibility and Private Profit,* Office of Legislative Oversight and Analysis, New York State Assembly, November 15, 1976.

15. "NYC Fund a Maverick on Voting GM Proxies," *Pensions & Investments*, June 31, 1974; and "Public Employee Funds Should Vote on Social Issues: NYC Controller," *Pensions & Investments*, July 15, 1974.
16. "City Leaders Seek Policy on Depositing D.C. Funds," *Washington Post*, March 7, 1977.
17. Telephone interview with Bill Brennan of Education/Instrucción, August 24, 1977; statements supplied by two Hartford banks to Hartford city council; see also Education/Instrucción Report #9, February 7, 1977, "Redlining: Fair Housing at Its Worst in Hartford, Connecticut" (Education/Instrucción, PO Box 12245, Hartford, CT, 06112). Hartford City Counselor Nick Carbone (telephone interview, August 24, 1977) introduced the resolution requiring full disclosure and examination of city general funds and pension moneys. He says: "We want to look at the portfolio in its entirety and see if we can handle it in a different way which will have a greater benefit to Hartford residents. . . . You're not only talking about redlining of mortgages, you're talking about redlining in terms of jobs, investments, the whole bit."
18. Kohlmeier, *op. cit.*, pp. 12–13, 38–39; and *New York Times Magazine*, July 11, 1976, p. 31.
19. Telephone interview with Jack Kittredge, August 23, 1977. See Final Report of the Commission on State Investment, Massachusetts Social and Economic Opportunity Council, Boston, July 1976, "A Linked Deposit System for Massachusetts." Kittredge hopes that, after a couple of years' experience with the linked-deposit system, the same principles could be applied to the state's pension funds.
20. "Funds offer low-rate mortgage loans to participants," *Pensions & Investments*, March 14, 1977, p. 25; "Pressures Bend Public Fund Investment Goals," *P&I*, October 7, 1974.
21. Robert Tilove, *Public Employee Pension Funds* (New York: Columbia University Press, 1976), p. 220.
22. In an interview with Wallace Sullivan, executive director of the Teachers Retirement System of the City of New York, and Joe Russo (his assistant), Sullivan acknowledged that, in spite of the urgent need for capital and jobs in New York City, the Teachers' $3 billion was not at all geared toward reinvestment in companies operating in the city.
23. Newfield and DuBrul, *op. cit.*, pp. 11–49; New York Assembly Office of Legislative Oversight and Analysis, *op. cit.*
24. "Gotham's Creditors," Michael Brody, *Barrons*, August 22, 1977; *Pensions & Investments*, March 15, 1976, p. 8.

25. Sullivan, Russo, *op. cit.;* personal interview with Jack Begal, June 21, 1977; Jim Savarise, *op. cit.* Public employee pension funds have been blamed for the fiscal crises in many northern cities. According to Robert Tilove, *op. cit.*, public pensions are no more "generous" than private pensions when it is taken into account that most public plans require hefty contributions from the employee (usually one-third to one-half of total costs), while almost 80 percent of all private plans are noncontributory. The real problem with public pensions is that the employing governments have been either unwilling or unable to adequately fund the plan.

26. See Jack Begal, "Behold the Bond," *New York Times,* February 2, 1977, op-ed page.

27. *Directory of National Unions and Employee Associations—1975,* Bureau of Labor Statistics (1974 figures).

Chapter 19: The Legal Question

1. See *Pensions & Investments,* June 6, 1977, p. 11.

2. *Pensions & Investments,* April 25, 1977, p. 3.

3. During the course of conducting interviews for this book, it became clear that there is a tremendous amount of confusion as to what can and cannot be done under ERISA. This is true even with officials charged with administering the law. In a personal interview on August 4, 1977, Ian Lanoff, administrator of ERISA enforcement for the Labor Department, would give no specific indication of how his office would enforce the act as it relates to alternative pension-investment strategies. In fact, some of his responses on this issue contradicted each other. It will take years, says Lanoff, for both legal and administrative precedents to be thoroughly established.

4. Personal interview with Lawrence Smedley, July 5, 1977.

5. See *Pensions & Investments,* September 12, 1977, p. 54. *P&I* reports that union trustees are now more cautious than ever, to the point that they are reluctant to invest in anything but blue-chip stocks and bonds.

6. Personal interview with Russ Allen, June 30, 1977.

7. Personal interview with Ian Lanoff, August 4, 1977.

8. See Noel Arnold Levin, *Labor Management Benefit Funds,* Practicing Law Institute (New York: 1971), #4 in series, pp. 195–218; and "Public Employee Pensions in Times of Fiscal Distress," *Harvard Law Review,* Vol. 90: 992, pp. 1003–18. Levin, past president of the International Foundation for Employee Benefits, offers a carefully reasoned guide for the trustee of a multiem-

ployee plan, and the *Harvard Law Review* goes through a step-by-step test of prudence for public administrators that could easily be applied to private funds as well.

9. *The American Banker* (September 9, 1976, p. 2) reported that a survey of labor pension trustees found that 63 percent felt that their boards should take a more active interest in the management of companies in which they invest. Ironically, ERISA's fiduciary standards may end up pushing unions into direct involvement with company management. Going further, Richard Days, administrator of a small UAW fund in New York City, states: "We should assert ourselves as European workers do, where, by law, they have one-third representation on the board of directors of industry, and parity, 50 percent, in steel and coal. In our negotiations with Chrysler, we proposed having a union person on the board. That means that I have something to say about what we're going to do. If this concept were employed throughout the country, the outlook of America would be entirely different. The security of all individuals would be much greater" (personal interview, June 17, 1977).

10. *Pensions & Investments*, April 12, 1976, p. 21. See also Kenneth T. Rosen, *The Role of Pension Funds in Housing Finance*, Joint Center for Urban Studies, MIT/Harvard, Working Paper #35, June 1975. This report details how pension funds could increase the amount of money they currently make available to the mortgage markets. Although pension funds are not heavily invested in mortgages, the report concludes that such investments are actually better suited to pension funds' needs than many of the investments they now hold. Rosen concludes that the prime reason for low pension-fund investment in mortgages is that commercial bank trust departments dominate pension investment decisions, and these banks prefer corporate stocks and bonds to workers' housing.

Some unions, notably the IBEW and various carpenters' locals, invest heavily in housing mortgages, with guarantees that their money will be used to finance union-built structures.

11. Leonard Mactas, "How Private Pension Funds Can Help Troubled Cities and States," *Pension World*, October, 1976, pp. 49–51.

12. Speech by Michael Clowes, before the Association of Private Pension and Welfare Plans Conference, April 21, 1977.

13. *Pensions & Investments* (May 23, 1977, p. 1), quotes W. M. Valiant, the treasurer of Borg-Warner Corp., as saying, "The days of the corporate pension plan may be numbered. I think eventually the Social Security system may swallow the pension system." See

The Future of Private Pensions, by Merton C. Bernstein (London: The Free Press of Glencoe, 1964), for a comprehensive proposal in this vein.

14 See "Social Security Still Facing a Deficit," by Brooks Jackson, *Washington Star,* December 20, 1977; "Social Security: Original Confusion," by Robert J. Samuelson, *Washington Post,* December 6, 1977; *Pensions & Investments,* May 23, 1977, pp. 1, 32; *P&I,* June 6, 1977, p. 8. The business community was also frightened by Carter's original proposal to pay some of the Social Security costs out of general revenues rather than from an earmarked payroll tax.

15. The American Medical Association vehemently opposed Medicaid as the first step toward socialization of medicine. Now, the AMA is one of Medicaid's staunchest defenders, since it has meant a bonanza for doctors and hospitals.

16. See "My Case for National Planning," by Thornton Bradshaw (president of Atlantic Richfield), *Fortune,* February 1977, p. 100 ff.

17. Personal interview with Reese Hammond, July 15, 1977.

18. Personal interview with William Winpisinger, July 18, 1977.

19. *Ibid.*

20. The Carter Administration offers a glimpse of what unions and the Graybelt can probably expect from Washington in the decades to come—just enough to prevent a total erosion of the President's support in these areas and an open revolt among northern and labor Democrats. But no more.

Chapter 20: Laying the Base

1. See *Public Policy Readers,* Conference on Alternative State and Local Public Policy, Institute for Policy Studies (1901 Que St., NW, Washington, D.C. 20009) for a collection of some of the more imaginative proposals and critiques of existing policies.

2. See *New Directions in State and Local Policy,* Conference on Alternative State and Local Public Policy (Washington, D.C., 1977).

3. Telephone interview with Ohio State Senator Mike Schwartzwalder, August 24, 1977.

4. *New Directions, op. cit.,* pp. 79–89.

5. James Rowan, "Public Control of Public Monies," *Progressive,* February 1977, p. 51.

6. Personal interview with Sam Brown, August 15, 1977; and *New Directions, op. cit.,* p. 314. Brown, former Colorado State Treasurer and now director of ACTION, feels that the crucial issue for the remainder of this century will be the distribution of capital. "In the long term, that's the way the coalition of the future will

be built. The question of democratizing control over limited resources and limited wealth and capital will be central to the politics of the future."

7. Rowan, *op. cit.*, p. 49; Jeff Faux and Robert Lightfoot, *Capital and Community*, Exploratory Project for Economic Alternatives (Washington, D.C., 1976).

8. James Rowan in *New Directions, op. cit.*, p. 299; and Lynette Benton and Carl Sussman (with the assistance of David Smith), "The Community Development Finance Corporation," Center for Community Economic Development, reprinted in *Northeast Cities Conference Reader*, December 1976, sponsored by Hartford City Institute, National Conference on Alternative State and Local Public Policies.

9. "What Are CDC's?" Center for Community Economic Development, reprinted in *Northeast Cities Conference Reader, op. cit.*

10. See Faux and Lightfoot, *op. cit.*, pp. 55–64.

11. See Roger Neville Williams, "People's Banks," *New Republic*, December 4, 1976; *New York Times*, April 5, 1975; *New York Times*, April 25, 1975; *Business Conditions*, Federal Reserve Bank of Chicago, July 1976.

12. See Rowan, *op. cit.*

13. Testimony of Kenneth E. Buhrmaster, before the New York State Assembly Banking Committee, hearings on a proposed New York State bank, May 2, 1975, p. 1 of prepared transcript.

14. Initial hearings were held in September 1977 on a proposed state bank for California. Sponsored by State Senator John Dunlap, this bank, if created, could have upwards of $20 billion in assets (capitalized with general state funds and a portion of the state's public employee funds). Senator Dunlap hopes to have a series of hearings over the next several years and has already generated a considerable amount of support for the concept of a state bank for California (telephone interview, Sen. John Dunlap, August 23, 1977). See also "A Proposal for a California State Bank," by Ed Kirshner, in *Northeast Cities Conference Reader, op. cit.*, p. 69. Another proposal for a California state bank, by Derek Shearer, is available from the Conference on Alternative State and Local Public Policies.

15. William G. Shephard, "Re-Examining Public Enterprise," *Working Papers*, Summer 1973; and Andrew Kopkind, "Lemon Socialism," *Real Paper*, reprinted in *Programs and Proposals: A Reader on Public Policy*, New England Conference on Alternative State and Local Public Policy, 1975.

16. See Rowan, *op. cit.*

17. John Case, Leonard Goldberg, Derek Shearer, "State Business," *Working Papers*, Spring 1976, p. 24 ff.
18. *Ibid.;* and Leonard Goldberg, San Francisco State College, "Public Enterprise at the State Level," undated monograph.
19. Case, Goldberg, Shearer, *op. cit.*, pp. 71–73; and Faux and Lightfoot, *op. cit.*, pp. 92–95.
20. *Ibid.*, pp. 70–71.
21. Christine Lanigan, "Connecticut's Push for New Products," *New Englander*, February 1976, p. 31 ff; and Faux and Lightfoot, *op. cit.*, pp. 53–54.
22. Case, Goldberg, Shearer, *op. cit.*, pp. 67–74.
23. *The Brier Hill Unionist* (Newspaper of United Steelworkers Local 1462, Youngstown), October–November 1977.
24. Text of "A Religious Response to the Mahoning Valley Steel Crisis" (dated November 29, 1977), from press release by Diocese of Youngstown, December 12, 1977.
25. Throughout the northeast corridor, communities and workers have attempted to save jobs by buying out plants that were closing. In Clinton, Massachusetts, nearly 800 workers and townspeople turned out for a meeting to try to raise enough capital to save their jobs at the Colonial Press. A large bakery in Boston shut down, and again, employees, their unions, and state development officials worked to find a solution. The city of N. Tonawanda, New York, and the International Paperworkers Union have worked for over a year in an attempt to reopen a large papermill there. All of these efforts failed for one reason: lack of capital. City officials who normally would be expected to be horrified by the notion of public- or worker-controlled enterprises, along with union officials who have traditionally opposed worker ownership, shed their ideological blinders and opt for the obvious solution when faced with the choice of decisive action or economic disaster (source: Federation for Economic Democracy, Box 802, Ithaca, NY 14850). Another good source for recent developments on the West Coast is the Community Organizing Ownership Project (see the Fall 1977 issue of their publication, *The Public Works*)— 6529 Telegraph Ave., Oakland, CA 94609. Also on the West Coast, the New School for Democratic Management offers a wide range of courses for employees in worker-controlled concerns— 256 Sutter Street, San Francisco, CA 94108.
26. Jeremy Rifkin, *Own Your Own Job* (New York: Bantam, 1977), pp. 41–43; "Miners Buy Mine to Save Their Jobs; Then Business Booms," *Wall Street Journal*, August 25, 1975, p. 1.
27. William F. Whyte, "The Emergence of Employee-Owned Firms

in the U.S.," *Executive,* Spring 1977; and Richard G. Case, "Saving the LB," *Syracuse Herald-American, Empire* magazine, October 30, 1977.

28. Memorandum from William F. Whyte, New York State School of Industrial and Labor Relations, September 16, 1977; and "Rags to Riches," *Newsweek,* January 2, 1978, p. 50.

29. Clearly, if regulatory agencies are subject to corporate domination, public enterprise will be as well. See Gordon Adams, "Public Ownership for Private Benefit—the Case of Rolls Royce," *Working Papers,* Spring 1974.

30. See Derek Shearer, "The Salt of Public Enterprise," *The Nation,* February 21, 1976; Robb Burlage, ed., "Public Employees: Progressive Public Management and Public Employee Rights," in *New Directions, op. cit.,* pp. 223–74.

31. Interviews with IGP personnel, September–December 1975; interviews with Paul Bernstein, fall 1977.

32. Paul Bernstein, "Worker-Owned Plywood Firms Steadily Outperform Industry," *World of Work Report* (published by the Work in America Institute, 700 White Plains Road, Scarsdale, NY 10583), May 1977; interviews with Bernstein, fall 1977; see also his *Workplace Democratization: Its Internal Dynamics,* Kent State University Press, 1976; and Katrina V. Berman, *Worker-Owned Plywood Companies: An Economic Analysis,* Washington State University Press, 1967. J. J. Bautz Bonano, "Employee Co-Determination: Origins in Germany, Present Practice in Europe, and Applicability to the U.S.," Harvard Journal on Legislation, Vol. 14, #4, June 1977, p. 947 ff.

33. The full Hart Poll is reproduced in Rifkin, *op. cit.*

34. Erwin Knoll, letter to authors, October 27, 1977.

Chapter 21: Pensions, Politics and Power: A Strategy for the 1980s

1. One potential pitfall of various union pension "reform" movements is that, in the process of cleaning up the funds, they could permanently divorce the union's membership from control of their funds.

2. In our interviews with union pension officials, all expressed confidence that the membership would be supportive of prounion investment strategies, although most acknowledged that the degree of trust necessary is not now present.

3. Needless to say, this must be done deliberately and openly to generate membership and public support as well as to avoid any hint of self-dealing on the part of the trustees.

4. Many union funds are already more heavily invested in mortgages

than the average pension plan, but labor has done little to publicize this either to their own membership or the general public. Although "public relations" is only a small part of the battle, it can be an effective tool for developing a broad base of support.

5. "Money Is Muscle With '78 Labor," Victor Riesel, *Birmingham (Ala.) News*, January 3, 1978.

6. Henry Foner, personal interview, June 20, 1977.

7. I. Philip Sipser, personal interview, June 20, 1977.

8. For instance, the UAW has not vigorously pursued this course in the past because its leaders don't want to be blamed if the fund does poorly. They would rather be able to criticize, if need be, from the outside. Still, there are a number of influential officials in the union who would like to see much more direct UAW involvement with the fund's investment policies.

9. Union pension officials have indicated to us that, quite often, management trustees are more than willing to go along with policies that strengthen the unionized sector of the economy—the various union mortgage-investment trusts are a good example of this.

Chapter 22: The Upcoming Battle

1. *Labor Management Benefit Funds,* Noel Arnold Levin, Practicing Law Institute (New York, 1971), #4 in series, p. 217.

2. The experience of the New Democratic Party in British Columbia is also quite instructive. See Derek Shearer, "The North Moves Left, Politics in British Columbia," *Working Papers,* Spring 1974; and Ben and Emily Achtenberg, "British Columbia 3 Years Late," *Working Papers,* Winter 1977.

3. But even in Italy and France, the Left didn't make any decisive gains until it had succeeded in mobilizing support across a broad spectrum, not just among committed party members.

4. This is precisely the predicament that Great Britain is in now. Those who say that England is the harbinger of the American future will be correct if a patchwork approach to economic problems is continued.

5. Disturbances like the New York City blackout riots of 1977 could be touched off by any number of events.

6. A number of southern political leaders have openly discussed shutting off natural-gas supplies to the North in retaliation for continued price controls.

Index